Do Muslim Women Need Saving?

Lila Abu-Lughod

HARVARD UNIVERSITY PRESS
Cambridge, Massachusetts & London, England

First Harvard University Press paperback edition, 2015
Eighth Printing

Library of Congress Cataloging-in-Publication Data

Abu-Lughod, Lila.
Do Muslim women need saving? / Lila Abu-Lughod.
  pages cm
Includes bibliographical references and index.
ISBN 978-0-674-72516-4 (cloth : alk. paper)
ISBN 978-0-674-08826-9 (pbk.)
  1. Muslim women—Social conditions. 2. Muslim women—Civil rights. 3. Women's
rights—Islamic countries. I. Title.
HQ1170.A346 2013
305.48'697—dc23   2013005846

Do Muslim Women Need Saving?

For my mother,
———————————
who watched me struggle

CONTENTS

Do Muslim Women Need Saving?

Introduction
Rights and Lives

On a bright December day in 2010, I was having tea with Zaynab, a woman who lives in a village in southern Egypt.[1] I had known her for many years, and as we caught up on each other's news, she politely asked me about the subject of my new research. I explained that I was writing a book about how people in the West believe that Muslim women are oppressed. Zaynab objected, "But many women are oppressed! They don't get their rights in so many ways—in work, in schooling, in . . ."

I was surprised by her vehemence. "But is the reason Islam?" I asked. "They believe that these women are oppressed by Islam."

It was Zaynab's turn to be shocked. "What? Of course not! It's the government," she explained. "The government oppresses women. The government doesn't care about the people. It doesn't care that they don't have work or jobs, that prices are so high that no one can afford anything. Poverty is hard. Men suffer from this too."

This was just three weeks before the day that Egyptians took to the streets and the world watched, riveted, as they demanded rights, dignity, and the end of the regime that had ruled for thirty years. Zaynab had a particular reason for her anger that day. I had arrived that morning to find her household in distress. The café that had been made out of the old living room of her house was shuttered. Inside, her son lay on the couch, despondent. He was the one who ran the café; the youngest of her sons, he was practical and hardworking. He had been a bright and eager kid when we first met him, watching closely when my husband helped Zaynab fix her washing machine and delighting us with the motor-driven toys he made. He had always been the first to hitch the donkey cart to go off to get fodder for the sheep and water buffalo that Zaynab had kept for milk and income.

Zaynab had just returned from the police station and she was agitated. She had gone to find out why they had picked up the boy who helped her son in the café. She explained what had happened. The local security officer had come in demanding breakfast. Another customer was served first. It seems that the security officers and the military police came in regularly, or sent an underling to get them food. Zaynab dramatically described all the good food her son would prepare for them: fava beans smothered in real clarified butter, eggs, cheese, pickles, and a mountain of bread. They never offered the full price; sometimes they didn't pay at all. This time, they had the waiter arrested.

As she drank strong tea for her headache, I tried to cheer up the family by making a facetious suggestion. How about posting their menu and prices on a board so that everyone would know what things cost? And to shame the police and military, have a second column listing the special discounted prices just for them. Neither Zaynab nor her son was amused. They were tired of this harassment.

The problem, Zaynab explained, was that no one dared stand up to them. With just a word, these men could have her shop or café closed down. She already had to pay off the security police and the tourist police daily. I had seen Zaynab seethe when the uniformed men or plainclothes police came by asking for packets of cigarettes and then refused to pay. They saw her as an ignorant peasant, her face dark with years of work in the fields, her black robes marking her as uneducated. They knew she was powerless. No wonder she blamed the government for women's oppression.[2]

I had been close to Zaynab and her family for almost twenty years. Her youngest child was the same age as my twins; we had met when they were infants. I admired the way Zaynab had raised her children and run the household more or less on her own. Her husband had left to find work in Cairo, as did so many from this depressed region, and only returned for short vacations.[3] Intelligent and knowledgeable about everything from poetic funeral laments to the economics of farming, she had been indefatigable in building a good life for her family. In recent years, when her children were old enough to help, she finally was able to capitalize on her location, which was near the buses that brought tourists to her hamlet to visit a well-preserved Pharaonic temple. She set up a small kiosk selling cigarettes, batteries, and chewing gum, and then expanded to sell bottled water, sodas, and snacks. Endlessly moving things indoors and out, serving customers, arranging for supplies, applying for permits, and paying bribes and fines, the headaches were regular and the income inconsistent.

Zaynab's individual circumstances are unique, of course. She lives in a poor region of Egypt. Her marriage had not been ideal. Active and independent, she had a head for business and managed a complicated farming enterprise more or less on her own for years. She regretted that she had never gone to school—many girls didn't when she was growing up—but she was sharp and wondered why she seemed to understand more about the world than her children, all of whom had gone to school.

Yet her reaction to the subject of my book on "the Muslim woman" confirmed something I had seen across the Arab world. She lived with hardships, but she was always thinking about how to do the best for her family. She was keenly aware of the political circumstances that shaped her life and her possibilities, whether they came from a security state or from being part of the international tourist economy. Her shock at my suggestion that anyone would think she was oppressed by her religion was significant. Like so many women I have known across the Arab world—from university professors and businesswomen to villagers—her identity as a Muslim is deeply meaningful to her, and her faith in God is integral to her sense of self and community.

Thinking like an Anthropologist

Because I have known women like Zaynab through my years doing ethnographic research, I am often bewildered by what I read or hear about "the Muslim woman." It is hard to reconcile my experiences with the women I have met in rural Egypt with what the American media present, or with what people say to me casually at dinner parties, in doctors' offices, and on the sidelines at my children's soccer games when they learn that I write about the Middle East. I am surprised by how easily people presume that Muslim women do not have rights.

This book is the result of my intellectual journey to make sense of the disjuncture between my experiences and these public attitudes. When defending the rights of Muslim women was offered as part of the justification for U.S. military intervention in Afghanistan in 2001, I had already spent twenty years writing about women's lives in various communities in Egypt. In the late 1970s, I lived for two years in a Bedouin community in Egypt's

Western Desert. I was then a graduate student in anthropology doing fieldwork for my dissertation. The book I eventually published based on this experience was called *Veiled Sentiments*.[4] It presented the surprising things that the poems so precious to women in this community could tell us about how they felt— about men, relationships, and life. The women who expressed themselves through poignant oral poetry first taught me just how complicated cultural and moral life was in at least one Arab Muslim community.

Worried that the academic style and arguments of my first book had stood in the way of conveying the liveliness of the women I had come to know, not to mention the nuances of their social relations and attitudes, I returned again to live in this community for about six months in the mid-1980s. Based on this research, I wrote a second book that was composed only of narratives. In *Writing Women's Worlds,* I used the everyday stories of individual women to try to capture something of the spirit of their world.

By presenting women's dreams, desires, anger, and disappointments—in their own words—I hoped to lay to rest some stereotypes. Some of the women longed desperately for children; others were frazzled by having too many. Some wanted to marry; others shied away—or pretended to. Some had husbands who were close life partners; others had husbands who hurt their feelings. Some escaped bad marriages; others were bound to them, as so many women are, by love of their children. The stories were about jealousies, arguments, deep interdependencies, and the changes women underwent as they grew older. Some of the women I wrote about clearly felt embraced by their large families and were confident and powerful; some were lonely and poor. Some women were defiant and proud; others were resigned to what fate had brought them. Some young women wanted to escape what they perceived as their community's flaws, even if they fiercely defended central values and argued in terms of becoming better Muslims. All had a keen sense of their rights.

The individuality of these women's experiences and their reflections on life and relationships challenged what I felt was anthropology's tendency to typify cultures through social scientific generalizations. I imagined feminists as another audience for my second book; I hoped that the narratives would persuade them that it is not so easy to talk about "patriarchy" or to put one's finger on how power works. I wanted my years of research to offer something unusual to a public that had little understanding of, but strong views about women in the Middle East. Trying to remain true to my experiences of living in this small community in Egypt for so many years—watching children grow up, women struggle to build families, people figure out how to realize their dreams, relationships and roles shift, and hopes sometimes turn to resignation—I did my best to convey the texture of "life as lived."[5]

I called what I was doing "writing against culture." I was convinced that generalizing about cultures prevents us from appreciating or even accounting for people's experiences and the contingencies with which we all live. The idea of culture increasingly has become a core component of international politics and common sense.[6] Pundits tell us that there is a clash of civilizations or cultures in our world. They tell us there is an unbridgeable chasm between the West and the "Rest." Muslims are presented as a special and threatening culture—the most homogenized and the most troubling of the Rest. Muslim women, in this new common sense, symbolize just how alien this culture is.

Western representations of Muslim women have a long history.[7] Yet after the attacks of September 11, 2001, the images of oppressed Muslim women became connected to a mission to rescue them from their cultures. As I explore in this book, these views rationalize American and European international adventures across the Middle East and South Asia. The media enthusiastically took up stories about the status and suppression of women. Feminists joined the cause. Popular memoirs by Muslim women who exposed the plights of their benighted sisters in Iran, Afghanistan, and Saudi Arabia became best sellers in the West. Women's organizations headed off to Afghanistan alongside a battery of humanitarians and legal experts. Later, these groups set up shop in Iraq, a country in which, ironically, women had previously enjoyed the highest levels of education, labor force participation, and even political involvement in the Arab world.[8]

The line between progressives and right-wingers has blurred in this shared concern for Muslim women. Some conservatives accuse American feminists of failing to protest "glaring injustices," including especially the "subjection of women in Muslim societies."[9] They accuse feminist scholars of being so consumed by a toxic anti-Americanism or so obsessed with a patriarchy that prevails everywhere (not to mention being wary of femininity, antifamily, and hostile to traditional religion) that they don't criticize "heinous practices beyond our shores." On the other side, observers of the U.S. feminist movement have argued that the revitalization of American feminism in the 1990s came with a shift from domestic to global issues. Farrell and McDermott, for example, attribute the stagnation of U.S. feminism after the 1970s to the conservative backlash that challenged earlier gains in affirmative action, education, employment, and sexual rights (at the same time that minority criticisms of U.S. feminism for racism were debilitating it). The mainstream turn to global or international feminism, they say, was a "strategic diversion from a fragmented domestic politics." American feminists began to focus on spectacularly oppressive practices that were easy to mobilize around: female genital cutting, enforced veiling, or the honor crime. Promoting causes far from home, they could secure themselves "a niche in larger political discussions around the role of United States as the beacon of humanitarianism."[10]

As an anthropologist who had lived for so long with women in communities where everyone was Muslim, I was forced by all these developments to reflect on what I could or should do with the perspective my ethnographic work had given me. The first principle of ethnography, which involves participating in daily life over a long period, is to listen and watch. I had already spent twenty years trying to understand something about women's lives in what now was being homogenized as "the Muslim world," where women's rights needed defending. So I embarked on a project to articulate why the emerging Western common sense about the plight of Muslim women did not capture what I knew from experience and from reading history. This book is my attempt to figure out how we should think about the question of Muslim women and their rights.

I do not just analyze or criticize media representations. Nor do I only study the ways popular rhetoric is put to political use. I am committed to taking seriously the lives of individual women I have known.[11] Each of the women whose lives I introduce in this book forces us to question dogmas. Each taught me something important about the inadequacy of contemporary understandings of the rights that Muslim women enjoy (or don't), even as they taught me that women live deeply gendered lives. Some face restrictions on mobility. Most have strong ideals of comportment and morality, work with laws and norms that distinguish men's and women's rights and responsibilities, and struggle with choices. I use their cases to bridge the gulf between the specific dilemmas and hardships they face in particular places and times and the common Western story of the hapless Muslim woman oppressed by her culture.

Alternative Voices

I am not alone in raising doubts about the images of Muslim women we are offered in the West. Nor am I the only one to question the connection between these images and the prevailing politics of violence. Informed interventions and sensible dissenting voices can be found in the American public sphere. On April 13, 2011, a website called Muslimah Media Watch that monitors representations of Muslim women uploaded a striking poster from a German human rights campaign.[12] At first glance, one sees plastic trash bags lined up against a mud wall; some are black, some are blue. A closer look reveals that hunched up among these bags is a figure shrouded in a blue burqa (Afghanstyle full covering). The German rights campaign slogan reads: "Oppressed women are easily overlooked. Please support us in the fight for their rights." A writer on another feminist website picked up the poster and retorted that "agency is easily overlooked if you actively erase it."[13] The feminists, Muslim and non-Muslim alike, who drew attention to this campaign poster are among those who ask us why so many, including human rights campaigners, presume that just because Muslim women dress in a certain way, they are not agentic individuals or cannot speak for themselves. These feminists are not ignoring the abuses the women suffer; to the contrary, they are suggesting that we ought to talk to them to find out what problems they face rather than treating them as mute garbage bags.

Martha Nussbaum, a feminist philosopher, also publicized the problems with presuming that veiling or covering might signal oppression. In a 2010 article in the *New York Times* blog

about the proposed bans of burqas in several European countries, she framed her arguments against the ban around the principle of freedom of conscience that is so central to American law
and historical values and on the human rights principle of equal
respect.[14] Her erudite demolition of the usual arguments put
forward in support of banning an item of women's clothing was
not just persuasive but amusing.

First, she dismissed arguments that the burqa is a symbol of
male domination and coercion by pointing out that those who
criticize this item of dress neither know the first thing about Islamic symbols nor would they support banning most practices
commonly associated with male domination in our own society.
These include commercial exploitation of women, plastic surgery, and fraternity violence, to name a few familiar examples.
Nussbaum offered some everyday examples to show the inconsistencies in the other two arguments in favor of the ban: (1) "security requires people to show their faces when appearing in public
places" and (2) "the kind of transparency and reciprocity proper
to relations between citizens is impeded by covering part of the
face." She wrote: "It gets very cold in Chicago—as, indeed, in
many parts of Europe. Along the streets we walk, hats pulled
down over ears and brows, scarves wound tightly around noses
and mouths. No problem of either transparency or security is
thought to exist, nor are we forbidden to enter public buildings
so insulated. Moreover, many beloved and trusted professionals
cover their faces all year round: surgeons, dentists, (American)
football players, skiers and skaters."

In a later post, Nussbaum responded to readers who objected
that the burqa was different because it portrayed women as non-
persons (think trash bags). Much of our poetry treats eyes as the
windows of the soul, she noted. Then she again described her
own experience. During a construction project in her office at

the University of Chicago she had to cover everything but her eyes because she wanted to protect her singing voice from dust. Students soon got used to it, she said: "My personality did not feel stifled, nor did they feel that they could not access my individuality."[15] She concluded that if we accept that human beings are entitled to equal dignity, we have to recognize that each of the arguments put forth in support of these bans is discriminatory. As she later elaborated in her book *The New Religious Intolerance: Overcoming the Politics of Fear in an Anxious Age*, what motivates these proposals to ban "covering" is not any problem with face covering but a fear of Muslims.[16]

None of those speaking out against the stereotyping of Muslim women is silent on the issue of women's suffering. Nussbaum herself has drawn attention to the gross inequities that are based on gender and the repugnant violence against women that occurs around the world.[17] I share the sentiments of all those who want to see a world in which women do not suffer as much as they do now—whether from hunger, poverty, domestic abuse, sexual exploitation, or practices that compromise their health or dignity. Anyone concerned with women's well-being must pursue moral and political ideals, however utopian. Yet as a scholar and someone who has lived with the kinds of women most often held up as prime and even exceptional examples of the grossly oppressed, I insist that we must analyze carefully the nature and causes of women's suffering. A good place to begin is to take seriously the insights of women like Zaynab.

Where Is Feminism?

The last two decades have been momentous for the development of new international instruments of women's rights and for the consolidation of feminist concern about women worldwide. In the 1990s, with the Fourth World Conference on Women in

Beijing in 1995 and the successful campaign to claim women's rights as human rights, we entered a new era of international exchange among women, activism by nongovernmental organizations devoted to women's empowerment, a growing feminist elite in other parts of the world, and the involvement of Western feminists in other regions. The UN Convention on the Elimination of All Forms of Discrimination against Women (CEDAW) provided an important framework and set of ancillary institutions for pursuing gender equality.[18] In the academy and elsewhere, lively debates have taken place. Liberal feminists who condemn patriarchy in other cultures and advocate universal standards of gender equity have been confronted by third world feminists and women of color in the West who insist that racial difference, class position, and geographic location shape women's experiences differently.[19] How can we treat women as an undifferentiated category?

The sharp debate within feminist circles about whether women share enough to constitute a singular category ("woman") has implications for the subject of this book. Should we be working with the similarly homogenized subcategory of "the Muslim woman"? I have taken her as my subject because others, some outside and some inside Muslim communities, are framing women's rights issues this way. Yet all of the cases of particular women I analyze in this book are drawn from the Arab world, and most are from the rural communities in Egypt where I have done research. This leap from the general to the particular requires explanation.

Muslim women live on all continents. More Muslims live in South and Southeast Asia, by far, than live in the Middle East. Many important developments in law and culture have emerged from these regions. Scholars have written about gender issues in all the nations in which Muslim women live. Women's experiences living in these other contexts can teach us different lessons than I can, with my focus on Egypt. Each country in which Muslims live has inherited a different history. In some countries, Muslims are minorities; in others, they are majorities. In a few countries, most are wealthy; in others, they are poor. The careful ethnographies that anthropologists and sociologists have written; the vivid documentary films that have been produced; the historical studies that those who work in the archives have published; the fiction, poems, and essays that women from these communities have created; the studies of law and legal reforms that experts have contributed—all confirm the tremendous diversity.

If I were a specialist on India, I would have drawn on a vast variety of experiences and situations—dating back hundreds of years and differentiated by region—to bring home this diversity. The dynamics that shape Muslim women's rights and lives in the subcontinent are dizzying. From their vulnerability in the tragic communal riots in Gujarat to their earlier use as pawns during Partition, when they (like Hindu and Sikh women) were booty of war and then reclaimed in the aftermath of independence for national honor, their identities as Muslims were key to what happened to them. Battles over a proposed Uniform Civil Code for family law in India have been pitched for years. Mobilized by a divorce case taken up by Indian feminists (mostly Hindu), the Muslim community protectively entrenched itself by insisting on preserving Muslim personal status law.[20]

Some of the more sensationalized abuses of Muslim women that have garnered world attention come from parts of the world other than where I have lived and worked. Because troops have been on the ground in Afghanistan since 2001, U.S. newspapers have regularly featured the problems that women in Afghanistan face. The focus has tended to be on "cultural practices" rather than war injuries or other consequences of militarization or the dislocations of war, as I explore in Chapter 1. It is important to look behind the headlines.

Bangladesh entered the limelight with publicity about incidents in which acid has been thrown at women, notably a major American television documentary called "Faces of Hope." Elora Chowdhury, who studied both the problem and the publicity, discovered that the issue of acid violence had been tackled in local campaigns by dedicated Bangladeshi feminists for years. They had set up organizations and laid the groundwork for providing services for survivors. Bangladeshi campaigners and victims (some the same) mobilized international support for their work, but then, as Chowdhury shows, the efforts of these groups were erased in the award given to the American documentary by the international rights organization Amnesty International.[21] More disturbingly, she traced how the incidents and the shifting demographics of the problem were simplified to fit a narrative of progress in which downtrodden Muslim women were given new lives by enlightened "saviors" who rescued them from "savages."[22] The messiness of the facts—who the acid throwers were and why the victims were attacked (for anything from rejection of sexual advances to family or land disputes)—were set aside. Even more worrying was what had happened to the victims whose causes were adopted by well-meaning benefactors. Interventions transformed their lives, but subjected them to novel pressures including Christian proselytizing. Some girls were criticized for making choices that went against the rescuers' scripts for them. In short, the story behind the news was complicated. It did not fit the story of Muslim women oppressed by their culture.

Muslim women's issues regularly stir up international debate in ways that concerns about women elsewhere in the world do not. Dina Mahnaz Siddiqi's meticulous research into the high-profile legal cases of rape in Bangladesh that were taken up by international women's rights groups shows neatly how stories get distorted when they go global. Siddiqi discovered that in many of the controversial cases where judges ruled that women should marry their rapists, women's testimonies and lawyers' explanations revealed that what we had instead were consensual relationships gone awry. The charges of rape or seduction were being brought forward when a pregnancy had exposed a relationship or when a relationship did not end in a promised marriage. Portraying the women as innocent victims of rape saved face and social respectability, and brought pressure on men to marry their girlfriends. International human and women's rights groups portray such resolutions as hideous violations of girls' rights when the problem is that the social ideals of female respectability, the stigma of sexuality, and the narrowness of the legal system limit women's options. Such gendered limits should not be confused with hideous "crimes against women." They also have nothing to do with Islamic law because the legal system in which the cases are pressed is the secular state court system.[23]

In recent years, Shari'a—the term people use loosely to refer to law that derives from Islamic legal traditions—has become an international symbol of Muslim identity and, to many in the West, a dreaded and traditional enemy of women's rights. The impact and implications of imposing "Shari'a law" are sharply debated.[24] In Southeast Asia, something called Shari'a law was imposed in Aceh after a protracted conflict with the Indonesian state and in the wake of autonomy and post-tsunami wealth.[25] Its violation of local gender norms and its connection to the political conflict reveal it to be anything but traditional. In nearby Malaysia, however, an innovative group of Muslim feminists calling themselves Sisters in Islam emerged to challenge conservative

interpretations of Islamic law. In 2009 an international movement for legal reform of Islamic family law grew out of this
organization.[26]

These examples from different parts of the Muslim world il-
lustrate the variety of situations in which Muslim women find
themselves, the sorts of debates and strategies they engage, and
how frequently their experiences are misunderstood and the
complexities of their situations ignored. These analyses of what's
wrong with the simple story of Muslim women's oppression
hold cautionary tales for us. Abuses and infringements of wom-
en's rights must be acknowledged. This is true everywhere they
occur, whether in sex trafficking in Seattle, Tel Aviv, or Dubai;
rape in Belgium, Cambodia, or Bosnia; or domestic violence in
Chicago, Capetown, or Kabul. At the same time, we have to recognize the everyday forms of suffering that women endure—
from insecurity to hunger and illness—that are not always gendered or specific to particular cultures or religious communities.
We have to keep asking hard questions about who or what is to
blame for the problems that particular women face. What responses might be most effective for addressing problems that we
do find, and who is best situated to understand or respond to
these problems? Muslim women activists have been addressing
gender issues in their communities for more than a century in
places like Egypt, Syria, and present-day Bangladesh. As Elora
Shehabuddin notes, these reform movements were initially led by
men, but "by the late nineteenth and early twentieth century . . .
Muslim women themselves were making passionate pleas for
change."[27]

For the past decade, I have been trying to think through both
the politics and the ethics of the international circulation of discourses about "oppressed Muslim women." Inspired less by debates in my discipline of anthropology than by what is happening

in the world, I have been following the very active social life of "Muslim women's rights." If the prominent use of the sad figure of the oppressed Muslim woman for a war in Afghanistan in 2001 set me on the path to thinking through the issues, I have nevertheless felt that the best way to approach the problem is to go deeply into the specifics and what I know. That is why I draw heavily on my experiences living in some small communities in Egypt. I do not claim that the women whose lives I analyze are representative or can stand in for all others. Instead, I use them to suggest that intimate familiarity with individuals anywhere makes it hard to be satisfied with sweeping generalizations about cultures, religions, or regions, or to accept the idea that problems have simple causes or solutions. I am more drawn to the detail and empathy of the novelist than to the bold strokes of the polemicist.

Confounding Choices

Even if many are willing to set aside the sensationalized stories of oppression that capture media attention and contribute to the widespread sense of certainty about the direness of the situation of "the Muslim woman," most people still harbor a stubborn conviction that women's rights should be defined by the values of choice and freedom, and that these are deeply compromised in Muslim communities. This obsession with constraint is shared by outsiders and secular progressives within the Muslim world. It is expressed perfectly in persistent worries about the veil (hijab/niqab/burqa/head scarf). Women who cover themselves are assumed to be coerced or capitulating to male pressure, despite the fact that wearing an enveloping cover is mandatory (in public) in only a few settings and that educated Muslim women in the past thirty years have struggled with the opposite problem: They must defy their families and sometimes the law to take on what they value as pious Islamic dress. Women's decisions to take on the veil in what Leila Ahmed has called "a quiet revolution" are shaped by a long history of controversy over its meanings.[28] Can dress symbolize freedom or constraint? How can we distinguish dress that is freely chosen from that which is worn out of habit, social pressure, or fashion? A cartoon on a 2007 cover of the major New York literary magazine the *New Yorker* captures this dilemma wonderfully. Three young women sit side by side in a New York subway car. One is in full black niqab with just her eyes showing. Next to her sits a blond who is wearing large sunglasses, shorts, a bikini top, and flip-flops revealing painted toenails. Next to her sits a kindly looking, bespectacled nun wearing a habit. The caption reads: "Girls will be girls."

Because of the terms in which Muslim women's lives are represented and debated in the West, no book about women in the Muslim world can avoid confronting the question of how to think about choice and what it means to assert freedom as the ultimate value. I return again and again to these issues that lie at the heart of the matter. Born into families, we all find ourselves in particular social worlds. We are placed in certain social classes and communities in specific countries at distinct historical moments. Our desires are forged in these conditions and our choices limited by them. This is not to say that some individuals and communities do not enjoy more choice and more power to choose than others—after all, Virginia Woolf taught us in *A Room of One's Own* that at least in Britain up until the Second World War, these have usually been men.[29] But is the relative power to choose defined solely by sex or by culture? We need to reflect on the limits we all experience in being agents of our own lives. And beyond that, we have to ask ourselves what we think about those for whom choice may not be the only litmus test of a worthy life. Most religious traditions are built on the premise that people do not fully control what happens to them. Even the ancient Greeks saw hubris—excessive pride or belief that one could defy the gods—as a tragic flaw.

Questions like these are crucial for thinking about Muslim women and their rights. In considering the strange idea that liberal democracies want to legislate what Muslim women should wear, Wendy Brown reminds us that secularism has not brought women's freedom or equality in the West. Our views, Brown says, are based on the "tacit assumption that bared skin and flaunted sexuality is a token if not a measure of women's freedom and equality."[30] The women who are going to the mosques to learn how to be better Muslims and who are embracing a new kind of veiling as religious duty would be nonplussed.[31] My friend Zaynab, in her black overdress and head covering, would be shocked by this assumption. Our convictions about Muslim women's relative lack of choice, Brown concludes, ignore "the extent to which all choice is conditioned by as well as imbricated with power, and the extent to which choice itself is an impoverished account of freedom."

How such simplistic ideas about freedom are maintained is a running theme of this book. I look both at political rhetoric and popular culture. Ayaan Hirsi Ali, the Somali émigré whose voice has been so crucial in the past decade to defining North American and European views on women and Islam, refers to Muslim women as "caged virgins." She presents herself as a Muslim woman who has freed herself from the cage, rejecting the "tribal sexual morality" that she ascribes to Islam and emancipating herself through atheism.[32] She gives step-by-step advice to young Muslim girls about how to run away from home.[33] Mass-market paperbacks about abused Muslim women buttress such views with metaphors of caged birds, trapped flies, and spiders in jars.

The Wounded Bird

The contrast between the free and unfree is at the core of contemporary American feminism, drawing on a powerful national ideology and political philosophy. One of the most poetic and familiar evocations is the title of Maya Angelou's classic memoir, *I Know Why the Caged Bird Sings.* Her autobiographical story of emancipation from both racism and sexual abuse turns on a contrast between the caged bird and the free. The caged bird's shadow, in Angelou's poem, "shouts on a nightmare scream."[34]

I want to set beside this classic contrast another song about a nightmare scream, one that I heard in Jordan. This other song invites us to think differently about women and freedom because it speaks to the new context in which we live, a context dominated by a popular discourse like Ayaan Hirsi Ali's, which pits Western freedom against imprisonment by Islam. This song is a sober reminder that we must situate such images and ground our thinking about the meanings of freedom in the everyday lives of individuals, on the one hand, and the imperial politics of intervention, on the other. We will find that it is rarely a case of being free or oppressed, choosing or being forced. Representations of the unfreedom of others that blame the chains of culture incite rescue missions by outsiders. Such representations mask the histories of internal debate and institutional struggles over justice that have occurred in every nation. They also deflect attention from the social and political forces that are responsible for the ways people live.

I heard this song from one of my favorite aunts (technically my father's first cousin, but we called her "aunt"). Widowed a decade ago, she had decided to move to Jordan to be near her brother and sisters. The family was scattered after their expulsion from Palestine in 1948, but her siblings were gathering again after they, like many Palestinians, were driven out of Kuwait in the first Gulf War. I had not seen her for many years, but when a conference took me to Jordan, I got in touch. In her late seventies now, she remained beautiful and glamorous. She still wore tasteful makeup and had her hair pulled up in a bun with a colorful clip. Wearing an elegant, long black skirt and trendy ankle boots, she also carefully draped a chiffon scarf loosely over her head when we went to pay a call on some relatives.

As long as I'd known her, she had been punctual about prayers, and on her lips were the same entreaties to God and expressions of faith that are familiar to anyone who has spent time in the Muslim world. But my aunt also loved to sing. That day, she wanted to sing for us. Of the many songs she had written, this plaintive song was the one, she said, that best expressed her feelings. It was intriguing to me that it played on the same images as the poem in Angelou's book on freedom.

> I'm a wounded bird
> Living in the world, a stranger . . .
> I search, search for my country
> I find nothing but my laments . . .
>
> The wound in me is deep
> And will need years to heal . . .
> I am screaming inside
> But no one but me can hear

She interpreted her song for me, not sure I would understand the Arabic or the deep meaning. Everyone, she said, thinks she is happy because she is so warm and fun-loving on the outside. Vivacious and funny, she is indeed a lively raconteur and someone who appreciates people's foibles. When she complained about her bad knee or her failing eyesight, she would say with a twinkle, "You know how hard it is when you get to be thirty-seven and a

half years old!" She confided to me that she had composed this
song after her daughter (who was about my age and had been
dear to me, too) was killed in a car accident with college friends
in Wisconsin. She didn't leave the house for months. But she
sings the song with new feeling now—shortly after her husband
passed away, she lost her eldest son to cancer.

My aunt has not had the life she deserved. With her talents
and intelligence, and her origins in a good family from Jaffa, she
had what looked initially like a good marriage. She married a
man who was considerably older but well educated by the Jesu-
its. He had a respectable job working for the British customs office at Lydda (now Ben Gurion) Airport. In the black-and-white
studio photograph of her on their wedding day, which she had
enlarged and hung in her bedroom, she sits demurely on a chair,
her hair in curls, and a white pearl necklace around her neck, her
young body feminine in a long, white lace dress. But their life took
an unexpected turn.

A few years after they were married, fighting broke out in
Jaffa with the settlers in Tel Aviv who wanted Palestine as a Jewish state. During the troubles, her husband took her and their
two young sons "on holiday" to Egypt. They had two suitcases
with them. She tells the story of what happened when they got
the news that Jaffa had fallen to the Zionists. They were in a ho-
tel in Cairo when they learned that the Zionist settlers had taken
by force what, even under the partition plan imposed by the
United Nations (UN), belonged to the part of Palestine to have
been left to the Palestinians. The state of Israel was declared and
it included Jaffa. Her husband beat his head against the wall.
Never able to return, they spent the next twenty years living a
modest life in a lower-middle-class neighborhood in Cairo.

I got to know them in the late 1950s, when my father took a
job working for the United Nations Educational, Scientific, and

Cultural Organization (UNESCO) in Egypt. We loved to play with our cousins, her children. My aunt would cook us delicious food, sing as she worked around the house, and let us play pranks on the neighbors. She kept the household going without much companionship from her husband. As a refugee, her husband found it hard to find work and was often forced to be away. He was a dour man anyway, at least by the time I knew him, proud that he spoke many languages (Arabic, French, English, and Hebrew) and often buried in a book. He did not share her zest for life or music. They raised four children, sending them off, one by one, to the United States for college. The eldest became an engineer and eventually sent for his parents, setting them up in a Midwestern suburb.

There is so much in her life that seems unfair. As a girl growing up in Jaffa in the 1930s and 1940s, she married too early to get an education. As a refugee, like hundreds of thousands of Palestinians who lost everything, she was cut off from her family in 1948. As someone who spent more than fifty years married to a man who was not a good match for her, she could not flourish, though she made the best of it. Singing kept her going. The song about herself as a wounded bird, though, was about more than her personal plight. She explained to me, "I am like Palestine. My wounds are deep. We Palestinians are all wounded and strangers in this world." There was no way to separate her personal situation from the particular historical and political circumstances that gave it shape and limits.

My aunt finds comfort in her songs and takes pleasure in family. But I noticed when we talked that she also finds inner peace through prayer. She struggles to read a part of the Qur'an every day, even though she did not have the benefit of an education that would make this easy. With her eyes bright, she tells me that in the Qur'an she has found marvels. She comments, "You begin to be philosophical about life. You have to accept what life brings you."

My aunt has had it easier financially than Zaynab has. She never had to work in the fields or confront security police. She now lives in middle-class comfort in her own apartment decorated with dried flower arrangements and framed photographs of those she has loved and lost. Yet no more than the village woman in her black robes living in a mud brick house would my aunt recognize herself in that figure of the popular American imagination: the Muslim woman who submits slavishly to an uncaring God and accepts abject confinement and harsh treatment by men because of some verses from the Qur'an. Love of family and faith in God keep her going.

These women's lives show us just how varied and complicated the sources of any one woman's suffering might be. From the abuse of power by security police in Egypt in 2011 to the injustices of colonial British support for Zionist expulsion of Palestinians from their land and homes in 1948, we see that the most basic conditions of these women's lives are set by political forces that are local in effect but national and even international in origin. Neither woman had a husband who was able to help her flourish, whether because of personality or precarious financial and political circumstances. The confidence of these women and even their public face was sometimes shaken by these men, who nevertheless did their best to provide for their families, burying their own humiliations and insecurity. Is it because they are Muslim men that they were less than perfect husbands?

And how are we to account for these women's resilience and initiative? Both threw themselves into making good lives for their children, living for and through them. My aunt's losses anguished her; she tried to manage this grief through her faith in

God. Zaynab has been consumed by the struggles and failings of her sons, by her eldest daughter's loneliness, and by her youngest daughter's diabetes. Zaynab's trust in God gives her strength and perspective.

The lives of women like Zaynab and my aunt reveal terms like oppression, choice, and freedom to be blunt instruments for capturing the dynamics and quality of their lives. Such terms do little to help us understand the tireless efforts of these women, their songs of loss and longing, and their outbursts about rights. Both women would find it bizarre to imagine that people could think they were caged by their culture or oppressed by their religion, even though they have not had easy lives and some of what they suffer is indeed gendered. Images of caged birds and trash bags by the side of a road obscure their social realities and their creative responses to hard situations.

Politics of the Everyday

This book seeks answers to the questions that presented themselves to me with such force after September 11, 2001, when popular concern about Muslim women's rights took off. I worry about the ways that representations of Muslim women's suffering and arguments about their lack of rights have been working politically and practically. I follow the concept of "Muslim women's rights" as it travels through debates and documents, organizes women's organizations and activism, and mediates lives in refugee camps and the halls of the United Nations. I try to uncover what this framework that describes distant women's lives only in terms of rights, present or absent, hides from us about both everyday violence and forms of love. I ask what evaluating lives in terms of rights does for (and against) different kinds of women. Along the way, I uncover how key symbols of Muslim women's cultural alienness—from the veil to the honor crime—are deployed in twenty-first-century political projects, and why these symbols grip us.

Trying to understand people's lives is for me a passion. It is also my vocation as an anthropologist. That is why I seek answers to these big questions through the lives of particular women I know. These are women who are trying to lead good lives and who are making choices that are sometimes hard, limited by the constraints of the present and the uncertainties of the future. I have known them for many years, as individuals living in families, communities, countries, and the world. How do they see the problems they are facing? What do they say they want? How should this make us think about that mythical place where Muslim women, undifferentiated by nation, locality, or personal circumstance, live lives that are totally separate and different from our own? What can thinking about their circumstances teach us about values like choice and freedom in the context of human lives—any human lives?

These women, I believe, can help us reflect critically on the groundswell of support for global women's rights that has emerged in the past decade, and the special concerns about the rights (or wrongs) of "the Muslim woman." How is the current moral crusade to save Muslim women authorized? What worldly effects do well-meaning concerns have on the suffering of women elsewhere in the world? How does the proposition that such women live caged in their cultures undergird fantasies of rescue by "the world community"?[35] These are questions that troubled me because I knew from experience how surprised women like Zaynab and my aunt would be by the contours of this concern.

CHAPTER 1

Do Muslim Women (Still) Need Saving?

Commentators noted the political timing of *Time* magazine's cover story about a beautiful young woman from Afghanistan whose nose had been cut off. The unsettling photograph of Bibi Aysha, whose Taliban husband and in-laws had punished her this way, appeared on newsstands in August 2010. Eight months earlier, President Obama had authorized a troop surge, but now there was talk about bringing some Taliban into reconciliation talks. The juxtaposition between the photograph and the headline—"What Happens if We Leave Afghanistan?"—implied that women would be the first victims. Unremarked was the fact that this act of mutilation had been carried out while U.S. and British troops were still present in Afghanistan.[1]

Time had selected this photograph from a large number of possible images. The talented South African photographer who took it explained the backstory at the award ceremony when it was declared World Press Photo of the Year. Jodi Bieber had been on assignment in Afghanistan taking portraits of women. She had photographed politicians, documentary filmmakers, popular television hosts, and women in shelters and burn hospitals.[2]

Time's managing editor defended his decision to feature this shocking photograph in both moral and political terms. Even if it might distress children, he wrote (and he had consulted child psychologists), they needed to know that "bad things happen to people." The image, he also argued, "is a window into the reality of what is happening—and what can happen—in a war that affects and involves all of us." He was not taking sides, he said, but he would "rather confront readers with the Taliban's treatment of women than ignore it." He continued: "The much-publicized release of classified documents by WikiLeaks has already ratcheted up the debate about the war . . . We do not run this story or show this image either in support of the U.S. war effort or in opposition to it. We do it to illuminate what is actually happening on the ground . . . What you see in these pictures and our story is something that you cannot find in those 91,000 documents: a combination of emotional truth and insight into the way life is lived in that difficult land and the consequences of the important decisions that lie ahead."[3]

Bibi Aysha had been photographed in a shelter in Kabul run by an American organization with a large local staff, Women for Afghan Women (WAW). She was waiting there to be sent to the United States for reconstructive surgery, thanks to the generosity of donors and the Grossman Burn Foundation. Both the photographer and WAW were broadsided by the publicity following the *Time* cover. WAW tried to protect Bibi Aysha from the glare, eventually preventing all interviews and photographs. By then they were sheltering her in New York, hoping she would recover enough from her trauma for surgery to take place.

A member of WAW's board nevertheless echoed *Time*'s political message. She predicted "a bloodbath if we leave Afghanistan."

Bibi Aysha's plight was to remind the public of the atrocities the Taliban had committed. Esther Hyneman rejected the suggestion made by Ann Jones in the *Nation* that the Taliban were being singled out for demonization when they were not much different from other misogynous groups in Afghanistan, including those in the U.S.-backed government. If the Taliban were to come to power, she warned, "the sole bulwarks against the permanent persecution of women will be gone." These bulwarks were the international human rights organizations and "local" organizations like her WAW.[4]

The controversy over Bibi Aysha indicates how central the question of Afghan women's rights remains to the politics of the War on Terror that, almost from its first days in 2001, has been justified in terms of saving Afghan women.[5] As an anthropologist who had studied women and gender politics in another part of the Muslim world for so many years, I was not convinced at the time by this public rationale for war, even as I recognized that women in Afghanistan do have particular struggles and that some suffer disturbing forms of violence.

Like many colleagues whose work focuses on women in the Middle East and the Muslim world, I was deluged with invitations to speak at the time of heightened interest in 2001. It was the beginning of many years of being contacted by news programs, as well as by departments at colleges and universities, especially women's studies programs. I was a scholar who had by then devoted more than twenty years of my life to this subject, and it was gratifying to be offered opportunities to share my knowledge. The urgent desire to understand our sister "women of cover" (as President George W. Bush had so marvelously called them) was laudable. When it came from women's studies programs where transnational feminism was taken seriously, it had integrity. But I was uncomfortable.

Discomfort with this sudden attention led me to reflect on why, as feminists in or from the West, or simply as people concerned about women's lives, we might be wary of this response to the events and aftermath of September 11, 2001. What are the mine-fields—a metaphor sadly too apt for a country like Afghanistan (with the world's highest number of mines per capita)—of this obsession with the plight of Muslim women? What could anthropology, the discipline whose charge is to understand and manage cultural difference, offer us as a way around these dangers? Critical of anthropology's complicity in a long history of reifying cultural difference, linked to its ties with colonial power, I had long advocated "writing against culture." So what insights could I contribute to this public discourse?

Cultural Explanations and the Mobilization of Women

In an essay I published in 2002, less than a year after I gave it as a lecture at Columbia University, I argued that we should be skeptical regarding this sudden concern about Afghan women. I considered two manifestations of this response: some conversations I had with a reporter from the *PBS NewsHour;* and the radio address to the nation on November 17, 2001, given by then first lady Laura Bush. The presenter from *NewsHour* first contacted me in October 2001 to see if I would be willing to provide some background for a segment on Women and Islam. I asked her whether they had done segments on the women of Guatemala, Ireland, Palestine, or Bosnia when the show covered wars in those countries. But I agreed to look at the questions she was going to pose to panelists. I found them hopelessly general. Do Muslim women believe X? Are Muslim women Y? Does Islam allow Z for women? I asked her if she would ask the same questions about Christianity or Judaism. I did not imagine she would call me back. But she did, twice. The first was with an idea for a segment on the meaning of Ramadan, which was in response to an American bombing during that time. The second was for a program on Muslim women in politics, following speeches by Laura Bush and Cherie Blair, wife of the then British prime minister.

What is striking about these three ideas for news programs is that there was a consistent resort to the cultural, as if knowing something about women and Islam or the meaning of a religious ritual would help one understand the tragic attack on New York's World Trade Center and the U.S. Pentagon; how Afghanistan had come to be ruled by the Taliban; what interests might have fueled U.S. and other interventions in the region over the past quarter of a century; what the history of American support for conservative Afghan fighters might have been; or why the caves and bunkers out of which Osama bin Laden was to be smoked "dead or alive," as President Bush announced on television, were paid for and built by the Central Intelligence Agency (CIA).

To put it another way, why was knowing about the culture of the region—and particularly its religious beliefs and treatment of women—more urgent than exploring the history of the development of repressive regimes in the region and the United States' role in this history? Such cultural framing, it seemed to me, prevented the serious exploration of the roots and nature of human suffering in that part of the world. Instead of political and historical explanations, experts were being asked to give religious or cultural ones. Instead of questions that might lead to the examination of internal political struggles among groups in Afghanistan, or of global interconnections between Afghanistan and other nation-states, we were offered ones that worked to artificially divide the world into separate spheres—re-creating an imaginative geography of West versus East, us versus Muslims, cultures in which first ladies give speeches versus others in which women shuffle around silently in burqas.

Most troubling for me was why the Muslim or Afghan woman was so crucial to this cultural mode of explanation that ignored the complex entanglements in which we are all implicated in sometimes surprising alignments. Why were these female symbols being mobilized in the War on Terror in a way they had not been in other conflicts? As so many others by now have pointed out, Laura Bush's radio address on November 17, 2001, revealed the political work such mobilization accomplished. On the one hand, her address collapsed important distinctions that should have been maintained. There was a constant slippage between the Taliban and the terrorists, so that they became almost one word—a kind of hyphenated monster identity: the "Taliban-and-the-terrorists."[6] Then there was the blurring of the very separate causes of Afghan women's suffering: malnutrition, poverty, class politics, and ill health, and the more recent exclusion under the Taliban from employment, schooling, and the joys of wearing nail polish. On the other hand, her speech reinforced chasmic divides, principally between the "civilized people throughout the world" whose hearts break for the women and children of Afghanistan and the Taliban-and-the-terrorists, the cultural monsters who want to, as she put it, "impose their world on the rest of us."

The speech enlisted women to justify American military intervention in Afghanistan and to make a case for the War on Terror of which it was a part. As Laura Bush said, "Because of our recent military gains in much of Afghanistan, women are no longer imprisoned in their homes. They can listen to music and teach their daughters without fear of punishment . . . The fight against terrorism is also a fight for the rights and dignity of women."[7]

These words have haunting resonances for anyone who has studied colonial history. Many who have studied British colonialism in South Asia have noted the use of the woman question in colonial policies. Intervention into *sati* (the practice of widows immolating themselves on their husbands' funeral pyres) and child marriage were used to justify rule. As Gayatri Chakravorty Spivak famously put it, "white men saving brown women from brown men."[8] The historical record is full of similar cases, including in the Middle East. In turn-of-the-century Egypt, what Leila Ahmed has called "colonial feminism" governed policy on women.[9] There was a selective concern about the plight of Egyptian women that focused on the veil as a sign of their oppression but gave no support to women's education. The champion of women was the same English governor, Lord Cromer, who had opposed women's suffrage back home.

Marnia Lazreg, a sociologist of Algeria, has offered vivid examples of how French colonialism enlisted women to its cause in Algeria:

Perhaps the most spectacular example of the colonial appropriation of women's voices, and the silencing of those among them who had begun to take women revolutionaries . . . as role models by not donning the veil, was the event of May 16, 1958 [just four years before Algeria finally gained its independence from France after a long struggle and 130 years of French control]. On that day a demonstration was organized by rebellious French generals in Algiers to show their determination to keep Algeria French. To give the government of France evidence that Algerians were in agreement with them, the generals had a few thousand native men bused in from nearby villages, along with a few women who were solemnly unveiled by French women . . . Rounding up Algerians and bringing them to demonstrations of loyalty to France was not in itself an unusual act during the colonial era. But to unveil women at a well-choreographed ceremony added to the event a symbolic dimension that dramatized the one constant feature of the Algerian occupation by France: its obsession with women.[10]

Lazreg gives memorable examples of the way in which the French had even earlier sought to transform Arab girls. *The Eloquence of Silence* describes skits at the award ceremonies at the Muslim Girls' School in Algiers in 1851 and 1852. In the first skit, written by "a French lady from Algiers," two Algerian girls reminisce about their trip to France with words including: "Oh! Protective France: Oh! Hospitable France! . . . Noble land, where I felt free Under Christian skies to pray to our God: . . . God bless you for the happiness you bring us! And you, adoptive mother, who taught us that we have a share of this world, we will cherish you forever!"[11]

These girls are made to invoke the gift of a share of this world, a world where freedom reigns under Christian skies. This is certainly not the world the Taliban-and-the-terrorists would "like to impose on the rest of us."

Just as we need to be suspicious when neat cultural icons are plastered over messier historical and political narratives, so we need to be wary when Lord Cromer in British-ruled Egypt, French ladies in Algeria, and First Lady Laura Bush, all with military troops behind them, claim to be saving or liberating Muslim women. We also need to acknowledge the differences among these projects of liberating women. Saba Mahmood points particularly to the overlap today between the liberal discourses of feminism and secular democracy; the missionary literature from earlier eras, like the Algerian school skit, show instead that the earlier language was not secular.[12]

Politics of the Veil

Let us look more closely at those Afghan women who were said to be rejoicing at their liberation by the Americans. This necessitates a discussion of the veil, or the burqa, because it is so central to contemporary concerns about Muslim women. This sets the stage for some thoughts on how anthropologists, feminist anthropologists in particular, contend with the problem of difference in a global world and gives us preliminary insights into some of what's wrong with the rhetoric of saving Muslim women.

It is commonly thought that the ultimate sign of the oppression of Afghan women under the Taliban is that they were forced to wear the blue burqa. Liberals sometimes confess their surprise that women did not throw off their burqas after the Taliban were removed from power in Afghanistan in 2001. Someone who has worked in Muslim regions would ask why this should be surprising. Did we expect that once "free" from the extremist Taliban these women would go "back" to belly shirts and blue jeans or dust off their Chanel suits? We need to be more sensible about the clothing of "women of cover," and so there is perhaps a need to make some very basic points about veiling.

First, it should be recalled that the Taliban did not invent the burqa. It was the local form of covering that Pashtun women in one region wore when they went out. The Pashtun are one of several ethnic groups in Afghanistan and the burqa was one of many forms of covering in the subcontinent and Southwest Asia that had developed as a convention for symbolizing women's modesty or respectability. The burqa, like some other forms of cover has, in many settings, marked the symbolic separation of men's and women's domains, part of the general association of women with family and home rather than public spaces where strangers mingle.

Hanna Papanek, an anthropologist who worked in Pakistan in the 1970s, has described the burqa as "portable seclusion." She notes that many saw it as a liberating invention because it enabled women to move out of segregated living spaces while still observing the basic moral requirements of separating and protecting women from unrelated men.[13] Ever since I came across her phrase "portable seclusion," I have thought of these enveloping robes as "mobile homes." Everywhere, such veiling signifies belonging to a particular community and participating in a moral way of life in which families are paramount in the organization of communities and the home is associated with the sanctity of women.

The obvious question that follows is this: If this were the case in Pakistan or Afghanistan, why would women suddenly want to give up the burqa in 2001? Why would they throw off the markers of their respectability that assured their protection from the harassment of strangers in the public sphere by symbolically signaling to all that they were still in the inviolable space of their homes and under the protection of family, even though moving about in public? In fact, these forms of dress might have become so conventional that most women gave little thought to their meaning.

To draw some analogies (none of them perfect), why should we be surprised that Afghan women did not throw off their burqas when we know perfectly well that in our society it would not be appropriate to wear shorts to the Metropolitan Opera? At the time these discussions of Afghan women's burqas were raging, a wealthy friend of mine was chided by her husband for suggesting that she wanted to wear a pantsuit to a wedding: "You know you don't wear pants to a WASP wedding," he reminded her. New Yorkers know that the beautifully coiffed Hasidic women, who look so fashionable next to their somber husbands in black coats and hats, are wearing wigs. This is because religious belief and community standards of propriety require the covering of the hair. They also alter boutique fashions to include high necks and long sleeves. People wear the appropriate form of dress for their social communities and their social classes. They are guided by socially shared standards and signals of social status. Religious beliefs and moral ideals are also important, including as targets for transgressions to make a point (one thinks of Madonna here). The ability to afford proper and appropriate cover affects choice. If we think that U.S. women live in a world of choice regarding clothing, we might also remind ourselves of the expression, "the tyranny of fashion."

What happened in Afghanistan under the Taliban was that one regional style of covering or veiling—associated with a certain respectable but not elite class—was imposed on everyone as "religiously" appropriate, even though previously there had been many different styles that were popular or traditional with different groups and classes. There had been different ways to mark women's propriety or, in more recent times, piety. Even before the Taliban, the majority of women in Afghanistan were rural and non-elite. They were the only ones who could not emigrate to escape the hardship and violence that has marked Afghanistan's recent history. If liberated from the enforced wearing of burqas, most of these women would choose some other form of modest head covering, like those living across the region who were not under the Taliban—their rural Hindu counterparts in the North of India (who cover their heads and veil their faces from in-laws) or their fellow Muslims in Pakistan.

Even the New York Times carried a good article in 2001 about Afghan women refugees in Pakistan, attempting to educate readers about this local variety of modes of women's veiling.[14] The article described and pictured everything from the now-iconic blue burqa with embroidered eyeholes, which a Pashtun woman explains is the proper dress for her community, to large scarves they call "chadors," to the new Islamic modest dress that wearers refer to as "hijab." Those wearing the new Islamic dress are characteristically students heading for professional careers, especially in medicine, just like their counterparts from Egypt to Malaysia. One wearing the large scarf was a school principal; the other was a poor street vendor. The telling quote from the young street vendor was, "If I did [wear the burqa] the refugees would tease me because the burqa is for 'good women' who stay inside the home."[15] Here you can see the local status in the Afghan refugee community that is associated with the burqa—it is for good, respectable women from strong families who are not forced to make a living selling on the street. It has nothing to do with being mute garbage bags by the side of the road, as the German human rights poster described in the introduction was to insinuate a decade later.

The British newspaper the *Guardian* published an interview in January 2002 with Dr. Suheila Siddiqi, a respected surgeon in Afghanistan who held the rank of lieutenant general in the Afghan medical corps.[16] A woman in her sixties then, she came from an elite family and, like her sisters, was educated. Unlike most women of her class, she had chosen not to go into exile. She was presented in the article as "the woman who stood up to the Taliban" because she refused to wear the burqa. She had made it a condition of returning to her post as head of a major hospital when the Taliban came begging in 1996, just eight months after having fired her along with other women. Siddiqi is described as thin, glamorous, and confident. But further into the article, it is noted in passing that her graying bouffant hair is covered in a gauzy veil. This is a reminder that though she refused the burqa, she had no question about wearing the chador or scarf. Over the past decade, the demographics and meaning of wearing (and not wearing) the burqa in public have changed, varying especially between the cities and countryside.[17]

Veiling must not be confused with, or made to stand for, lack of agency. Not only are there many forms of covering, which themselves have different meanings in the communities where they are used, but veiling has become caught up almost everywhere now in a politics of representation—of class, of piety, and of political affiliation. As I describe in *Veiled Sentiments,* my first ethnography of a Bedouin community in Egypt in the late 1970s and 1980s, for women I knew there, pulling the black head cloth over the face in front of older, respected men was considered a voluntary act. One of the ways they could show their honor and assert their social standing was by covering themselves in certain contexts. They would decide (and debate) for whom they felt it was appropriate to veil.[18]

To take a radically different case, the modest Islamic dress that so many educated women across the Muslim world have been adopting since the mid-1970s both publicly marks their piety and can be read as a sign of educated urban sophistication, a sort of modernity.[19] For many pious women in the Islamic revival, this new form of dress is embraced as part of a bodily means, like prayer, to cultivate virtue. It is, as Mahmood has described, the outcome of their professed desire to be close to God.[20] Lara Deeb, who has written about the public piety of women in Lebanon who are associated with Hizbollah, described how these women see themselves as part of a new Islamic modernity, an "enchanted modern."[21] In some countries, and not just Europe, women have to violate the law to take on this form of dress. In other countries, like Iran, women's play with color or tightness, or the revelation of a shoulder, a belly button, an ankle, or a wisp of hair mark political and class resistance.[22]

So we need to work against the reductive interpretation of veiling as the quintessential sign of women's unfreedom, even if we object to state imposition of this form, as in Iran or with the Taliban. (It must be recalled that earlier in the twentieth century, the modernizing states of Turkey and Iran had banned veiling and required men, except religious clerics, to adopt Western dress and wear European hats.) What does freedom mean if we accept the fundamental premise that humans are social beings, raised in certain social and historical contexts and belonging to particular communities that shape their desires and understandings of the world? Is it not a gross violation of women's own understandings of what they are doing to simply denounce the burqa as a medieval imposition? One cannot reduce the diverse situations and attitudes of millions of Muslim women to a single item of clothing. And we should not underestimate the ways that veiling has entered political contests across the world.[23]

The significant political-ethical problem the burqa raises is how to deal with cultural "others." How are we to deal with difference without accepting the passivity implied by the cultural relativism for which anthropologists are justly famous—a relativism that says it's their culture and it's not my business to judge or interfere, only to try to understand? Cultural relativism is certainly an improvement on ethnocentrism and the racism, cultural imperialism, and imperiousness that underlie it; the problem is that it is too late not to interfere. The forms of lives we find around the world are already products of long histories of interactions among those living far from each other.

I suggest that we approach the issues of women, cultural relativism, and the problems of "difference" from three angles. First, we need to consider what feminists should do with strange political bedfellows.[24] I used to feel torn when I received the e-mail petitions circulating in defense of Afghan women under the

Taliban. I was not sympathetic to the dogmatism of the Taliban; I do not support the oppression of women. But the provenance of the campaign worried me. I do not usually find myself in political company with the likes of Hollywood celebrities.[25] I had never received a petition from such women defending the right of Palestinian women to safety from Israeli bombing or daily harassment at checkpoints, asking the United States to reconsider its support for a government that had dispossessed them, closed them out from work and citizenship rights, and refused them the most basic freedoms. Maybe some of these same people were signing petitions against sensational "cultural" practices, for example, to save African women from genital cutting or Indian women from dowry deaths. However, I do not think it would be as easy to mobilize so many of these American and European women if it were not a case of Muslim men oppressing Muslim women—women of cover, for whom they can feel sorry and in relation to whom they can feel smugly superior. Would television diva Oprah Winfrey host the Women in Black, the women's peace group from Israel, as she did the Revolutionary Association of Women of Afghanistan (RAWA), which was also granted the *Glamour* magazine Women of the Year Award?

To be critical of this celebration of women's rights in Afghanistan is not to pass judgment on any local women's organizations such as RAWA, whose members have courageously worked since 1977 for a democratic secular Afghanistan in which women's human rights are respected, against Soviet-backed regimes or U.S.-, Saudi-, and Pakistani-supported conservatives. Their documentation of abuse and their work through clinics and schools have been enormously important. It is also not to fault the campaigns that exposed the dreadful conditions under which the Taliban placed women. The Feminist Majority campaign helped put a stop to a secret oil pipeline deal between the

Taliban and the U.S. multinational corporation Unocal that was going forward with U.S. administration support.

Western feminist campaigns must not be confused with the hypocrisies of the colonial feminism of a Republican president who was not elected for his progressive stance on feminist issues, or of a Republican administration that played down the terrible record of violations of women by U.S. allies in the Northern Alliance, as documented by Human Rights Watch and Amnesty International, among others. Rapes and assaults were widespread in the period of infighting that devastated Afghanistan before the Taliban came in to restore order. (It is often noted that the current regime includes warlords who were involved and yet have been given immunity from prosecution.)

We need to look closely at what we are supporting (and what we are not) and think carefully about why. How should we manage the complicated situation of finding ourselves in agreement with those with whom we normally disagree? In the introduction to this book, I talk about the blurring between Left and Right on the issue of Muslim women's rights. How many who felt good about saving Afghan women from the Taliban are also asking for a radical redistribution of wealth or sacrificing their own consumption radically so that Afghan, African, or other women can have some chance of freeing themselves from the structural violence of global inequality and from the ravages of war? How many are asking to give these women a better chance to have the everyday rights of enough to eat, homes for their families in which they can live and thrive, and ways to make decent livings so their children can grow? These things would give them the strength and security to work out, within their communities and with whatever alliances they want, how to live a good life. Such processes might very well lead to changing the ways those communities are organized, but not necessarily in directions we can imagine. It is unlikely that such changes would not include being good Muslims, and debating, as people have for centuries, how to define a good Muslim, or person.

Suspicion about bedfellows, I argued in those early days of the U.S. presence in Afghanistan, was only a first step needed for our rethinking. To figure out what to do or where to stand, I suggested that we would have to confront two more issues. First, we might have to accept the possibility of difference. Could we only free Afghan women to be "like us," or might we have to recognize that even after "liberation" from the Taliban, they might want different things than we would want for them? What would be the implications of this realization? Second, I argued that we should be vigilant about the rhetoric of saving others because of what it betrays about our attitudes.

Accepting difference does not mean that we should resign ourselves to accepting whatever goes on elsewhere as "just their culture." I have already introduced the dangers of "cultural" explanations; "their" cultures are just as much part of history and an interconnected world as ours are, as I explore more fully in this book. Instead, it seems to me that we have to work hard at recognizing and respecting differences—but as products of different histories, as expressions of different circumstances, and as manifestations of differently structured desires. We should want justice and rights for women, but can we accept that there might be different ideas about justice and that different women might want, or even choose, different futures from ones that we envision as best?[26] We must consider that they might be called to personhood, so to speak, in different languages.

Reports from the Bonn peace conference, held in late November 2001 to discuss the rebuilding of Afghanistan just after the U.S.-led invasion, revealed significant differences among the few Afghan women feminists and activists who attended. RAWA's position was to reject any conciliatory approach to Islamic governance. According to one report, though, most women activists, especially those based in Afghanistan who are aware of the realities on the ground, agreed that Islam had to be the starting point for reform. Fatima Gailani, a U.S.-based adviser to one of the delegations, was quoted as saying, "If I go to Afghanistan today and ask women for votes on the promise to bring them secularism, they are going to tell me to go to hell."[27] Instead, according to one report, most of these women looked to what might seem a surprising place for inspiration on how to fight for equality: Iran. Here was as a country in which they saw women making significant gains within an Islamic framework—in part through an Islamic feminist movement that was challenging injustices and reinterpreting the religious tradition.

The constantly changing situation in Iran has itself been the subject of heated debate within feminist circles, especially among Iranian feminists living in the United States or Europe.[28] It is not clear whether and in what ways women have made gains and whether the great increases in literacy, decreases in birthrates, presence of women in the professions and government, and a feminist flourishing in cultural fields like writing and filmmaking are despite or because of the establishment of an Islamic Republic. The concept of an Islamic feminism itself is also controversial. Is it an oxymoron or does it refer to a viable movement forged by brave women who want a third way? In the decade since that conference in Bonn, as we see in Chapter 6, Islamic feminisms have been thriving and developing well beyond Iran.

One of the things we have to be most careful about is not to fall into polarizations that place feminism, and even secularism, only on the side of the West. I have written about the dilemmas faced by Middle Eastern feminists when Western feminists initiate campaigns that make them vulnerable to local denunciations by conservatives of various sorts, whether Islamist or nationalist, for being traitors.[29] As some like Afsaneh Najmabadi have argued, not only is it wrong to see history simplistically in terms of a putative opposition between Islam and the West (as is happening in the United States now and has happened in parallel in the Muslim world), but it is also strategically dangerous to accept this cultural opposition between Islam and the West, between fundamentalism and feminism. This is because there are many people within Muslim countries who are trying to find alternatives to present injustices—those who might want to refuse the divide and take from different histories and cultures, who do not accept that being feminist means being Western, and who will be under pressure, as we are, to choose: Are you with us or against us?

We need to be aware of differences, respectful of other paths toward social change that might give women better lives, and recognize that such options are set by different historical experiences. Can there be a liberation that is Islamic? Does the idea of liberation, as I explore more fully in this book, capture the goals for which all women strive? Are emancipation, equality, and rights part of a universal language or just a particular dialect?[30] To quote Saba Mahmood again, writing about the pious Muslim women in Cairo: "The desire for freedom and liberation is a historically situated desire whose motivational force cannot be assumed a priori, but needs to be reconsidered in light of other desires, aspirations, and capacities that inhere in a culturally and historically located subject."[31] Might other desires be as meaningful for people? Might living in close families be more valued? Living in a godly way? Living without war? I have done ethnographic fieldwork in Egypt for more than thirty years and I cannot think of a single woman I know—from the poorest rural peasant like Zaynab to the most educated cosmopolitan colleagues at the

American University in Cairo—who has expressed envy of women in the United States, women they variously perceive as bereft of community, cut off from family, vulnerable to sexual violence and social anomie, driven by selfishness or individual success, subject to capitalist pressures, participants in imperial ventures that don't respect the sovereignty or intelligence of others, or strangely disrespectful of others and God. This is not to say, however, that they do not value certain privileges and opportunities that many American women enjoy.

Saba Mahmood has pointed out a disturbing thing that sometimes happens when one argues for respecting other traditions. The political demands made on those who write about Muslims are quite different from demands made on those who study secular-humanist projects. Mahmood, who studies the piety movement in Egypt, is constantly pressed to denounce all the harm done by Islamic movements around the world. Otherwise, she is accused of being an apologist. Yet there is never a parallel demand on those who study modern Western history, despite the terrible violences that have been associated with the Christian West over the past century, from colonialism to world wars, from slavery to genocide. We ought to have as little dogmatic faith in secular humanism as in Islamism, and as open a mind to the complex possibilities of human projects undertaken in one tradition as the other.

Beyond the Rhetoric of Salvation

My discussion of culture, veiling, and how one navigates the shoals of cultural difference should put First Lady Laura Bush's self-congratulation about the rejoicing of Afghan women liberated by American troops in a different light. It is problematic to construct the Afghan or Muslim woman as someone in need of saving. When you save someone, you imply that you are saving her from something. You are also saving her *to* something. What violences are entailed in this transformation? What presumptions are being made about the superiority of that to which you are saving her? Projects of saving other women depend on and reinforce a sense of superiority, and are a form of arrogance that deserves to be challenged. All one needs to do to appreciate the patronizing quality of the rhetoric of saving women is to imagine using it today in the United States about disadvantaged groups such as African American, Latina, or other working-class women. We now understand them to be suffering from structural violence. We have become politicized about race and class, but not culture.

We should be wary of taking on the mantles of those late nineteenth-century Christian missionary women who devoted their lives to saving their Muslim sisters. One of my favorite documents from the period is a collection called *Our Moslem Sisters,* the proceedings of a conference of women missionaries held in Cairo in 1906.[32] The subtitle of the book is *A Cry of Need from the Lands of Darkness Interpreted by Those Who Heard It.* Speaking of the ignorance, seclusion, polygamy, and veiling that blight women's lives across the Muslim world, the missionary women assert their responsibility to make these women's voices heard: "They will never cry for themselves, for they are down under the yoke of centuries of oppression."[33] "This book," it begins, "with its sad, reiterated story of wrong and oppression is an indictment and an appeal . . . It is an appeal to Christian womanhood to right these wrongs and enlighten this darkness by sacrifice and service."[34]

One hears uncanny echoes of their virtuous goals today, even though the language is distinctly secular and the appeals are less often to Jesus than to human rights, liberal democracy, and Western civilization, as we explore in Chapters 2 and 3. Sometimes the appeals are even simpler: to modern beauty regimes and the rights to cut hair. This was the surprising message of a group of hairdressers who went to Kabul to open a beauty academy for Afghan women, teaching them "hair and make-up." These Australians, Americans, and exiled Afghans were part of an initiative called "Beauty without Borders," supported, not surprisingly, by the cosmetics industry and *Vogue*.[35]

The continuing currency of the missionaries' imagery and sentiments can be seen in the way they are deployed for even more serious humanitarian causes. In February 2002, a few months after coalition forces entered Afghanistan, I received an invitation to a reception honoring the international medical humanitarian network called Médecins du Monde/Doctors of the World (MdM). Under the sponsorship of the French ambassador to the United States, the head of the delegation of the European Commission to the United Nations, and a member of the European Parliament, the cocktail reception was to feature an exhibition of photographs under the clichéd title "Afghan Women: Behind the Veil." The invitation was remarkable not just for the colorful photograph of women in flowing burqas walking across the barren mountains of Afghanistan but also for the text, which read in part:

> For 20 years MdM has been ceaselessly struggling to help those who are most vulnerable. But increasingly, *thick veils* cover the victims of the war. When the Taliban came to power in 1996, Afghan Women became faceless. To unveil one's face while receiving medical care was to achieve a sort of intimacy, find a brief space for *secret freedom* and recover a little of one's dignity. In a country where women had no access to basic medical care because they did not have the right to appear in public, where women had no right to practice medicine, MdM's program stood as a stubborn reminder of human rights . . . Please join us in helping to *lift the veil*. (emphasis added)

Although I do not take up here the fantasies of intimacy associated with unveiling—fantasies reminiscent of the French colonial obsessions so brilliantly unmasked by Malek Alloula in his book, *The Colonial Harem,* about Algerian colonial postcards—I can ask, and try to answer in the chapters that follow, why humanitarian projects and human rights discourse in the twenty-first century need to rely on such stereotyped constructions of Muslim women.

It seems to me that it is better to leave veils and vocations of saving others behind. Instead, we should be training our sights on ways to make the world a more just place. The reason that respect for difference should not be confused with cultural relativism is because it does not preclude asking how we, living in this privileged and powerful part of the world, might examine our own responsibilities for the situations in which others in distant places find themselves. We do not stand outside the world, overlooking a sea of poor, benighted people living under the shadow—or the veil—of oppressive cultures; we are part of that world. Islamic movements have arisen in a world intimately shaped by the intense engagements of Western powers in Middle Eastern and South and Southeast Asian lives; so has Islamic feminism.

A more productive alternative might be to ask ourselves how we could contribute to making the world a more just place—a world not organized around strategic military and economic demands; a place where certain kinds of forces and values that we consider important could have a wide appeal; a place where there is the peace necessary for discussion, debate, and institutional transformation, such as has always existed, to occur and continue within communities. We need to ask ourselves what kinds of world conditions those of us from wealthy nations could contribute to making, such that popular desires elsewhere will not be determined by an overwhelming sense of helplessness (or angry reaction) in the face of forms of global injustice. Where we seek to be active in the affairs of distant places, we might do so in the spirit of support for those within those communities whose goals are to make women's (and men's) lives better.[36] And we might do so with respect for the complexity of ongoing debates, positions, and institutions within their countries. Many have suggested that it would be more ethical to use a more egalitarian language of alliances, coalitions, and solidarity, rather than rescue.

Even members of RAWA, which was so instrumental in bringing to U.S. women's attention the excesses of the Taliban, opposed the U.S. bombings from the beginning. They did not see Afghan women's salvation in military violence that only increased hardship and loss. They called for disarmament and for peacekeeping forces. Spokespersons pointed out the dangers of confusing governments with people, or the Taliban with innocent Afghans who would be most harmed. They consistently reminded audiences to take a close look at the ways policies were being organized around oil interests, the arms industry, and the international drug trade. They were not obsessed with the veil, even though they were perhaps the most radical feminists working for a secular democratic Afghanistan. Unfortunately, only their messages about the excesses of the Taliban were heard, even though their criticisms of those in power in Afghanistan had included previous regimes.

As U.S. involvement in Afghanistan increasingly came to resemble the quagmire in which the Soviets found themselves in the 1980s, arguments of groups like RAWA have been proven prescient. In a comprehensive analysis of the situation in Afghanistan six years after the invasion, Deniz Kandiyoti drew attention to two key factors adversely affecting Afghan women.

Looking closely at the political history of the country and at the current political jockeying among groups in a weak and aid-dependent government, she noted easy threats to women's legal and social rights, which are readily pawned. As WAW's Esther Hyneman had warned in her defense of "the bulwarks" against retreats on women's rights, women have indeed become part of what Kandiyoti calls a "new field of contestation between the agenda of international donor agencies, an aid-dependent government and diverse political factions, some with conservative Islamist agendas."[37]

But this expert on gender in the Muslim world asks us to concentrate not on Kabul, with its politicians, technocrats, and international experts (including transnational feminists), but on what the war economy has done to people's social lives across the country. In the shift from subsistence agriculture and herding to opium production and arms smuggling, this criminal economy has funded and emboldened local warlords, including the Taliban, while putting most rural households into debt. Families and communities have been stripped of their autonomy and live in a constant state of insecurity. In the rural areas, Kandiyoti notes, we see "corrosive interactions between poverty, insecurity, and loss of autonomy." These create new forms of vulnerability with serious consequences for women. As I describe in the introduction for Zaynab in southern Egypt, women's options in places like Afghanistan are "conditioned by the fortunes of the communities and households in which their livelihoods and everyday lives are embedded."[38] They are distant from the government and formal legal systems, Islamic or secular. A disturbing development has been a new pattern of commodification of women. Like Bibi Aysha, who was given to her husband's family allegedly to settle a murder debt, daughters are now regularly given by their impoverished or frightened families to militia commanders and drug traffickers. Kandiyoti heard stories of young girls being offered to old men in "distress sales" or sent away to save them from roving bands of Taliban youth.[39]

These abuses are not extensions of local custom or traditional culture. They are reactions to the current situation in Afghanistan. Kandiyoti says, "What to Western eyes looks like 'tradition' is, in many instances, the manifestation of new and more brutal forms of subjugation of the weak made possible by a criminal economy, total lack of security and the erosion of bonds of trust and solidarity that were tested to the limit by war, social upheaval and poverty."[40] Traditions built on mutual obligations have been undermined by rapidly changing, desperate economic circumstances and by political instability. Men are no longer able to meet their obligations to women or fulfill their ideals of honor, protection, or generosity. This is the problem; this is the situation on the ground.

Yet Afghanistan, with its thirty-year legacy of conflict, continues to be understood as traditional. In the 2010 *Time* magazine article that accompanied the photograph of Bibi Aysha, we find a typical example of a seamless move between Islam and tradition. A timeless culture appears directly following a quote from the minister of the economy, leader of an Islamist party who expressed his views against coeducation: "That is in accordance with Islam. And what we want for Afghanistan is Islamic rights, not Western rights." The article comments that "traditional ways, however, do little for women. Aisha's family did nothing to protect her from the Taliban. That might have been out of fear, but more likely it was out of shame. A girl who runs away is automatically considered a prostitute in deeply traditional societies, and families that allow them back home would be subject to widespread ridicule . . . In rural areas, a family that finds itself shamed by a daughter sometimes sells her into slavery, or worse, subjects her to a so-called honor killing—murder under the guise of saving the family's name."[41]

I have much more to say about so-called honor killing in Chapter 4. For now I want to suggest that rather than resorting to such general cultural statements, we owe it to women in Afghanistan to look at their history and its impact on their current situation. With its power rivalries and its war economy, Afghanistan's circumstances are thoroughly tied up with the West, its everyday worlds embedded in a global economy and an international War on Terror. Militarization always has hidden consequences for women; these surely have more force than "culture" or "tradition."[42]

So a first step in hearing the diverse voices of Afghan women and the political message of groups like RAWA, which even in 2001 expressed concern about military intervention, is to break with the language of (alien) cultures, whether to understand or to change them. Missionary work and colonial feminism belong in the past. We should be exploring what we might do to help create a world in which those poor Afghan women—for whom First Lady Laura Bush said "the hearts of those in the civilized world break"—can have safety, decent lives, and a range of rights. What we have learned since the United States and its allies intervened is that conflict, insecurity, impoverishment, and international drug trafficking do not bring them closer to having such lives.

CHAPTER 2

The New Common Sense

We seem to be living in remarkable times. Ever since women's rights served as a respectable reason to support military intervention in 2001 in Afghanistan, the language of human rights has not only been on (almost) every tongue, but the call for women's rights has gone mainstream. The abuses women suffer are no longer considered private matters, swept into dark corners, or dismissed as insignificant in the international public sphere. Fifty years ago, no one could have imagined this development. The feminists who labored so hard on legislation, health, education, consciousness raising, and international conventions should feel gratified, even if the term "feminism" carries a taint and is rarely claimed by those today making universalistic calls for women's rights.

Signs of this seismic shift are everywhere, but nowhere more apparent than in some very well-received books by writers in the United States who address a broad, educated public. The *New York Times* columnist Nicholas Kristof and the Somali émigré Ayaan Hirsi Ali are excellent examples of writers who have made strong public cases for global women's rights. What

developments—in institutions, culture industries, and politics—
have enabled the public to find the arguments they put forward
in their best-selling books so convincing and plausible? How has
this new common sense about the urgency of going to war for
women taken hold? A close reading of their arguments, along
with those of Kwame Anthony Appiah, a Princeton philosopher,
gives us some clues—clues that take us back to Afghanistan.

Going to War for Women

*Half the Sky: Turning Oppression into Opportunity for Women
Worldwide,* a book by Nicholas Kristof and Sheryl WuDunn, is
billed as "a call to arms against the most shocking and widespread human-rights violation of our age—gender inequality."[1]
Published by the venerable U.S. publisher Alfred Knopf and endorsed by movie stars like George Clooney and Angelina Jolie,
the book was recently made into a television series. The vivid
stories that Kristof and WuDunn tell in *Half the Sky* are about
the sufferings of women in different parts of the world. The
husband-wife journalist team has captured the public's interest
for the cause of women's rights, something that decades of resolutions by the United Nations (UN) and bureaucratic covenants
declaring the moral and legal wrongs of discrimination against
women could not.

Half the Sky brings alive for readers the disturbing experiences—
sometimes brutal, sometimes banal—that women and girls endure. The book seeks to move and motivate, and is dedicated to
"all those on the front lines around the globe, saving the world,
one woman at a time."[2] Kristof and WuDunn believe that their
persuasive power derives from the ways they tell their stories:
they talk about individuals, not statistics. *Half the Sky* is popu-
lated by women who have survived against the odds, the most
admired being those "who have overcome unimaginable hurdles

in order to change the world."[3] Readers are asked to open their hearts and their pocketbooks to them.

The moral mainstreaming of global women's rights is also evident in a more scholarly but nevertheless quite visible book that appeared a year after *Half the Sky*. Written by a well-regarded philosopher and public intellectual who had not previously commented on women's rights issues, it is confident in tone, vivid in illustrative case studies, and humane in its vision. *The Honor Code* by Kwame Anthony Appiah appeals to our human potential to do the right thing. A philosopher and cultural critic born in Ghana, educated at Cambridge, and now teaching at Princeton, Appiah reflects on the way a sense of honor has led societies to shift, time and again, their understandings of what is right and wrong. Looking back over key moments in history, he shows that people could and have come to condemn as inhumane and dishonorable practices that previously had seemed not just normal but noble.

Two of the four case studies in his book about moral revolutions involve practices that harm women specifically. Appiah informs us that the moral hurdle our human desire for esteem must lead us to overcome now is to learn to find violence against women repugnant. Just as dueling in Europe, foot binding in China, and the slave trade in Britain came to an end when people began to feel these practices were shameful, so we must get men (in places like Pakistan) to find shameful the particular mistreatment of women known as the "honor crime."[4] In identifying this as the most urgent moral cause we face today, Appiah joins a chorus that includes hundreds of dedicated organizations around the world, scholars mounting academic conferences about this "form of violence against women that has existed throughout history and in a range of societies," and charitable foundations

that invite us to "shop honour." For a donation, you choose between an "Honour" tote bag and a men's tie.[5]

From yet another corner of the American public sphere comes
proof that women's freedom and equality have come to be idealized across the political spectrum. Working out of a major American conservative think tank after irregularities in her asylum
application to the Netherlands made her situation there uncomfortable, Ayaan Hirsi Ali, the outspoken and rebellious daughter
of the second wife of a former Somali opposition leader, has
made her name defending women's rights. Listed by *Time* magazine as one of the most influential people in the world, she has
been recognized by many awards, including *Glamour*'s Woman
of the Year. She has established a foundation to defend and protect the rights of women. This celebrity has become so familiar
that her publishers decided a portrait of this striking woman,
looking straight out at readers, should supplant the clichéd image that marketed her first book: her shrouded nemesis, the fully
veiled Muslim woman.[6]

These significant voices from the liberal and conservative public spheres suggest that there has been a leap forward in the
public recognition of the seriousness of gender discrimination
and women's suffering. Their perspectives and positive reception
mark the emergence of a new common sense that gender injustice
is a legitimate concern, not a fringe issue. Building on the work of
historians, social researchers, political theorists, and philosophers,
these writers are promoting a new way of thinking: a global approach that acknowledges women's issues as major social and
moral problems, not just the concerns of feminists. Writing clearly,
simply, and directly, they turn our attention to particular places
around the world that many know little about—Somalia, Cambodia, India, the Netherlands, Pakistan, the Congo, China, and

Afghanistan. They amplify, clarify, and bring to life what feminist researchers, local and transnational human and women's rights organizations, and grassroots feminists have struggled for so long to analyze and publicize.

The optimism of these interventions into popular public discourse makes them especially effective. They shine a harsh light on gender oppression and then they call out to us to live up to our highest moral values and our political ideals. They presume that people, once they *know*, will not stand by, silent and apathetic. Narrating stories of progress—from bondage to freedom, from despair to hope, from sexual enslavement to small-scale entrepreneurship through microcredit financing—they ask us to join a collective moral struggle to improve the lives of women.[7]

But how do these writers make their case that we ought to enter what Appiah calls "the war on women"? One way they do so is by calling up the ghost of Atlantic slavery—as analogy, as instructive case study, and as subliminal referent. This comparison is worth pausing over because a look at what historians and social researchers have taught us about Atlantic slavery and its aftermath leads to some cautionary questions regarding the new consensus about women's rights. How do these writers construct their objects and their arguments? What silences might make us suspicious?

For Kristof and WuDunn in *Half the Sky*, abolition stands as the unambiguous sign of our capacity to move beyond moral evil. They declare: "In the nineteenth century, the central moral challenge was slavery. In the twentieth century, it was the battle against totalitarianism. We believe that in this century the paramount moral challenge will be the struggle for gender equality around the world."[8] Abolition is a key case in the study of moral revolutions in Appiah's *The Honor Code*. Slavery also makes cameo appearances in Hirsi Ali's work; her first book is subtitled "An Emancipation Proclamation for Women."

Our historical understanding of modern slavery is still unfolding as scholars struggle to grasp how the horror of the Atlantic slave trade could have lasted for hundreds of years and involved the death or uprooting of millions of human beings; what it meant for the various groups and people involved, from British merchants to North American plantation owners, Christian missionaries and Africans of the coastal kingdoms and the interior, and the men and women enslaved; and what its legacy is today, including an underclass of technically free but disposable human beings. But three lessons from the studies of slavery help us pinpoint the contours and limits of posing the new challenge regarding women as "a call to arms for the emancipation of women."[9]

Half the Sky tells a simple story about abolition. Some good moral people in England struggled valiantly and finally persuaded and pressured others, including Parliament, to go against national and economic interests and abolish the slave trade.[10] Credit is given to the actions of ordinary individuals who signed petitions and boycotted sugar from the West Indies. The real hero, though, was Thomas Clarkson, who, like a present-day journalist, documented in the 1790s the grim conditions on British slave ships. The authors agree that he could be considered "the founder of the modern human rights movement."[11]

In *The Honor Code*, Appiah focuses on these same forces and people, including Christian moralists, in the struggle against slavery. But he gives more credit to the middle class and working men who were insulted by the devaluation of human labor that slavery implied. Appiah expresses a debt to the historian Christopher Leslie Brown, but he does not actually take up the key argument that Brown makes in *Moral Capital*. Brown notes that "antislavery opinion" in Britain had many sources: some sympathized with individual slaves, some pitied enslaved nobility, and some were horrified by the conditions of the enslaved, while others detested the principle of slavery. Some considered slavery unchristian or worried that it impeded the spread of Christianity in the Americas; others worried that slavery fostered immoral behavior. Some hated the new planter class and some agonized over the contradictions between the ideals of liberty and the realities of colonial slavery. Some feared armed rebellions—though the European story of abolition rarely acknowledges the agency of the enslaved.[12]

However, Brown's key point is a historical one. "Before the American Revolution," he argues, "no one had attempted to impose antislavery values through parliamentary legislation."[13] For him, the key question is: What actually enabled an organized antislavery campaign to develop? What contingent historical conditions led moral virtue to accrue to what had been, before, scattered antislavery sentiment? If the American colonies had not broken away, he ventures, and this sentiment and activity had been occurring instead in a "united empire," things might well have turned out differently. In short, a number of factors came together to make abolition not just possible, but suddenly unquestionably right. Brown gives us a real history of moral action that builds on a complex analysis of slavery, capitalism, imperial expansion, and the tensions between metropolitan ideology and colonial practice. Appiah barely mentions these factors.

What *Half the Sky* and *The Honor Code* also barely mention in the progress story they tell about abolition in Britain and its former slaveholding colonies is how other forms of labor exploitation replaced unfree labor. Institutionalized racism was substituted for slavery. In the United States, the color line was drawn by the "one drop [of black blood]" rule and was used to contain blacks in the American South in a kind of apartheid known as Jim Crow. Almost 150 years after emancipation, African Americans still struggle for equality of opportunity. Banished into informally segregated and underfunded schools and neighborhoods; largely excluded from good jobs, respectability, and upward mobility; often sexualized and degraded; ghettoized and criminalized, their suffering is either made invisible or blamed on them. Mass incarceration, described by Michelle Alexander as "the new Jim Crow," has shaped a cohort of men and women.[14] Ending slavery was a milestone in the history of the struggle against human barbarity, but emancipation has not yet produced equality.

Given this history, what lessons should we draw from the analogy between gender oppression and slavery? First, it is not so obvious how moral revolutions actually happen. They seem to depend on many voices, multiple social and political factors, and contingent historical events. Appiah, like the great German sociologist Norbert Elias, shows us that morality, like manners, actually has a history.[15] Part of our job is to reflect on what might account for, and what could stabilize, the new moral currency of "going to war for women."

Second, we must look at where the analogy breaks down. On the one hand, gender relations are different from relations between the free and enslaved. Women and girls everywhere are more entangled with men and boys—in complex ways, including through kinship and love—than slaves were with their masters. On the other hand, abolition was undertaken by the people and communities directly responsible for the enslavement of others, even if they disavowed and sought to undo the history of their violence through the moral claims of abolition.[16] It was the British people who convinced their *own* government to abolish the slave trade. Abraham Lincoln's Emancipation Proclamation was addressed to his fellow Americans. In contrast, the consensus in opposition to the kind of violence against women that Appiah deplores is about persuading men in *other* places to end their violence toward *their* women.

It Feels Transcendent

For all these writers, the wrongs and suffering of women—whether "sexual slavery" or "mental slavery," rape or maternal mortality, so-called honor killings or confinement to homes and brothels— are to be found in distant lands. Their arguments about gender discrimination and inequality take a global perspective. The stories they tell are from Africa, Asia, and the Middle East, or immigrant enclaves in Europe. The strange thing that happens along the way is that women's rights issues become pertinent *only* elsewhere.

The only American or European women who appear in the 280 pages of *Half the Sky* are altruistic high school students who raise money to build schools in Cambodia, or women who give up their jobs to devote themselves to working in health clinics in Africa. Some of the small organizations these American women started are now multimillion-dollar operations. The only American men who appear are those like Kristof himself, who rescues prostitutes from brothels, or those, like the late dean of Columbia University's School of Public Health, who devote themselves to fighting maternal mortality.

These are all good people. The cause of women does need to be higher on the agenda. But how does this focus on global good works erase the fact that the problems that should concern us are not only "over there"? In defending their choice to make gender issues a priority given all the pressing problems in the world, Kristof and WuDunn say something revealing: "This kind

of oppression feels transcendent."[17] Gender injustice feels transcendent to them, I would suggest, because they do not ground it
in the world they know. An occasional jarring statistic (for example, U.S. maternal mortality rates are much higher than Italy's
and are shocking compared to Ireland's) sits unelaborated. *Half
the Sky* tells no stories about overworked lawyers who defend
women in U.S. prisons who have been convicted of killing their
abusive lovers or husbands. No quotes appear from reports like
that of the U.S. Justice Department, whose national survey indicates that one in every six American women has been raped in her
lifetime, usually by an intimate or someone she knows.[18] They do
not mention Peggy Sanday's research on the white, middle-class
culture of college fraternities, where getting women drunk so the
guys can "score," even gang-raping their guests and boasting
about it the next day, is acceptable.[19] Nothing is said about the
alarming rates of domestic violence and murder of their spouses
that shadow returning veterans of the wars in Afghanistan and
Iraq. The only kind of problem American women face, according
to Kristof and WuDunn, is "unwanted touching from a boss" or
"underfunded sports teams."[20] In order to make their (legitimate)
case for concern about lethal sex discrimination, they trivialize
gender issues in the United States and Europe.

Like Cynthia Enloe, the pioneering feminist political scientist
who did so much to help us see the role of gender in international relations, Kristof and WuDunn recognize and applaud the
existence of feminist activists in other countries.[21] So does Appiah, who relies on the work of Pakistani women lawyers and
feminist activists. But the overriding message of *Half the Sky*,
like the other popular books discussed here, is that Westerners
are the ones who must change the world, even if it has to be, as
they say, not by "holding the microphone at the front of the rally
but by writing the checks and carrying the bags at the back."[22]

Appiah offers us a positive precedent for such intervention. He attributes the eradication of foot binding in China to the positive influence of Western shaming. A painful and hobbling practice that lasted for eight centuries and affected the majority of the female population of China, foot binding is now considered revolting. In its heyday, it was the subject of exquisite erotic elaboration by learned gentlemen and widely accepted by women as a beauty ideal and a prerequisite for a good marriage. As Appiah tells the story, the end of the practice came because outsiders— Western missionaries and merchants, along with educated Japanese—shamed a local elite into turning against it and becoming fervent reformers. When the literati abandoned the practice, confronted by "the advancing industrializing world, at a time when some of the literati had lost confidence in their own traditions to defend them from modernizing strangers," as Appiah puts it, there was "inevitably a cascade downwards of unbinding."[23]

The leading specialists on foot binding tell the story somewhat less benignly. Dorothy Ko roots the late nineteenth- and early twentieth-century reformers' efforts in the colonial condition of "humiliation by the West on a global stage."[24] Like Appiah, she ties reform to an emerging desire for modernity, but understands their concern about freedom as a response to a deep political crisis induced by military defeat first by the British, then by the French and the Japanese. The collapse of the empire in 1911 marked this total defeat. The manifestos against foot binding followed on the heels of the European imposition of treaty ports for "free trade" (theirs).

Ko argues, moreover, that there can be no simple explanation for the end of foot binding because there was "not one but many" foot bindings, in different eras, regions, villages, and classes.[25] Although the modernizing campaigns of the "natural feet" movement by embarrassed Chinese men were important, scholars have explored many other factors that must be part of any historical account of the practice and its demise. Some have made structural economic arguments, linking the decline of foot binding to the rise of factory-based textile production that replaced home-based spinning and weaving. Some observe that the practice did not actually disappear in the interior until after the Communist Revolution. This brought gender politics derived from Marx and Engels's theories, including attention to women's status, an ideology about the dignity of labor, links between forms of oppression (ruler and ruled, landlord and peasant, ancestral deities and ordinary people, and men and women), and an attempt to overturn the gendered division between production and reproduction that was seen as the prime cause of women's subordination. Early legal reforms by Mao, like the 1957 Marriage Act, outlawed concubinage and granted women the right to divorce. Socialist ideology gave women a language to name their oppression as "feudal." Foot binding was included.[26] A vast political mobilization sent cadres to villages across China to establish conformity of practice.[27]

Historical research shows, therefore, that even if it paved the way, more was needed to end the practice than the influence of Western missionaries and invaders that shamed early twentieth-century literati into binding their honor to the unbinding of women's feet. And in a poignant analysis, Ko has shown that the most immediate effect of the early reformers' campaigns for most Chinese women was a social bifurcation that humiliated and exposed them.[28] In this earlier period, the honor of the enlightened men and the few liberated women came at the price of silencing women by speaking for them about their pain. The reformers' honor depended on distinguishing themselves from the worthless backward majority.[29] Like today's German human rights campaigners who relegate Afghan women to mute trashbags, these reformers did not see Chinese women as "moral and political agents." And, as it happened, their campaign was temporarily forgotten by 1940, with the war and Japanese occupation.

This discussion of Western influence brings us back to the sentence in *Half the Sky* about why the cause of gender inequality feels transcendent. "This kind of oppression feels transcendent," say Kristof and WuDunn, "and so does the opportunity. We have seen that outsiders can truly make a significant difference."[30] The opportunity that women's oppression presents is for outsiders. The audience for their book and the recruits to their battle against gender inequality are, ultimately, those who want to end problems elsewhere. *Half the Sky*, like Hirsi Ali's *The Caged Virgin* and *Nomad*, and even Appiah's *The Honor Code*, is an invitation to Westerners to do something elsewhere.[31] These books do not ask us to examine the role Westerners already play—whether in their everyday practices, their governments' actions, or their economic strength—in perpetuating global inequities that exacerbate (and sometimes cause) the sufferings of women elsewhere. This is particularly the case in places like Pakistan or Afghanistan, where the War on Terror seriously complicates moral persuasion.

Fervent concern about suffering elsewhere that neither looks close to home nor attempts to unpack the complicated dynamics that produce suffering is worrisome. Also troubling are arguments that do not ask us to look at the privileges so many of us in the global North enjoy by virtue of a long history of global inequality. Among these privileges are vast consumption, safety from military incursion, advanced medical care, the relative ability to nurture our children and have hopes for them, and educations that should give us the tools we need to analyze these inequalities. We seem to accept shocking inequalities in the distribution of world resources as inevitable.

What is the effect of this insistence that we focus our gaze elsewhere? Such arguments allow those they hail to feel innocent, moral, and purposeful. In contrast, many radical global activists now ask us to seriously consider our responsibilities for this situation, as individual consumers and citizens, as part of nations with enormous military spending, and as beneficiaries (though increasingly also as victims) of corporate greed.[32] Offering $80 and donating some blood to try to save a dying pregnant African woman, as Kristof did, is better than turning away. Offering a $25 loan to a microcredit lender so that a woman in a village can borrow it (at 20–30 percent interest, which is better, Kristof and WuDunn assure us, than the rate of local moneylenders)[33] may not be harmful. But these amounts are less than those who feel good giving them would pay for a meal at an ordinary restaurant.

Acknowledging that "cynics" might criticize projects that send American high school students abroad to build schools for girls (saying the money they have raised through bake sales and soliciting rich relatives could be better spent on building more schools), *Half the Sky* defends such practices. One purpose is "to expose young Americans to life abroad so that they, too, can learn and grow and blossom."[34] In *Half the Sky*, we learn that "aid projects have a mixed record in helping people abroad, but a superb record in inspiring and educating donors."[35] The trip to Cambodia was for the students of one private school "an essential field trip and learning opportunity."[36] The learning opportunity though, was for privileged private school students who have had and will have many other opportunities to grow and blossom.

It is, of course, better that the privileged learn to care about the world than be self-centered and selfish. It is better to know than to be ignorant. And such trips abroad may prod students to want to know more and to become better adults. They might begin to ask how the failure to produce good state schooling and health care in so many parts of the world might be connected to them in systemic ways. Or they may question, even in their own towns and cities, why everyone does not receive the same learning opportunities they do. Yet books like *Half the Sky* and *The Honor Code* do not ask these questions. Instead, they induce sentiments of horror and pity about women elsewhere, mixed with patronizing admiration for some activists abroad.

"IslamLand"

If the first clue to the commonsense appeal of this popular battle for women's rights and equality can be found in the gaze that doesn't look back at itself, the second clue can be found most clearly in Ayaan Hirsi Ali's writing. She is a complex figure. Although her autobiographical book, *Infidel,* is fascinating and rich in detail, in other works she traffics in the ideological certainties of the Right, using the catchphrases they have commandeered. She invokes freedom and reason in her Manichean depiction of world affairs. She adopts Samuel Huntington's formulation of world politics as a "clash of civilizations" and Bernard Lewis's most famous sound bite about Muslims: "What went wrong?"[37] She disparages the soft liberalism of multiculturalism. Free and easy with her facts, eclectic in her references, and inconsistent in her arguments, she enjoys political patronage from the Right as a "moderate Muslim."[38] She appears to be the opposite of a liberal scholar like Appiah.

Yet Hirsi Ali shares something with these others who are shaping a new common sense about going to war for women besides a passionate hope that the present dangers for women can be overcome. She constructs a fantasy space that gives force to the popular groundswell of support for global women's rights on which these other writers build. We can see this most clearly in her third book, *Nomad,* which is characterized as a personal journey "from Islam to America." This is an odd phrase. She has actually come from Somalia in East Africa. She spent her childhood and youth in Saudi Arabia, Ethiopia, and Kenya because her father was in exile, and then she sought asylum in the Netherlands. Finally, she moved to the United States after causing a firestorm in Europe.

Islam is not a place from which one can come. Yet "IslamLand," as I would call this mythical place, annoints the call to arms for women with transparent goodness.[39] IslamLand enables those who advocate for women's rights to accrue moral capital. Kristof, WuDunn, and Appiah may be gentler in their politics, more humane in their liberalism, more civil and measured in their language, and more sympathetic in their hopes and humanism than Hirsi Ali. Their intellectual armature may be sounder. But they share two certainties with her. First, they identify with the moral "we," who know what's wrong in the world and must do something about it. Second—and this is what allows their certitude to be accepted so easily—they agree that IslamLand is the place where things are most wrong today, even if each of them offers disclaimers to disavow any direct blame of the religion of Islam. Hirsi Ali says, for example, "I do not despise Islam. I am thoroughly conscious of the noble values that the religion promotes, such as charity, hospitality, and compassion for the weak and poor."[40] Kristof and WuDunn say, "We don't blame Ellaha's difficulties on the Prophet Muhammad or on Islam as such."[41] Appiah writes authoritatively, "It is widely agreed across the world of Islam that neither the Koran nor the

Sunnah . . . nor the hadith . . . endorse the killing of women by men in their own family."[42] Yet each of these authors follows such statements with a figurative "but . . ."

IslamLand is the problem and Islam is condensed in the figure of the victimized Muslim woman. *Half the Sky*'s heroines and victims are not all Muslims, it is true. They come from Cambodia, South Africa, India, the Cameroons, the Congo, and Sri Lanka. The book opens with the redemption of Rath, a Cambodian girl who had been forced into brothels in Malaysia and Thailand. Kristof tells her story in gruesome detail. She was raped by the gangster brothel owners, then beaten and drugged until she complied. She and her fellow prostitutes were "kept naked to make it more difficult for them to run away or keep tips or other money . . . They were battered until they smiled constantly and simulated joy at the sight of customers because men would not pay as much for sex with girls with reddened eyes and haggard faces."[43] Kristof does not shy away from (porno)graphic details. This is his formula.[44]

Yet he seems to share the perspective that it is the men in IslamLand who most need to undergo a moral revolution—and that they will do so only if induced by Western moral pressure and shaming. Either they should redefine the bases of their right to esteem, their honor, as Appiah encourages Pashtun men and other fellow travelers in Muslim countries to do, or they should be forced to live in more gender-equal societies so that they stop acting out their "testosterone-laden values," as Kristof and Wu-Dunn recommend.

But just as Ko had to insist that there was no (single) foot binding in China because its patterns shifted, women experienced it differently, its purposes and rationales were multiple, and its meanings varied, so I suggest that there is no "Muslim woman" and no IslamLand. The situations of individuals, regions, countries, and classes differ. In Chapter 1, I describe just how many forms of cover there are in the Muslim world. In the introduction, I discuss the diversity of Muslim women's lives. Religious traditions mean different things to different women and men. These kinds of complexities are wiped out when you homogenize with a chapter title like the one found in *Half the Sky:* "Is Islam Misogynistic?" The chapter itself shows what is wrong with the question. There are so many contradictions. On the one hand, the Prophet Muhammad was progressive for his time, his wife Aisha was a leader in passing on the Islamic tradition, and several first ladies of Muslim countries are now leaders in education; Muslim women had property rights long before European women; 98 percent of people surveyed in Morocco, Lebanon, Egypt, and Jordan believe girls have educational rights equal to boys; Islamic feminists are reinterpreting the Qur'an; and outspoken Saudi women scold Kristof for being patronizing. On the other hand, women's testimonies carry less weight in court, a quarter of Egyptians in one survey thought women could not be president (this was long before there were free elections in 2012), and suicide bombers apparently believe they will have virgins in heaven—not realizing, says Kristof, that they have actually been promised grapes.[45]

Kristof (and I cite him as being the author of the chapter because it is based on his journalism) cannot answer the question he poses because it is impossibly broad. Imagine posing this question about more-familiar religious traditions. If you asked, "Is Christianity misogynistic?" many feminist theologians who have complained bitterly about God the Father would say yes. Historians like Elaine Pagels have found evidence of the way the church turned patriarchal in its early centuries, suppressing earlier visions such as those carried in the Gnostic Gospels buried in Egypt.[46] But by Christianity, would one mean Calvinists, Catholics, or the Anglicans now converting madly to Catholicism to flee the ordination of women? Would one be referring to Salem Puritans with their witch trials, Mother Teresa, or Hillary Clinton? Would one be asking about evangelists zealously working against sex trafficking or joining Quiverfull? Christian women in Quiverfull (backed by the American Council on Biblical Manhood and Womanhood, which was founded in 1987 to fight feminist influences in the evangelical church and spreads its message through the sixteen-million-member Southern Baptist Convention and the Campus Crusade for Christ) seek fulfillment through self-abnegation to husbands and having as many children as possible.[47] On the home page of the movement's website are quotes from the Bible.

Similarly, the lack of specification would be obvious if we asked if Judaism is "misogynistic." A chapter of *Half the Sky* opens with a passage from Deuteronomy that prescribes the stoning of non-virgin brides. Appiah introduces several similar quotes from the Old Testament.[48] But none of these authors has taken up the cause of oppressed Jewish women, or questioned proud proof of the continuity of Judaism that is pinned on genetic markers passed down from father to son among the priestly group known as Cohens.[49] Nor did they think we should intervene on behalf of Hassidic women who cover their hair with wigs and their legs with thick tights, even while small groups of nonreform women push the boundaries of Jewish law by leading prayers in New York basements. Everyone knows that many of the most radical twentieth-century American feminists have been Jewish, or half-Jewish.[50] There is variety. There are internal debates. History is everywhere. Outsiders don't assume they should dictate.

The simple substitution reveals the question to be wrong. So why do so few blanch when Hirsi Ali blames Islam for every violence suffered by a Muslim woman whether she is in Amsterdam or Nairobi, Kuala Lumpur or Sweden? Proudly announcing her atheism as critical to her own freedom, Ayaan Hirsi Ali even proposes, in an odd moment, that "Christian leaders now wasting precious time and resources on a futile exercise of interfaith dialogue with the self-appointed leaders of Islam should redirect their efforts to converting as many Muslims as possible to Christianity, introducing them to a God who rejects Holy War,"[51] presumably, the God of the Crusades.

What Muslim Woman?

IslamLand does not exist. Since I was five, I have been spending time in places that would fall on that other side of the great divide between IslamLand and the West. As an anthropologist, I have done fieldwork in several communities in Egypt. I have visited relatives in Jordan. I have gone to school in Lebanon. In the women I have known, I do not recognize "the Muslim woman" of Hirsi Ali's books or what miriam cooke has, tongue in cheek, called "the Muslimwoman."[52] Would it be Hirsi Ali's mother, frail and old now, living on handouts back in Somalia, surrounded by desert scrub and nieces who cook for her and sweep her house? Would it be the current president of Bangladesh or the Oxford-trained former prime minister of Pakistan, who was assassinated in 2007? Is it the filmmakers of Palestine or the writers of Lebanon, the Bedouin women in Egypt who weave rugs of extraordinary beauty and sing poignant songs about love, or the fashion bloggers of Qatar featured in *Harper's Bazaar Arabia?* The glossy spread about them in 2010, titled "Abaya Accessories," reported on the young women who reach into their own closets for the latest designer wear about which to blog. Their elegant black abayas are set off by leopard platform heels by Christian Louboutin. Their Chanel sunglasses vie for attention with their Alexander McQueen rings and "limited edition" Fendi two-tone python peekaboo bags. Are these the

Muslim women Hirsi Ali implores her readers to think about when she pities "the *others* . . . still locked in the world I have left behind"?[53]

There are many suffering women who are Muslims. Zaynab, in the village in Upper Egypt, has to deal with police harassment. My aunt suffers silently a great injustice and sings about deep personal losses. Refugees beg on the streets in Beirut and Amman. The suffering of some of these women is not totally unconnected to expectations about gender enshrined in the Qur'an or cultures in the Muslim world, or sometimes justified in terms of interpretations of Islamic law. But in all cases, their suffering has more complex causes. These are the sorts of causes we should explore.

I think of Amal, for example, another village woman in Egypt whom I have known for twenty years.[54] I always stay in the hamlet where she lives when I am there. Our daughters are close friends. If a foreign journalist had come on assignment to her village a few years ago, he might have written a dire column about her. He would have found her barely able to walk. Wan and in pain, she had just undergone what they call a "woman's operation." The doctor had told her she needed an operation that would cost 1,050 Egyptian pounds, the equivalent of $200. She explained to me quietly, "You know that wasn't possible for us." She put off seeing a doctor for too long and then finally had to have the operation. She had it done at the ramshackle local public hospital. People believe the conditions in the local hospital there are worse than in the private clinics. With structural adjustment, the Egyptian government has been forced to reduce funding of public health care so that patients now have to pay for the medicines and the anesthetic. Amal's husband defensively minimized the difference between the free surgery at the hospital and the costly one at the private clinic. "It's just the hands that cut," he insisted. "And it's just a few cuts." He was embarrassed that they could not afford the clinic, so he went on about the expensive medicines he had bought to care for her. He talked about how much time he had spent at the hospital in the seven days she was there.

Amal had spent a month in bed. She was just able to get up, but would have to take it easy for three months. And she was not to lift anything heavy for nine months, she explained. The rest of her family had picked up her responsibilities. Fleetingly, I thought about the impact on her conjugal life. She had a hard time mustering a smile when her husband joked that he'd have to take a second wife. Was this, finally, a sign of Islam's oppression of women?

Amal had been married for about twenty-three years at the time. She and her husband had distinct roles and responsibilities. Since I had known her, Amal had worked hard. She cut fodder for her sheep; fed and milked the water buffalo; raised chickens, geese, and rabbits; did the weekly marketing; washed clothes; cleaned house; and cooked—not to mention raising five children. Could this be seized upon as a sign of her suffering as a *Muslim* woman?

I thought about her husband. He too worked very hard. I almost never saw him idle, except when he showered and shaved to get ready for Friday prayers at the mosque. For more than twenty years, he had worked in archeological restoration with a foreign mission. They still had not given him any social security, health insurance, or benefits. Paid a tiny fraction of what his European colleagues with the same masonry skills got in salary, he set off on his bicycle every morning at 6:00 A.M. for a trip that took him an hour. Burnished by the sun, his muscles bulged from the heavy stonework of his job and the hoeing, irrigating, harvesting, and house building he did every day after work and on his days off. While Amal takes care of the animals and the house and does a bit of sewing on the side, he does the plumbing and electricity, makes his own rope from palm fiber to tie up the harvest, and makes bricks by hand from mud and straw. For ten years, he and Amal have been working surreptitiously to reclaim a bit of desert land to grow vegetables for the family and to lay the foundations for a house for his eldest son. The work for both of them was especially hard in the days when their children were too young to help, all in school.

A journalist meeting Amal the day I returned to the village to find her in pain might have seized on Amal's pain, her inadequate medical attention, or her husband's heartless joke. They disturbed me too. But I know that her medical and financial problems have complex causes, not simple gender discrimination and certainly not any kind of "war on women." As we talked, I discovered that she had been forced to sell one of her own sheep to help pay for the medical expenses. It is worth pointing out that the sheep are hers to raise and profit from. And this was not the first occasion on which I had heard her husband joke about taking another wife. Sometimes as my husband and I were sitting and drinking tea with the family after they'd invited us to supper, Amal's husband would ask if we could find him one of those rich European women who support other young men in his tourist region. Did Amal take this request seriously? She knew as well as we did that every time he said something like this, his daughters would pounce on him and pretend to pummel him, teasing him that they'd beat him up and run his new wife out of town if he dared. It was empty talk, even though technically his right. What lay behind his comment was sheer exhaustion and frustration about how unfair it was that others in this unequal world had it easier.

Like most women in the community, Amal says her prayers regularly and covers her hair. She does not often go places without her husband's knowledge, though she never has to ask permission. Social obligations in this tight-knit community are demanding. Women drop whatever they are doing when they hear of a death, an illness, a return from the hospital, a family crisis, an engagement party, a wedding, or a welcome party for those returning from the pilgrimage. The moral ideal that women belong in the home is trumped by the value of caring about kin and neighbors. Their reputations, and those of their family, are on the line. No husband would dream of standing in the way.[55]

So why is Amal not appropriate as a representative of "the Muslim woman" of IslamLand? She suffers. She has troubles. She has to make compromises. She is poor and hardworking. But it is clear that she and her husband are close, despite the jokes. They are not unusual in this village, though each couple's circumstances are as unique as their personalities. Amal and her husband work hard and share in all family decisions. He is protective of her. His children proudly tell the story of how he had beaten with a stick a large snake that was dripping venom on their mother's face as the two of them slept out in the unfinished house they are building across the field from the family home. They also put their children's well-being first. Not long before Amal's operation, someone came to ask for their eldest daughter's hand. They had outfitted her with everything a bride is expected to bring into the marriage—the kitchen appliances being the most expensive. They went into debt making sure she had a great wedding, complete with a DJ. That was why they were especially short of money for the surgery. A couple of years later, I found them delighted by their first granddaughter. Amal's husband posed proudly for my camera, kissing the baby on her cheek. Raising this family, the center of their lives, was a team effort. It had not always been easy and they did not always get along perfectly. But they had sacrificed for each other and for their children.

Superficial vignettes and extreme cases tell us little about the variety of ways women experience their lives and the contexts we must appreciate in order to make sense of their suffering.[56] The exceptions, the aberrations, and the signs of what for good reason we call "inhumanity" are disturbing everywhere. We are right to want to see them disappear. It is feminism's achievement to have shown that they are often gendered. But it must not be forgotten that such abuses of women are distributed across cultural, national, and religious boundaries. The war for women should not be selective.

Hirsi Ali claims to speak from her own experience as "a Muslim woman"—one who has managed to escape this role. Her experiences are instructive. They teach us something about Somalis in exile and about immigrants in Europe, but not about "the Muslimwoman." She is exceptional in more than her acumen, determination, and rejection of family and religion. Her life, as she tells it in her autobiographies, has been difficult. Her mother was erratic and angry that her politically active husband had abandoned her to raise the kids on her own. She suffered skin diseases and often hit her children. Hirsi Ali's brother is by her own admission manic-depressive; her younger sister died after several years of depression and psychotic attacks. Many of her aunts and uncles, she reports, had what Somalis call "madness." She lays all problems at the door of Islam and polygamy. But her own contingent personal story tells us that there is much more to it than religion.[57]

Primed for Moral Crusades

To understand why the new common sense about going to war for women's rights seems so right despite the flaws I have laid out—whether its reliance on the myth of a homogeneous place called IslamLand or its selective and moralizing imperative to

save others far away—we need to look sideways. Two other
popular ways of talking about violations of women's rights that
have emerged in the past few decades lend support to the kinds
of representations of women's suffering that writers like these
present. On one side is a political and moral enterprise with tremendous legitimacy in our era: international human rights. Wom-
en's rights language and the institutional apparatus that has developed in tandem have been associated with human rights since
the 1990s: feminists began to campaign with the slogan "women's
rights are human rights." Their successes have led some in legal
studies to detect the emergence of governance feminism (GF), the
domination by radical feminists of legal, bureaucratic, and political institutions around the world.[58] At the center of this set of
institutions is a claim to universal values.

On the other side is a more sordid industry. This is the world
of mass-market commercial publishing. This industry commissions and promotes a genre of books that one can identify, and
judge, by their covers. We see them at airport bookstores. The
copycat images are of women wearing black or white veils, showing only their eyes—or sometimes one eye. The titles are variations on a theme: *A True Story of Life behind the Veil in Saudi
Arabia; Sold: One Woman's True Account of Modern Slavery; My
Forbidden Face; Without Mercy; Burned Alive; Married by Force.*
They are often personal stories "as told to." Disdained by respectable writers like the ones I consider in this chapter, I would argue
that this genre underwrites their work.

How have these two institutions molded the imaginations of
the women being recruited to *Half the Sky*'s battle against "the
most shocking and widespread human-rights violation of our
age"? Wildly different as they are, these two adjacent discourses
have paved the way for the enthusiastic reception of the new
common sense about the transcendent rightness of going to war

for women, especially Muslim women. Some historians of the
Anglo-American world at the time of abolition argue that there
is a link between an emerging "pornography of pain" that took
shape in the late eighteenth and early nineteenth centuries and
humanitarian reform efforts. Karen Halttunen sees such images
of suffering as an "integral aspect of the humanitarian sensibility."[59] In the twenty-first century, I argue in Chapter 3, it is a genre
of "pulp nonfiction" about the abused Muslim woman and girl
that links up with the utopian discourse of universal human
rights to help create the new common sense and sensibility.[60]

Authorizing Moral Crusades

How do the architects of this new common sense about going to war for women gain such authority? Why have so many come to agree with their arguments— which manufacture consent for international engagements across the Muslim world—when there are flaws in their reasoning, silences in their stories, partiality in their representations of women's problems, and when a myth lies at their core?

These writers make their premises unassailable by drawing on a language of human and women's rights that now has tremendous currency. This language insists that people around the world must learn how to be just and to measure up in a universal metric of humanity that is defined, in part, by aspirations for gender equality and women's freedom. If the authority for this moral crusade to rescue women in other parts of the world, and usually from their cultures or traditions, depends on associating itself with the high ground of universal rights talk that has been forged in a range of international institutions, its emotional persuasiveness derives from the bedrock on which such advocates build. This is best expressed in a massively popular genre of writing about the wrongs other women suffer—particularly Muslim women. The genre is graphic, even pornographic.

The two languages, one abstract and disinterested, the other affective, bleed into each other in the new common sense about rescuing women. Key to the vocabularies of both are consent, choice, and freedom. The central drama is the difference between those who choose and those who do not, between those who are free and those who live in bondage. The way this drama unfolds has consequences for the crusade.

We need to consider both of these languages. But the popular genre of writing on the abused Muslim woman is particularly fascinating. We can think of it as a form of trafficking: literary trafficking. The weakness of the analogy between Atlantic slavery and today's gender oppression that I discuss in Chapter 2 is overcome here by some surprising similarities between slave plantation pornography and this genre. I therefore reflect in this chapter on the political contexts in which these books are produced and ask how they might be affecting those who consume them. I also read against the grain of their dark titillations and strange alchemy—in which the exceptional becomes general—to glimpse even in such formulaic stories another way of thinking about the victim/heroines who are the objects of such intense concern.[1]

The Utopian High Ground

We live in an era in which the idea of universal human rights has been broadly accepted. The very success of the institutionalization of the concept in myriad organizations and its virtual monopoly on the high ground of global morality led feminists beginning in the 1980s to try to link the struggle for women's rights and well-being to human rights. Activists working in the international arena waged a successful campaign to declare women's rights as human rights. They did so through drafting conventions, installing themselves in vast bureaucratic institutions, and putting in place mechanisms of accountability. If the evils of gender discrimination now seem so obvious and the language of women's rights has such authority, we have to thank these conventions and campaigns. Among the heroines of the new common sense about global women's rights are the women activists involved in grassroots and international institutions dedicated to promoting rights.[2]

To get a sense of what the campaigns linking women's and human rights entail, we can take a quick look at some key arguments put forth by influential feminists.[3] One prominent legal scholar who invokes universal rights in campaigns against pornography and rape actually begins in a surprising way. She criticizes the Universal Declaration of Human Rights (UDHR), faulting it and the institutions that support it, both national and international, for being patriarchal. Her plaintive question, "When will women be human?" is meant to challenge not only the failure to apply the UDHR universally but also its partial or exclusionary vision of the human. After melodramatically cataloging in the first person plural all the abuses women in particular suffer in what she sees as a global war against women (the same sorts of abuses Nicholas Kristof and Sheryl WuDunn cover so well in *Half the Sky* and to which Anthony Appiah's *The Honor Code* gestures), Catherine MacKinnon asserts, "Women need full human status in social reality. For this, the Universal Declaration of Human Rights must see the ways women distinctively are deprived of human rights as a deprivation of humanity . . . for human rights to be universal, both the reality it [the UDHR] challenges and the standard it sets need to change."[4]

Charlotte Bunch, who articulated most clearly the connection between women's and human rights, mobilized some of the same arguments. In spearheading the campaign in the 1990s, she argued that women's issues should not be treated as separate issues; they are more properly understood as neglected aspects of global agendas for human rights and development. Governments should be committed to women's equality as a basic human right. Sex discrimination and violence against women, she charged, had been excluded from the human rights agenda until the 1990s because people had failed to see the oppression of women as political; instead, they took it as natural.[5]

Both of these advocates of women's rights called for a universally applied standard of gender equality. They did so by appealing to the universal rights of the human. One of the most intelligently debated statements on the urgency of making gender equity a universal social priority—a goal promoted by *Half the Sky*'s "call to arms"—is Susan Moller Okin's essay, "Is Multiculturalism Bad for Women?" In this essay, which Ayaan Hirsi Ali found persuasive but many others have contested, Okin pits feminism against any and all arguments for group rights or cultural rights. She lines up the liberal ideal of sex equity, defined as the possibility for women to "live as fulfilling and as freely chosen lives as men can"[6] (which she grants is not yet fully realized anywhere) against culture. She locates culture only outside the West—only outside of liberal states.[7] Although Okin does not appeal explicitly to universal human rights, as do the other two, her argument rests on the assumption that liberal culture is the acultural norm and should be the universal standard by which to measure societies. Those who fall short are the barbarians outside the gates and even some who have breached the gates—immigrants. They are, unfortunately for women, in thrall of their cultures or religions.[8]

Okin accuses all cultures of being patriarchal—defined by men's control over women. Discrimination against women in the home and family is especially pernicious, she argues, because such practices "are never likely to emerge in public, where courts can enforce their rights and political theorists can label such practices as illiberal and therefore unjustified violations of women's physical or mental integrity."[9] But she adds that "while virtually all of the world's cultures have distinctly patriarchal pasts some—mostly, though by no means exclusively, Western liberal cultures—have departed far further from them than others."[10] She implies that the lives of women of the non-West, where communities or governments fail to support their rights or to allow them a flourishing life (in the terms defined), are particularly deficient. Here we see an overlap with the new common sense. There is little doubt about who has the right answers for women and who should lead the moral crusade for gender equality or for the end of violence against women.

Another strand of liberal feminist thought that Martha Nussbaum represents invokes universality differently. The best way to promote gender justice, Nussbaum argues, is to insist that there are basic human capabilities and that our task is to reform societies and nation-states so that they will promote human flourishing in terms of these capabilities. She subscribes to what she calls the Aristotelian position on "the proper function of government, according to which its task is to make available to each and every member of the community the basic, necessary conditions of the capability to choose and live a fully good human life, with respect to each of the major human functions included in that fully good life."[11] She wants to extend this function of government to modern nation-states in an international regime of governance.

Nussbaum distinguishes her approach from the rights approach, explaining that "capabilities . . . have a very close relationship to human rights, as understood in contemporary international discussions. In effect they cover the terrain covered by both the so-called first-generation rights (political and civil liberties) and the so-called second-generation rights (economic and social rights)."[12] Alert to the criticisms that have been raised about rights talk, Nussbaum then argues that the strategic advantage of talking instead about capabilities is that it "bypasses the troublesome debate" about the derivation of "rights" talk from the Western Enlightenment.[13] The capabilities approach, she maintains, "is not strongly linked to one particular cultural and historical tradition, as the language of rights is believed to be."[14]

Appealing to universals is a powerful tool, whether by invoking the *Universal* Declaration of Human Rights of the United Nations,[15] that authorizing document for the discourses and practices of human rights, or by insisting that our obligation is to promote (and judge countries and societies on the basis of their success in enabling) the functioning of human capabilities. What is universal should or does apply or exist uniformly in a geographic sense. It is not something local. What is universal seems neutral in that it belongs to everyone and anyone, not to someone particular. The opposite would be something partisan that favors one group or grows out of its interests or traditions. In these everyday meanings, the universal is understood through a distinction from another term. It is the stronger, more encompassing, more general term. It is also the more abstract term because universals stand above particulars, and therefore lend tremendous authority to those who claim them.

The new common sense borrows from this powerful discourse of universal rights that appears not to represent special interests.[16] However, the "silent referent," as Dipesh Chakrabarty has put it, for the universal in schemas like Okin's and Nussbaum's is an imagined and idealized liberal democracy along with a form of modern culture and reason that, through the language of universalism, it helps create.[17] One must be critical of gender subordination. As I argue in Chapter 1, however, we need to consider how women's desires and ideals of the human are formed differently, and formed by a long history of geopolitical entanglements among the specific groups that are represented today as so separate. How have they produced and shaped each other such that they stand now in particular relationships to each other? The language of universals and the dialects of women's human rights and human development are part of this set of long historical relationships; they do not stand neutrally above, nor do the values they promote.[18]

The Fantastic World of "Pulp Nonfiction"

If the new common sense about the urgency of battling for women's rights and equality gains authority through its association with this international consensus on "universal" rights and the value of "choosing freely," it draws surreptitiously on a different discourse of the American and European public spheres for its emotional appeal. Published by trade presses, reviewed widely, and adopted by book clubs and women's reading groups, a lurid genre of writing on abused women—mostly Muslim—exploded onto the scene in the 1990s and took off after 9/11.

The recurrent and defining themes of this genre are force and bondage. At one end are gentle memoirs like Azar Nafisi's *Reading Lolita in Tehran,* journalistic accounts like Asne Seierstad's *The Bookseller of Kabul,* and polemics like Ayaan Hirsi Ali's *The Caged Virgin* and its sequels. These have been met with critical acclaim. At the less respectable end are books with an even wider readership. The literary scholar Dohra Ahmad has called this genre "pulp nonfiction," which may be a misnomer. Here, we are plunged into dystopic worlds of violent abuse, our guides the Muslim girls who have suffered and escaped. In a study of the lighter books in this genre, Ahmad faults the public for regularly mistaking these literary productions for ethnographies of actual people and places; readers presume they are finding out something about other cultures when they read such books. Sometimes these books are even assigned in schools. Although there is some variety within the genre, even the few works that are sensitively attuned to the particulars of a place and sympathetic to their heroines, Ahmad argues, get absorbed by readers into a generalized vision of what, in Chapter 2, I call "IslamLand."

There is a long tradition of representing Muslim women in the West. Scholars give it a name: gendered Orientalism. Pictorial as well as literary, what is constant is that Muslim women are portrayed as culturally distinct, the mirror opposites of Western women.[19] In the nineteenth century, the depictions took two forms: women of the Orient were either portrayed as downtrodden victims who were imprisoned, secluded, shrouded, and treated as beasts of burden or they appeared in a sensual world of excessive sexuality—as slaves in harems and the subjects of the gaze of lascivious and violent men, not to mention those looking in. Christian missionary women appealed for support by decrying the oppression of their Muslim sisters in the first register. Artists and writers, and even the colonial postcard photographers of the early twentieth century, preferred the sensual and sexual.[20]

The late twentieth- and early twenty-first-century mass-market paperbacks echo these themes but have their own distinct style and character. Their protagonists are, as Ahmad notes, "plucky individualists" with feminist ideals who do not want to remain trapped in their strange and sordid worlds. They want freedom, like the "native informant" celebrities such as Ayaan Hirsi Ali and Irshad Manji, whose denunciations of Islam as causing the oppression of women have been so warmly welcomed and whose careers have been bolstered by powerful institutions. Their personal stories are, as Saba Mahmood notes, always told in terms of emancipation.[21] In the darker versions, these books contain graphic scenes of violence and abuse, much of it sexualized.

It is hard to know whether to treat these "memoirs" as non-fiction; that is how they are billed. Some are unreliable because they are based on repressed memories. Many of the protagonists are known only by first names. Some books are based on "secret knowledge." Some, such as Norma Khouri's *Honor Lost,* which I discuss at length in Chapter 4, have been exposed as hoaxes. Almost all the books are cowritten with journalists or professional ghostwriters. They are, at the least, mediated in complex ways. To the extent that they may reflect real experiences or incidents, they are as disturbing as any incidents of abuse that we read about in our newspapers, legal cases, or psychology case studies of pathological behavior.

But the books work hard not to let us make these comparisons. Although they are told in the first person of individual women, the traumas and abuses they catalog do not present themselves to readers as unique to these individuals. They are always contextualized by culture—the authenticating details of eking out a living on a bare mountaintop in Yemen; the exotic color of Moroccan weddings and exorcisms; the cloistered opulence of Saudi Arabian palaces; the damp cellars of Pakistani immigrant communities in the north of England; the fields of rural Palestine. It does not seem to matter that many of the details of geography or tradition are wrong, or that foreign words are misspelled. The placement in these locations marks the abuses as cultural or collective. The bad men who abuse our heroines are Muslim—even if Moroccan, Pakistani, Jordanian, or Yemeni. Without offering a general picture of the communities in which our heroines live, since these are just personal stories, these memoirs cannot give readers any indication that such abuses—whether incest, rape, beatings, or other cruelties—might be exceptional, or might be considered as horrifying in those communities as they would be in ours. Without the contextual information we draw on to judge similar stories of abuse and violence in North America or Europe, we are led to attribute these abuses to the culture at large. This is the selective process that Leti Volpp has called "blaming culture for bad behavior."[22]

Contrary to the message of uniformity that their copycat covers convey and this cultural framing implies, to someone like me who is familiar with the kinds of communities or the countries in which they are set, the stories seem radically specific. When one reads against the grain, there are plenty of hints that they are unsettling and exceptional, if based on truth. Take the trilogy of memoirs beginning with *Sold* that tell the terrible tale of two girls "sold" into marriage in Yemen. These are daughters of a British working-class mother and a violent, gambling Yemeni immigrant father. Although the villain is the heartless Arab man (this was pre-9/11, so Muslims had not yet become the obligatory enemy), the memoirs mention that the families who "bought" the underage brides were from a despised group. In the third book, it is remarked in passing that this is a poor country where three-quarters of the men leave home to look for work. Surely this must produce an unusual situation for women, not to mention the minority of men left behind. The unhappy grooms to whom these miserable girls were "sold" via their émigré fathers live in a peculiarly isolated, demanding part of Yemen.

What might such details tell us? As with poor farmers in remote areas in other parts of the world, it may be hard to find wives. In Korea, for example, they must import them because few local women want the hard work and traditionalism of such communities.[23] It would seem from the story of Zana and

Nadia, and the other British/Yemeni girls whose stories the books allude to, that the most desperate of the Yemenis may be forced to draw on a pool of girls of Yemeni parentage who know little about the place beforehand. For someone like me, it is puzzling that the girls are totally ignorant about the basics of Islamic marriage. They have not given their consent, they have not received their marriage gift (mahr), and they never had wedding celebrations. This is quite shocking for anyone who knows the Middle East, where weddings are the highlights of social life, even among the poor, and marriage is regulated and recognized.

These stories each use a peculiar situation without marking its radical specificity or lack of representativeness and without giving much context. (The girls discover later, for example, that in the cities, women dress well, eat well, are educated and have leisure, and some are feminists.) The result is that these best sellers that trade on images of bondage—Zana's *Sold;* its sequel, *A Promise to Nadia;* and their mother's *Without Mercy: A Mother's Struggle against Modern Slavery*—lead readers to surmise that forced marriage is normal in the Yemeni community, that this is Yemeni culture,[24] and these women must be rescued.

A Taste of (for) Force

The genre is characterized by consistent themes: coercion and lack of consent, absence of choice, and unfreedom. To give the flavor of these works and to suggest how the peculiar play with force may affect readers of the genre, I begin with a typical scene. It is from a sequel to *Sold,* the story of these two British girls "sold" into marriage in Yemen by their father. Writing her own account, the girls' mother Miriam, who lives in Birmingham, explains why she had to escape from the brutal Arab father of her seven children. She has just chosen to be sterilized. Her husband comes home drunk, and she confronts him again about her two missing daughters. He tells her to forget them and locks her in the room. Miriam recounts:

> He was close now, leaning towards me, his beery breath engulfing me. I sat, terrified, on the sofa. He came closer and held out his hand. I slapped at it furiously, hoping he would go away. Instead he pulled me up, his good thumb and middle finger around my throat. I fought him off, pushing him to the floor. He grabbed at my dressing-gown in a vain effort to save his fall, pulling the material apart, tearing it down its length . . . "Take your clothes off! All of them!" Muthana growled deeply.
>
> . . . Well, if he thought I was going to make this into some fantasy trip, he was mistaken. I flung my nightie into a heap on the floor, contemptuously. His eyes travelled over my body, settling on the scar from the operation to sterilize me. He reached out and touched the scarred flesh. Instinctively I slapped his hand away. He laughed and touched it again. I went to slap at his hand again when, suddenly, he grabbed my hand by the wrist and pulled me sharply to the floor, rolling me over onto my back and jumping on top of me immediately in a quick movement.
>
> I scrunched my eyes shut and clanged my fists at my side. I lay rigid on the floor as he indulged himself, crying out in his pleasure as I cried out in my shame.[25]

Marital rape epitomizes absence of consent, just as does forced marriage, the fate of her daughters. It is the latter that has captured the attention of women's groups and government officials across Europe.[26] One of the fullest treatments in "pulp nonfiction" comes from France.

Married by Force by Leila (no last name) is even more graphic in its violence than Miriam's account. The story of a troubled French girl of Moroccan parentage, the book recounts incidents of violence and terrible cruelty in the family in which Leila grows up. Her father is a disciplinarian; her brothers are abusive. She wants to be like French girls, but they won't let her. Her parents force her to marry a man from Morocco, a husband she hates. She has a frightening encounter with a sex maniac imam hired to exorcise her because she objects. The book is written (with a journalist, of course) in the aftermath of Leila's suicide attempts and stays in a psychiatric hospital. Like Zana, *Sold*'s heroine, Leila finally escapes her forced marriage and finds freedom. It is then that she tells us her story.

The reader is treated to some horrific scenes between husband and wife. Trying desperately to provoke him to divorce her, Leila goads her husband and insults him mercilessly. She makes him sleep in the lounge and won't let him touch her. They argue all the time. She recounts the turning point: "One evening, at midnight, I was quietly taking a bath to relax and I'd forgotten to lock the bathroom door. He began to start a fight, me in the bath, him on the other side of the door, being spiteful."[27] They exchange insults until she reveals to him a secret about his own mother. He calls Morocco to confirm and then is "furious, his eyes popping out of his head. 'Bloody bitch, bloody tart, open this door!' "

He charges into the bathroom and shoves her head underwater. She scratches his face. He throws her onto the floor and punches and kicks her, yelling, "Is this what you want? Here, take that and that." She describes her feelings, lying naked on the floor and being beaten, with a weirdly out-of-place metaphor meant to position this bad marriage squarely in the specific context of Islamic barbarity: "It was the total shame, humiliation and horror of a woman being stoned to death."[28]

In another, more fanciful book, lightened by a likable heroine who has a weakness for whiskey and extravagant shopping at Bergdorf Goodman, the theme of force is also lashed onto Middle Eastern men. *Desert Royal* is the fourth in a series of popular books by Jean Sasson that are presented as the first person accounts (as told to) of "Sultana," a wealthy feminist Saudi Arabian princess who wishes to expose to the world what is really going on in her society. It includes incidents that capture the essential unfreedom of women there. A sexual charge runs through it.

The most sensational scene is a visit Sultana and her two teenage daughters pay to a distant cousin. They have heard rumors that he has built a spectacular palace to replicate Paradise, and they want to see it. Their visit is disastrous. Besides finding thousands of caged birds that one daughter madly rescues, they come across a pavilion that is signposted "Stallions." Looking for horses, the other daughter discovers a "harem" of sex slaves, "purchased" from their families in Asia. The young women in tawdry halter tops and negligees are guarded by an exotic and gnomic Sudanese eunuch. Our heroines wish to set these young women free but are thwarted when they learn that their passports have been taken.

As Sultana explains in her apparently evenhanded condemnation of patriarchy, "I knew that it was not a simple matter to come between men and their sexual desires. It is the natural inclination of many men, and not only in the Middle East, to seek out young girls or young women as sexual conquests."[29] Yet she surmises that their wealthy owner wants these girls for a special cultural reason. In his eyes, she suggests, "these young women were like the seductive virgins called 'houris' that are described in the Koran. I suspected that I was looking at a stage intended to provide untold delights for Faddel. Yet this must be the scene of unspeakable hell for these women held against their will."[30]

Like today's Islamic feminists, Sultana didactically asserts that most of these horrid practices involving force are violations of true Islam. Captives are to be treated well, even if animals, she comments in relation to the caged birds. On the question of consent, she says, "Our religion forbids the forcing of females into a union not of their liking, but, like much that is good in our Islamic faith, this is misinterpreted or simply ignored."[31]

In this short book, we are treated to other stories of forced sex, the most disturbing being the discovery by Sultana of her nephews' rape of a Pakistani girl in the servants' tent set up during a family outing in the desert. Hearing a woman's screams in the quiet night, Sultana and her sister go to investigate. In their flashlight beam, they surprise two men assaulting a woman while another stands by. Her description is (porno)graphic, hinting at pedophilia: "One man was covering the poor victim's mouth in an effort to silence her cries . . . the second man who was on top of the naked woman gradually turned to face us . . . The poor girl had been stripped of her clothing. She lay naked and defenceless before us. Her face was a frightful mask of terror, and her delicate frame was racked with sobs. She was so small that she appeared to be more a child than a woman."[32] As Sultana confides, she knew that some of her nephews had traveled to Thailand, the Philippines, India, and Pakistan for prostitutes, "but this was the first time I had heard of any of these nephews actually purchasing a woman to bring her into our kingdom as a sexual slave."[33]

Literary Trafficking
The public appetite for such depictions of sordid and brutal treatment of women by Muslim or Arab men is disquieting. Unlike the many good ethnographies written by anthropologists about women's everyday lives in these countries, these "memoirs" of suffering by oppressed Muslim women enjoy spectacular and strangely enduring popularity.[34] *Sold,* by the Birmingham girl who escaped from Yemen with her mother's help after thirteen

years, was published in 1991. Zana Muhsen and Andrew Crofts, a professional ghostwriter, are listed as coauthors. The book was picked up by two new publishers in 1994 and reprinted almost twice a year until 2010. A follow-up was published as *A Promise to Nadia* (the sister who stayed behind). And then their mother wrote her own story (with Jana Wain, with whom she set up an organization to rescue girls kidnapped and sent abroad by their foreign fathers), from which I quoted. Published in 1995, it has been reprinted almost annually, with spikes in 1996 and 2003. Jean Sasson's *Princess* trilogy and its sequel have sold millions.

More disquieting is the constant reference to sex. The focus on sexual abuse has made some of the memoir writers award-winning activists. Jasvinder Sanghera, the author of *Shame* and *Daughters of Shame*, who publicized the problem of forced marriage, has received many awards for inspiration and bravery, not to mention an honorary degree from the University of Derby. The most amazing case is that of Hannah Shah, author of *The Imam's Daughter*. She went public in 2009 with her gruesome story of sexual abuse by her father, an imam in North England of rural Pakistani origin. She says she speaks to gatherings of 5,000.[35]

What makes these books so appealing and their authors so celebrated when the writing is often appalling and the stories so extreme? To understand this, we have to place them in the contexts in which they are being read. These books are caught up in a charged international political field in which Arabs, Muslims, and particular others are seen as dangers to the West. Feminists praise these far-fetched books. Fay Weldon, for example, endorsed *Desert Royal* as "a book to move you to tears." On the back cover of *Without Mercy: A Mother's Struggle against Modern Slavery*, we find Weldon again: "What is astonishing about the book . . . is the account of how downtrodden, defeated Miriam [the kidnapped girls' mother] suddenly came to buoyant life." It should not surprise us to discover that Fay Weldon joined the right-wing Zionist Daniel Pipes on the board of an anti-Muslim Danish group that was formed after the controversy of the cartoons of the Prophet Muhammad.[36]

The "personal letter" from Sultana that prefaces *Desert Royal* openly engages international politics. Sultana frames her book as an invitation to the West: "I hope you are not weary of hearing our tragic tales, for we are gaining small freedoms here and there, and we continue to need your attention and your support for years to come. Without media attention and political intervention from other lands, most of our men would be most joyous to return to a time of utter darkness for the females living in Saudi Arabia. It is a sad truth that only when they are forced will our men allow light into our lives."[37]

That books about bad Arabs who force and enslave girls have a special place in the politics of European immigration is revealed by the enthusiastic reception of such books in France. Three of the classics I discuss in this book were first published or publicized there: *Burned Alive*, the memoir by "Souad" and Jacqueline Thibault of an honor killing survivor (discussed in Chapter 4); *Sold*, the book by Zana Muhsen and Andrew Crofts about the girls in Yemen, which became a best seller in France before it took off in England, fanned by Zana's dramatic appearances on the prime-time show *Sacrée Soirée* and the book's publication by a press owned by the son-in-law of the former French president Giscard-D'Estaing;[38] and *Married by Force*, by "Leila" and Marie-Thérèse Cuny. French anxieties about North African immigrants are particularly intense, as these Arab Muslims form a postcolonial underclass in the restless suburbs *(banlieues)*.[39]

Married by Force directs itself to a French audience troubled by immigrants. This native who wants to escape her community confirms their views of the backwardness of the North Africans they detest. Leila explains, for example: "I couldn't stand this life, but other girls who had been married by force like me put up with it . . . All the people who used to talk about integration could never rescue us: they didn't have all the necessary information. Even we girls from the schools and colleges would get hit up, claiming that our parents would 'never' do that to us. They'd never marry us by force to some North African immigrant, because we'd say 'no.' However, in most cases we were forced to say 'yes.' We were caught in a system . . . What can be done to make families adapt and evolve?"[40] In her study of the politics of humanitarianism in France, Miriam Ticktin draws a real-world parallel. She attributes the exceptional success of one territorial asylum case made for Zina, a Frenchwoman of Algerian background who had been forced into marriage, to "the sexually imbued cultural exoticism" that her personal story carried. In a country whose president, Nicolas Sarkozy, had dramatically offered France's protection "to each martyred woman in the world," only this sort of violence followed the proper format. The judge gave precedence to the French Civil Code over the bilateral accords that normally regulate family matters in the case of North Africans.[41]

Even the more sober memoir by Mukhtar Mai from Pakistan, cowritten with the same Marie-Thérèse Cuny who penned *Married by Force* and translated into English as *In the Name of Honor*, with a glowing foreword by Nicholas Kristof, was also first published in France. As her publisher Philippe Robinet explains, "When journalists reported that she had been condemned by her village tribal council to be gang-raped, the horrifying news made headlines around the world . . . My colleagues and I made the arduous journey to the remote village of Meerwàla, where we were welcomed by Mukhtar Mai and her friend Naseem

Akhtar. They were amazed that we had come all the way from France to suggest that we should write a book together, a book that would help her in her struggle."[42]

In Britain in the past decade—with troops stationed in Iraq and Afghanistan, eruptions of public hysteria about Shari'a arbitration courts and burqas, fears of homegrown fanaticism instigated by the 7/11 bombings, and feminist agitation leading to national legislation against honor crimes and forced marriage—it is Pakistanis, not Arabs, who have emerged as the new authors of these memoirs. Andrew Crofts's earlier success with the Yemeni story of Zana led to his involvement in writing another story of abuse and freedom about a British woman from the Pakistani community. The title of Crofts's 2009 book with Saira Ahmed carries the anachronistic flavor of nineteenth-century melodrama: *Disgraced: Forced to Marry a Stranger, Betrayed by My Own Family, Sold My Body to Survive, This Is My Story.*[43] The product description on Amazon.co.uk shouts all the familiar keywords of the genre: "Brought up in a *violent Muslim* household, where family *honour* is all, Saira is watched 24 hours a day. However, an innocent friendship with a boy is uncovered and Saira is sent to Pakistan, punished for dishonouring her family. There, the *nightmare* really begins. *Forced* to marry an older stranger who *rapes* her repeatedly and makes her his round-the-clock *sex slave*, she eventually plots her *escape* but, destitute, has to return to the family home in England . . . Disgraced is the true story of an innocence ruined and a life shattered. But it is also a tale of *survival* told by a woman who has finally discovered her true voice" (emphasis added).[44]

These are the terms of other memoirs in the genre, including *Shame* (2007) and *Daughters of Shame* (2009) by Jasvinder Sanghera, and *Unbroken Spirit: A True Story of a Girl's Struggle to Escape from Abuse* (2008) by Ferzanna Riley. Consider the description of Sameem Ali's *Belonging,* published in 2008. It is about a girl, neglected by her family, who also is sent off to Pakistan: "Aged just thirteen, Sameem was *forced* to marry a complete stranger. When pregnant, two months later, she was made to return to Glasgow where she suffered further *abuse* from her family. After finding true love, Sameem fled the violence at home and *escaped* to Manchester with her young son . . . Belonging is the shocking true story of Sameem's struggle to *break free* from her past and fight back against her upbringing" (emphasis added).[45] This description makes clear that the new genre capitalizes on the current humanitarian focus on the girl child as the exemplary victim, as it displaces onto racial others the lurking fears of pedophilia that are so much of our own everyday worlds where we constantly read reports of the cracking of another child pornography ring.

Slave Pornography

The pornographic element of these memoirs must be considered directly. The dynamics are clearest in one published in Britain in 2009 at the height of the controversy over the Shari'a family arbitration courts. This is the memoir that also most directly challenges the authority of Islam. It is damning, even if it is prefaced (for fear of libel suits?) with the formulaic disclaimer we have come to expect from crusaders of the new common sense. The author notes in her preface, "It is worth pointing out that there are many Muslims in Britain and around the world who have had only good experiences of growing up with their faith, including women who are free to live full, independent and liberated lives and Imams who practice lawfully and have an extremely positive influence on their communities. This book is in no way a denigration of Islam generally. It is a personal account of my own life experiences."[46]

Yet the villain is a horrid imam and the heroine his daughter, alternately described as a caged bird or shackled bride. Typical of its graphic scenes of the repeated rape and abuse of this little girl by her father, an apparent pillar of the Muslim community who locks her in the cellar for his work, is the following: "Dad was like a terrifying predator. I never knew when he would strike. Once I was in the bathroom, when all of a sudden Dad just barged in. He locked the door . . . He took down his shalwar kamiz baggy pants, and plunked himself down on the loo. He forced me to watch as he started touching himself and breathing heavily. I tried to look away, in disgust, but he grabbed me by the hair and forced my face towards him—so close that I could smell that horrible, musty smell that always made me feel so sick. Then he grabbed my hand and forced it around his flesh."[47]

Here we can see most clearly how these memoirs are meant to inspire horror and pity, followed by admiration for the heroine survivors' escapes into freedom. Freedom means escaping not just the Muslim men who torment them but their own communities and cultures. The memoirists confess their rage, self-loathing, and suicide attempts; they often describe themselves as having been rebellious teenagers. This is the feminist difference of the late twentieth century and into the twenty-first, where brown women seem to want to be rescued by their white sisters and friends, to adapt Spivak's famous formulation. If these Muslim girls and women were not portrayed as wanting what we want—love, choice, and sexual freedom (even Christianity or atheism, in the case of Shah and Hirsi Ali)—preferring instead to be dutiful daughters living in the bosom of their families, virgins at marriage, devoted wives partnering with their husbands, or pious individuals seeking to live up to the moral ideals of their religion and living according to its laws, it would be hard for Western readers to identify.[48] It would be hard for publishers to find such eager audiences if they offered us women and girls who challenged our assumptions about what they should want and what is good for them. Western women would no longer be the role models, nor would they feel needed.

The only pious women who appear in this genre of "oppressed Muslim women" stories are the hapless victims, grievously betrayed by their silent God, who appear in the most extreme and controversial examples. The mobilization of the pornography of bondage for anti-immigrant European politics is best seen in a short film that actually breaks with the conventions of faux-cultural and individual specificity of this dystopic genre. The context is the Netherlands in 2004. The writer is the Somali refugee and right-wing politician Ayaan Hirsi Ali. The work in question is the eleven-minute film called *Submission* that catapulted her to notoriety.[49]

Hirsi Ali's signature intellectual style of asserting direct causal connections between decontextualized verses from the Qur'an and abuses of women she has met in shelters or in her fantasies shapes the film. There are four characters: a woman repulsed by the husband chosen for her by her family, for whom marital sex feels like rape; a woman who must submit to beatings by a jealous but philandering husband because he supports her financially; a modest, veiled woman who is subjected to humiliating incest by her uncle; and a woman who fell in love but was abandoned by her lover and then lashed for fornication. The film implies that such abuses are sanctioned, if not directly caused, by Islam, ignoring centuries of interpretation—exegetical, judicial, and everyday—of the Qur'anic verses in question, and silent on the abhorrence of rape or incest in the Islamic legal tradition, not to mention all Muslim societies.

Dutch scholars, especially feminists, have had a lot to say about this film and Hirsi Ali.[50] Some have pointed out that *Submission* offers audiences "an intimate erotic-religious image, which, through the presentation of victims, serves to unveil the cruelty and injustice of Islam."[51] Annelies Moors calls it "hard core Orientalism." The effect of the film depends as much on its visuals as its voice-over.[52] The women are eroticized victims. One lies in the fetal position, her face bruised and her negligee ripped to reveal her breasts. Another stands on a prayer mat, draped only in the sheerest of black gowns. Another is seen from behind, the bare skin of her graceful back carved in a Qur'anic verse. Hirsi Ali proudly claims these images from sadomasochistic fantasy as her own idea, not those of the filmmaker Theo Van Gogh, who lost his life for them.[53]

If we want to appreciate the allure of this genre, we must finally confront this pornographic aspect. With Marcus Wood, we might want to ask, what are the effects of a genre of pornography—with its objectification of subjects and its depiction of violence, sexual force, and bondage—when it is tied to a racial politics and a legacy of colonial or racial domination? What Wood calls "plantation pornography" begins with the role of eighteenth- and nineteenth-century British writings and pictures, often placed in the context of abolitionist literature, that depict the abuse of black bodies in the Atlantic slave trade. It overflows into the present as "a huge business" that has infiltrated literature, fine art, popular publishing, film, video, and BDSM (bondage and discipline, domination and submission, sadism and masochism) cultures on the web.[54]

Wood shows how central this pornographic genre is to the misrepresentation of slavery. His subtle and complex reading of John Gabriel Stedman's 1790 classic text *Narrative of a Five Years Expedition against the Revolted Negroes of Surinam* reveals a troubling double effect: "For Stedman Surinam is a centre of decadence, vice, frivolity, cruelty, sensuality, and the unequal distribution of wealth. His stated aim, or one of them, is to go about and uncover the nature of this perversion and depravity. Yet his attitude is constantly shifting between a moral outrage that is rhetorically constructed and shrill, and an equally hysterical series of attempts to emotionally bond with the slave victim by attempting to appropriate their pain in order to demonstrate his own sensitivity."[55] In fact, he marries a slave, Joanna, whose narrative he makes famous.

We find a similar moral outrage in the pulp nonfiction about the Muslim woman or girl, incited (and, perhaps, excited) by the violations and violence of sex. But given the women authors (all "lapsed" Muslims) and the intended audience (largely female and mostly non-Muslim), we can see a slightly different dynamic of identification and appropriation of pain put into play. This is not the place to debate the virtues, meanings, or effects of pornography and its links to desire. Nor is it my intent to enter the debates in the literature on humanitarianism and the pornography of violence. Key works like Dean's *The Fragility of Empathy after the Holocaust,* ask whether exposure to representations of violence is numbing.[56] Bernstein asks whether the pornography of horror—the decontextualized contemporary images of atrocity that fascinate and repulse—serves the purposes of greater understanding and political orientation or just feeds liberal attachment to one's own moral sensibilities.[57]

All that needs to be noted here is that Western readers, mostly female, find these sensationalist books gripping enough to buy them in the millions. Their identification with Muslim women victims is a feminist one. This gives it a slightly different dynamic than the strangely mediated empathy of the slaver or ex-slaver with the abused slave woman victim that was found in late eighteenth-century works like Stedman's or circulated in the abolition literature. I argue in Chapter 4 on the seductions of "the

honor crime" that such books produce a horror that indeed underwrites a confident sense of moral distinction and Western feminist superiority.

A common enemy—patriarchy—supposedly affirms the sister-
hood. Yet in every set of acknowledgments, the memoirists thank
the English and French men who have been their editors, publishers, ghostwriters, boyfriends, or husbands. So it becomes clear
that it is actually the menacing and irremediably patriarchal Muslim man acting out his cultural script who stands as the clear evil
against which such a sisterly community can bond. Such men,
we know, are targeted as the enemies of our police forces and
our armies. So then we must ask how such identifications erase
readers' roles as perpetrators of violence (insofar as they belong
to a community involved in violence against Muslims abroad
and at home, which these books seem to justify), just as the eigh-
teenth- and nineteenth-century British men who empathized
with slave victims erased their racial and national culpability.
What kinds of emotional complicity do such books encourage
for women? And how do the affects these books induce in their
women readers lead them to support an imperial politics to
which they might not consciously assent if they imagine themselves to be progressive, or at least liberal?

If Wood concluded that the test of the sentimental man in the
eighteenth century was his ability to imaginatively experience the
pain of others, the production of this sublime experience slipping
into the commercial bondage fantasy in relation to slave women,
we might want to consider whether the empathetic responses of
women readers to the narratives of victimized Muslim women
confirm their own morality while shading into a commerce in
Muslims.[58] This commerce takes the form of the proliferation
of books in this genre, as well as the shadowy presence on the
web in sex and bondage sites of a revival of nineteenth-century

Orientalist paintings of harems and slave girls, including those of Jean-Léon Gérôme. The consumers of such books and websites come from the very communities that are involved in military exercises against Muslims around the world, egged on by hysterical hate and fear and accompanied by the criminal profiling of Muslim men even in their own countries. Does the genre help absolve these perpetrators, whose empathetic tears assure them of their morality even as fantasizing about abuse grips them? Does their imaginative suffering over others give them not just some kind of pleasure but the reassurance of utter distinction and separation from those who suffer?

Structuring Desires

Popular literary representations define views and structure feelings about Muslim women and their rights. Memoirs and other forms of pulp nonfiction are not just texts whose themes and tropes relate to earlier popular travel and missionary literature on Muslim women. They are commercial products that publishers market and readers receive in a very specific political context. In this regard, my analysis resembles Dabashi's critique of Azar Nafisi's more literate memoir, *Reading Lolita in Tehran*. Dabashi focuses on the role of the "native" who confirms the absence of rights for Muslim women in Iran by glorifying classics of Western literature, denigrating local culture and traditions. He shows how the cover photograph was cropped to elide its original context (active, politically engaged women students reading about the elections in newspapers) and to suggest instead veiled women secretly reading Western erotic classics.[59] Saba Mahmood describes Nafisi's memoir as "ruthless in its omissions," erasing all traces of the extensive internal social and political critique that has marked the period in Iran that Nafisi purports to chronicle in this "life-quenching portrayal."[60]

In our world of mass media, these iconic abused-but-defiant Muslim women are feted in elite New York circles, featured in glossy magazines, and funded lavishly through personal charity. They warm the hearts of those who promote them, sell their stories, and, as Sherene Razack puts it, "steal their pain" for profit and personal comfort.[61] As I have argued, these stories are key ingredients in the normalization of political and military hostility toward countries like Pakistan, Afghanistan, Iran, and Iraq.

But my analysis of the surprisingly pornographic nature of these memoirs suggests that their most substantial and important effects are the ways they cathect readers, especially Western women, to a fragile emotional truth. Do these readers take comfort in being above such sordid bondage? Blinded to similar stories that occur in our midst, do these books generate fantasies of the possibility of autonomy and freedom from such violence? Voyeurs of cruelty, do women readers feel that they are empathetic and moral subjects simply called to action by their sisterly feeling and their repugnance for those who violate innocent others, some only thirteen years old? Or ten years old? Like the sympathy toward those slave women whose lashings and rapes European humanitarians like Stedman deplored in titillating detail, the complex affects the genre inspires create a sense of virtue. They lend passion to the mission of saving women globally.

Critiques of representations always incite questions about how else we might understand the world. It does not matter so much whether these memoirs are truth or fiction; the question has been how they function in the world into which they are inserted. In this book, however, I do want to offer alternatives. And it is intriguing that one can find them even in adjacent genres, not just the lives of ordinary women such as Zaynab, Amal, and others whose personal stories I tell. It is uncanny, for example, how Ayaan Hirsi Ali's personal story is made to follow the script and feed this passion. The ideal heroine of this genre, she tells us she was beaten, oppressed, and forced into marriage. She then escaped to freedom. Granted asylum in the Netherlands, she discovered secular reason and renounced servitude to Islam. She seems to be the authentic embodiment of that abused victim caught between force and redemption.

Yet I want to use her autobiography, *Infidel,* to open up the story. In it, we discover evidence of how complicated women's lives and social worlds can be. *Infidel* can't be corralled into the story line Hirsi Ali champions in her public lectures and extreme statements. She is too intelligent for that. First, we learn that she was never raped or forced into marriage—on the contrary, she secretly ran off with and married briefly an attractive maternal relative while on her own in Somalia; and she passionately longed for and kissed a friend of her brother's in Kenya, deluding herself into thinking he was Muslim.

Her confrontation with "Islam" was ambivalent. As a young teen, she came under the sway of a fascinating Islamist teacher in her Kenyan school. She voluntarily threw aside her normal clothes to take on a voluminous black cloak. She explains, "It had a thrill to it, a sensuous feeling. It made me feel powerful . . . I was unique: very few people walked about like that in those days in Nairobi. Weirdly, it made me feel like an individual. It sent out a message of superiority: I was the one true Muslim . . . I was a star of God. When I spread out my hands, I felt like I could fly."[62] She prayed a lot and attended lectures to try to understand her religion. No one forced her. In this autobiographical account, she records in marvelous detail both the enormous differences between the Islamic ideals and practices of her Somali family and the Saudis they briefly lived among, and the specific tensions that arose in the 1980s and 1990s between more traditional forms of

Islam and the new Salafi movement brought by the Muslim
Brotherhood to Kenya, Somalia, and elsewhere.

Even more revealing of an alternative story about how Muslim women are regarded—with respect and acknowledgment of
the value of consent—is an incident Hirsi Ali describes in Hol-
land after she was granted asylum (on false grounds, we now
know). As soon as her father learned of her whereabouts, the man
he had earlier arranged for her to marry in Nairobi flew in from
Canada to find out why she had not come to join him. She told
him she would not go to Canada with him and be his wife. He
returned a few days later, saying he had consulted with her father and they agreed to set up a formal gathering of the most
prominent clan elders living in Europe. The husband arrived the
next day with ten dignified men, including the "Crown Prince" of
the clan. Each spoke in turn, she reports, about honor, marriage,
the civil war, and what values should be upheld. At the end, the
prince said, "Now we will pause so you can think about it." They
offered to reconvene the next day to hear her answer, but she was
ready to give it. Her refusal was followed by a set of questions
about why. Finally, borrowing a key concept from the Qur'an,
she said, "It is the will of the soul . . . The soul cannot be coerced."[63] The prince responded, "I respect this answer. I believe
all of us should respect it." And with that, her husband agreed to
a divorce. "All the men stood up then, and one after another each
man cupped my hands in their two hands, and left. They were full
of respect."[64]

This is a surprising procedure and resolution for a community
that Hirsi Ali would have us believe—in works like her film *Submission* and her first book *The Caged Virgin*—is under the sway
of an incorrigible religion that abuses and denigrates women.
Two visions are at war in *Infidel*. One is a closely observed and

keenly felt rendering of the uncertain and contradictory experiences of a particular girl in a particular Somali family with its unique circumstances, tensions, tragedies, vulnerabilities, and precarious struggles to maintain life and dignity in trying times. The second is a compulsive repetition of a formula that overlays these poignant struggles. The formula generalizes about what Islam means and does to people. Besides promoting a strangely decontextualized and ahistorical view of religion that relies on a simple literalist reading, the formula pits the enlightened and free West against backward and enslaved Muslim societies.[65] That story turns on simple oppositions between choice and bondage, force and consent.

It is important not to be seduced by the darkly appealing fictions of pulp nonfiction that underwrite the common sense that links itself publicly to the language of human rights. These accounts themselves contain hints that things are not so simple. One of the most poignant examples is found buried in the books Zana and her mother have produced about their experiences in Yemen, *Sold* and *Without Mercy*. The story of the younger sister, Nadia, who refused her mother's attempts to spring her from her "enslavement" in Yemen, gives us some clues about an alternative way to think about the key values of choice and consent. Although I take up this issue in more detail in the conclusion, I want to introduce here the observation that life is complicated for all of us. It is never easy to cleanly distinguish freedom and duty, consent and bondage, choice and compulsion. The determined older sister, Zana, leaves Yemen. She abandons her young son because custody goes to the father, both by religious and cultural tradition and by national law. She doesn't look back. But Nadia refuses to take her mother's offer of a ticket to freedom. The girls' mother, Miriam, can't seem to understand what her younger daughter, Nadia, is telling her again and again. She assumes that her daughter must be under the thumb of her domineering husband. She must be weighed down by her life and her stifling black robes.

Her mother cannot see that Nadia is deeply torn. She has five young children whom she would have to leave behind, the legitimate children of a Yemeni father. One is reminded of the painful stories that Das, Menon, Butalia, and other Indian scholars have told about the Indian and Pakistani states' decisions to "repatriate" the women "abducted" during Partition in 1948.[66] These women may or may not have come to love the husbands they had been living with for years. But it was clear from their tears and resistance that they were tortured by the forced separation from their children in the name of national honor.

In what ways had this life on a barren mountaintop become Nadia's real life? She was only thirteen when she left Birmingham. Her childhood was unhappy and included a brush with racism and the law. She lives in poverty in Yemen, it is true. But one has to consider the possibility that the reason she keeps resisting her mother's entreaties and the British consulate's intervention is that she would rather raise her children and be a married woman and part of her husband's community than move to the "freedom" of an unknown life in England, haunted forever by the loss of her children and the idea that they would grow up without the love of their mother. How many stories do we know of women, in any culture, choosing to stay in bad marriages or in miserable circumstances for their children because they love them? What does freedom or choice mean under such conditions?

The fiction that any of us can "choose freely" is maintained by conjuring up those in distant lands who live in bondage with no rights, agency, or ability to refuse or escape sex or violence. The fact that, in liberal democracies, the most contentious debates are about how choice should be balanced against the public good—in schooling, health care, welfare, or gun control—seems also to get lost in this story line.[67] That is why these popular memoirs have such a hold. That is why they seem to have come into our public imagination at the same time the new common sense emerged that we should save women globally.

Before taking a look at the framework of rights that gives shape and purpose to the efforts of activist women and their admirers, I want to unpack one of the most iconic symbols of the oppression of women in IslamLand: the honor crime. In the development of this culturalized category of abuse, we can see perfectly the ways narratives of choice come together with sexuality in liberal discourse and get imbricated in local and international institutions of care and punishment. In tracking this particular type of violation of Muslim women and girls, we see how people are led to suspend their critical faculties in the service of a moral crusade, and how blaming culture justifies intervention.

CHAPTER 4

Seductions of
the "Honor Crime"

One of the most iconic of the cultural-legal categories created to describe the deplorable state of women's rights in the Muslim world is the "honor crime." The deployment of this category makes clear just how inseparable the plight of Muslim women is from the politicized and polarized world in which we live. The 1990s marked the beginning of a strong era for international women's rights. Violence against women was successfully reconceptualized as a human rights issue and put on the agendas of various United Nations (UN) bodies. It now dominates the feminist agenda worldwide and is part of the new common sense. Naming and publicizing the honor crime, a category taken up eagerly by everyone from media makers to moral philosophers, marks humanitarian concern. Yet we must be wary—this category risks consolidating the stigmatization of the Muslim world and does not do justice to women.

Defined as the killing of a woman by her relatives for violation of a sexual code in the name of restoring family honor, the honor crime poses more starkly than any other contemporary category the dilemmas of rights activism in a transnational world.

It is marked as a culturally specific form of violence, distinct from other widespread forms of domestic or intimate partner violence, including the more familiar passion crime. Neither values of honor nor their enforcement through violence are ever *said* to be restricted to Muslim communities, nor are honor crimes condoned in Islamic law or by religious authorities. Yet somehow their constant association with stories and reports from the Middle East and South Asia, or immigrant communities originating in these regions, has given them a special association with Islam. Anyone concerned with representations of Muslim women, with the lives of actual women in the Muslim world, and with the global enterprise of "saving Muslim women" needs to look hard at this category. Insofar as the honor crime is designated a traditional or cultural practice and is introduced regularly into arguments about international affairs or the risks of multiculturalism, even being condemned in UN General Assembly resolutions, it deserves special attention from anthropologists and those trying to understand the new imperialism.[1]

Honor crimes are explained as the behavior of a specific ethnic or cultural community. The culture itself, or "tradition," is taken to be the cause of the criminal violence. So the category stigmatizes not particular acts of violence but entire cultures or communities. But can one acknowledge the seriousness of violence against women without contributing to the stigmatization of particular communities and their representation as exceptional? In the West today, Muslim communities are regularly portrayed as backward and prone to violence. In the new common sense, international conflicts are reduced to a "clash of civilizations" in which entire regions of the world are represented as rejecting values such as freedom and nonviolence. Western interventions have caused hundreds of thousands of deaths justified by the claim to bring freedom—and women's rights—to these other cultures.

Ambivalence or hostility in Europe and the United States toward immigrants from such regions is rationalized by the "uncivilized" practices they bring with them. Even within many Muslim-majority countries, elites look down on ordinary people from the countryside, the slums, and certain regions, blaming violence against women on the traditionalism and cultural backwardness of their less enlightened or "modern" compatriots.

Naming and criminalizing forms of violence may have positive effects. They may encourage legal reform and the education of judges. They might help governments and communities appreciate the seriousness of violence against women and justify the creation of shelters, training programs for police, and relief efforts for women. But are there ways to achieve such goals without defining some acts of violence against women as peculiar? The risk of this culturalization is that it will produce more animosity and violence. Women will be no safer.

Because moral horror about the honor crime was everywhere I looked in the media, in pulp nonfiction, and in serious academic work, I began to ask myself: What forces could be producing and maintaining this category of spectacular cultural violence? What elements of popular fantasy might be animating it? And what might the category prevent us from seeing about the social and political worlds in which violence against women is occurring?

In this chapter, I describe four problems with the way the category of the honor crime works. First, it simplifies morality and distorts the kinds of relations between men and women that exist in societies where honor is a central value. Second, defining honor crimes as a unique cultural form too neatly divides civilized from uncivilized societies, the West and the rest. Third, the obsession with honor crimes erases completely the modern state institutions and techniques of governance that are integral to both the incidents of violence and the category by which they are understood. Finally, thinking about honor crimes seems to be a sort of "antipolitics machine" that blinds us to the existence of social transformations and political conflict.[2]

Moral Puzzles

Rights activists, popular writers, and scholars have all contributed to raising the visibility of the honor crime in the past two decades. The sudden prominence of the honor crime in the late 1990s unsettled me. As an anthropologist who had lived and worked in particular communities of Muslim women in the Arab world, I had spent a long time trying to understand what people meant by honor and what honor meant to them. The subtitle of my first book is, after all, *Honor and Poetry in a Bedouin Society.* I was shocked when I read documents like Amnesty International's fact sheet on honor crimes. Called "Culture of Discrimination," it states: "So-called honor killings are based on the belief, deeply rooted in some cultures, of women as objects and commodities, not as human beings endowed with dignity and rights equal to those of men. Women are considered the property of male relatives and are seen to embody the honor of the men to whom they 'belong.'"[3]

Definitions such as this place honor crimes in types of societies where women are not just unequal to men but have no moral agency. By describing women as property, objects, or body parts controlled by men (as do some that reduce women to hymens),[4] these accounts trivialize moral systems and do not begin to do justice to the way women see themselves in such communities. They did not make sense to me. I had lived for years in a community that prided itself on its commitment to honor. I had a rich sense of women's and girls' lives in a community in which honor and sexual virtue were central to the social imagination. Honor and modesty were the subject of constant discussion.

These values were key to a shared and complexly lived moral code that inspired and obligated individuals. Women and men reflected on these values in an exquisite tradition of poetry and storytelling.

Veiled Sentiments, my first book, focuses on how modesty, the special entailment of honor that involved sexual propriety for women, was part of a widely shared but complex moral code. For my Awlad 'Ali Bedouin friends, honor helped define (and reproduce) social status. For the men and women I knew, honor was based on upholding personal ideals from valor to generosity, from trustworthiness to refusal to accept slights. For women and girls, as I describe in *Veiled Sentiments,* honor involved displaying most of these qualities of toughness and generosity expected of men and those from strong families (called "free") but in addition, forms of respect for others. Modesty, I show in my book, was one of the forms this respectfulness took, defining women as worthy of the respect of others. Modesty meant veiling for certain categories of men (and deliberately not others); it meant being reserved with, and even avoiding, members of the opposite sex who are not relatives. It had nothing to do with acting "feminine," according to our standards. For men, avoiding sexuality was equally important to honor; men were expected to keep a respectful distance from unrelated women and to treat them politely. They would never mention their wives or other women from their family in front of other men—out of respect. Sex outside of marriage was dishonorable for both men and women. And young men had little more choice in marriage partners than did young women. In a kin-based social order, marriages are far too important to be left to individuals.

Should this moral system that sets ideals for both men and women—shaped as it is by the social structure of patrilineal kin relations that organizes descent, inheritance, economy, and political and social relations—be understood (and judged) as simply a form of patriarchal oppression of women leading to violence? Must the restrictions on women's behavior be understood as constraints on their autonomy imposed by men? To begin to answer these questions, one would need to either ask how people involved in the system see it, or explore the complex ways the moral system plays out in actual social situations. I did both in two of my books, *Veiled Sentiments* and *Writing Women's Worlds*.

Awlad 'Ali girls I knew in the 1980s often complained about the unfair restrictions and suspicions to which they were subjected. Their aunts and grandmothers complained about increasing confinement, the result of leaving their nomadic life, along with some newer factors that I discuss later when considering how the Islamic revival that was transforming Egypt in the late twentieth century affected them. But I noticed that the girls chafed against new restrictions with a self-righteousness that came from their sense that they were, unfairly, not being trusted. They defended themselves not by saying they had the right to do whatever they wanted, but by asserting their own modesty and moral virtue, even if they did like bobby pins or lipstick. They spoke about themselves not as objects controlled by family or by men, but as persons who knew right from wrong.

To begin to understand that girls in this community see themselves as powerful agents of their moral standing, all we need to do is listen to some Bedouin wedding songs. The adversarial gender imagery of a couple of the many proud songs women would sing about brides in their families is striking: "They lived like falcons / The hunters of the wild couldn't touch them." "A bird in the hot winds glides / And no rifle scope can capture it."[5] Here are songs that, to return to a theme we've encountered before, use birds metaphorically to comment on women's lives neither in terms of emancipation (from the cage) nor grief about loss, but in terms of their pursuit of honor.

To appreciate how complex the system of morality is for individuals, one would have to talk about how everyday life proceeds. My ethnographies are full of stories about how girls dodge accusations, mothers worry about their daughters, brothers stand up for their sisters, and fathers support them against suspicion or accusations. They also recount men's stories of thwarted love or saving face after their sons or brothers have not acted honorably. At the heart of this community is the riveting and revealing interplay of women's and men's public displays of pride and independence and the poems they share with their intimates, poems of desire and pain that show their vulnerabilities and their attachments in their marriages and friendships. My Awlad 'Ali friends would find familiar the social constraints and demands of honor that produced the exquisite anguish of Romeo and Juliet; they themselves tell similar love stories about tragic, or near-tragic, desert lovers.[6]

Can this moral system of a community that jealously guards its independence from Egyptian state institutions be captured by the idea that men constrain women's freedom or own their bodies? This is what the Amnesty fact sheet suggests. What should we make of women's fierce commitments to the system? What kind of understandings of power, of people's social ties, and even of individual psychic life would lead us to think in such black-and-white terms about something as complex as gendered human life?

Compulsions of Liberal Fantasy

Besides the reductive way it presents societies in which honor is so central to morality, there is a second problem with the discourse on honor crimes. The tendency in the mutually reinforcing scholarship, popular culture, and legal campaigns is to treat the honor crime as a distinctive and specific cultural complex. This tradition continues in Kwameh Anthony Appiah's depiction of honor killings in Pakistan in his book *The Honor Code,* in which he calls for collective shaming or "carefully calibrated ridicule" to spur Pakistani men and those who engage in "honor killing" toward a moral revolution.[7] Even anthropologists like Unni Wikan have fallen into this trap, as demonstrated in her book on a spectacularly mediated honor crime that took place in Sweden in 2002, involving Kurdish immigrants. Her goal, she claims in the book, is to try to understand the culture that produced such an event. But the anthropological motive of understanding (without stigmatizing) is belied by rhetorical moves such as melodramatic chapter endings, consistent misreadings of evidence, and unremitting moral judgment.

Wikan's book examines the case of a father who killed his daughter, Fadime Sahindal, after years of estrangement; the trial, police, and media records were extensive and contradictory. Let me give one example of how Wikan misreads the evidence. One of Fadime's sisters explains that for their father, "everything went to pieces when the media got in on the case. He felt robbed of his dignity, his pride, his honor."[8] After the father had developed a heart condition that forced him to quit his job, he is reported to have told Fadime, "Don't show me up like this, to the media and the police! At least fifteen people spat at me!"[9] In the trial, he testified, "All these Swedes came by and threw stones at my window. They shouted things. 'Fucking blackhead, go back where you came from!' "[10]

Wikan, however, does not pick up on the lost dignity the sister mentions, the racism the father experiences, or the critical role the media and police played in the unfolding events. Symptomatically, she reverts to standard tropes about culture, seamlessly slipping among Kurdish, Middle Eastern, traditional, tradition-bound, and non-Western culture. Fadime's father, she insists, had a "mental outlook . . . anchored elsewhere; his roots were deeply sunk into a culture, or a set of traditions, with core values other than freedom and equality."[11] She says, "Many immigrants in European countries remain deeply rooted in rural cultures established several hundred years ago."[12] At her most sympathetic, she says that we must understand fathers like him as "victims of inhuman traditions"—against which valiant and enlightened daughters and organizations should struggle.[13] Her anthropological discourse meshes surprisingly well with popular discourses on the honor crime and the larger common sense about the problems of Muslim women.[14]

To get the full flavor of the unsavory politics of this conception of honor crimes, we need to turn to these more popular discourses. We have already seen how pulp nonfiction fixates on choice and freedom to paint its pictures of Muslim women's oppressions. The honor crime category also works through fantasy to attach people to a set of values they are made to associate strictly with modernity and the West. We can see this in two highly successful "memoirs" by honor crime survivors that found enthusiastic, if tearful, audiences in the wake of 9/11, the U.S. invasion of Afghanistan, and the impending military intervention in Iraq. The first is Norma Khouri's best-selling memoir from 2003 of the alleged honor killing of her best friend, Dalia, in Jordan. Called *Forbidden Love* in the United Kingdom and *Honor Lost* in the United States, it is structured as a classic romance novel, complete with a tall, dark, and handsome love object who is not a sexist brute. It pulses with chaste but throbbing mutual attraction. But this romance ends differently—with murder. And there is an Orientalist difference; the gripping plot is interlaced, as Harlequin romances and slasher films are not, with pedantic lectures on Islam. We are not allowed to forget that we are in IslamLand.

The story is organized by the standard themes of a long history of Western representations of the Muslim woman. In contrast to the free Western woman, she is imprisoned: "For most women," Khouri writes, "Jordan is a stifling prison tense with the risk of death at the hands of loved ones." She is also voiceless: "Women still pray that their silent cries will be heard," echoing the late nineteenth-century missionary women discussed in Chapter 1, who said, "They will never cry for themselves, for they are down under the yoke of centuries of oppression."[15] And then there is the stark contrast between patriarchal tradition and feminist modernity that we have encountered before in Susan Moller Okin's essay, "Is Multiculturalism Bad for Women?" Of her doomed friend Dalia, Khouri comments: "And yet there are a few rare women who risk their lives to try [to break the ancient code]. The whispers they hear are not from the desert, but from the winds of change."[16]

The memoir aligns itself with popular feminism. To lend credibility, the book ends with a page similar to the ones we encounter in *Half the Sky*. Titled "What Can You Do?," it urges readers to write letters opposing the practice of honor crimes and to donate money to the UN Commission on Human Rights.

The problem is that the book was a hoax. Norma Khouri, whose real name turned out to be Norma Bagain Toliopoulos, gained asylum in Australia on the basis of the events of the book. Investigative journalists then discovered that she had not lived in Jordan since she was three years old. Suspicious, the Jordanian journalist Rana Husseini tracked dozens of serious errors and anachronisms in the book, and the publisher withdrew it.[17] Rather than fleeing an honor crime, Khouri was a troubled woman (and compulsive liar) who had grown up in Chicago, had a police record, and was wanted for fraud.[18]

This piece of fiction masquerading as memoir reveals perfectly the fantasy and seduction of the honor crime. Self-righteous horror about the barbarism of "the other" is married to voyeuristic titillation, along the way facilitating the personalization of such powerful symbols of liberalism as freedom and choice. The freedom that honor crime books like this celebrate and that the scandalizing of honor crimes affirms turns out to be the freedom to have sex and to leave home. The choice that is cherished boils down to the right to make personal decisions based on love. So the book's warm and uncritical reception can be accounted for by the attractive way it affirms certain modern Western cultural values through an association of sexuality with liberation, and individual rights with public freedom.

Another "memoir," mentioned briefly in Chapter 3, confirms the erotic charge of the honor crime and its role in shoring up a sharp distinction between the liberated West and the repressive Muslim East. *Burned Alive: A Survivor of an "Honor Killing" Speaks Out*, published first in France in 2003, is a different kind of hoax, based on "repressed memories" (notorious for their unreliability) and filled with inconsistencies and errors.[19] It is the story of Souad (who has only a first name and lives "somewhere in Europe"). She is a Palestinian woman who was allegedly set on fire for being pregnant out of wedlock. Writing her memoir twenty-five years after the events were said to have taken place, this woman, who has been regularly made to act as a witness at conferences on honor crimes, testifies not just to the barbarism of her own society but also to the goodness of the mission of her European saviors. These include a woman named Jacqueline and a shadowy Swiss organization, SURGIR, whose Christian salvationist language is striking and whose appeal for money appears, as we have now come to expect, at the end of the book.

Souad admits she cannot write or read books, but that Jacqueline had assured her she could just "speak" the book. We are given no clues as to how the book was put together, except that the title page (though not the cover) indicates it was written in collaboration with Marie-Thérèse Cuny. This French writer had earlier helped "Leila," the French Moroccan whose memoir of forced marriage is analyzed in Chapter 3. As noted there, she would also soon help Mukhtar Mai (the Pakistani village woman whom Nicholas Kristof declares his heroine) write her memoir.

Burned Alive consists of Souad's disjointed, fragmented, first-person childhood memories, many of relentless cruelty at the hands of her father. She gives us vivid fragments of what she claims she had forgotten for twenty-five years—including a younger sister (whose name she cannot recall) being strangled by her brother with a black telephone cord. Souad's feelings toward her brother are wildly ambivalent—she insists again and again how much she loved him, and yet she depicts him as a murderer. Although Jacqueline describes Souad in the West Bank hospital where she found her as suffering intermittently from amnesia, Souad's "writing" becomes fluid and erotic when she describes her trysts with the handsome neighbor she believed would marry her, but who impregnated and then abandoned her. The breathless description of the first secret meeting with her would-be fiancé says it all: "I have never been so happy. It was so wonderful to be with him, so close, even for a few minutes. I felt it in my whole body. I couldn't think about it clearly, I was too naïve—I was no more educated than a goat—but that wonderful feeling was about the freedom in my heart, and my body. For the first time in my life I was *someone,* because I had decided to do as I wanted. I was alive. I was not obeying my father or anyone else . . . I was breaking the rules."[20]

These values of individual sexual transgression and personal autonomy are precisely the ones that anthropologist Unni Wikan honors in Fadime, the Swedish Kurdish honor crime victim. Fadime, she declares, is a symbol of the power of love. She stands for "an inclusive view of humankind, universal in its emphasis on the individual's irreducible value. She represented freedom and equality, regardless of gender, religion, and ethnicity,"[21] all because she defied her family by running off with a Swedish/ Iranian boyfriend and then condemned in front of Parliament immigrant communities that would not assimilate.

In all these narratives of popular fiction and bad anthropology, Western society and well-integrated immigrants are granted a monopoly on liberal and human values. The implication is that the West does not include in itself any illiberal values, whether chastity, religious moralism, intolerance, racism, incarceration, sexism, economic exploitation, or inequality. So it is worth considering the ideological role that the honor crime might be playing in a period when critics of American imperial interventions and of European anti-immigrant racism have questioned how liberal existing Western democracies actually are, not to mention thinking about how condemning the honor crime implies a sort of uncomplicated celebration of autonomy when a strong tradition in feminist political theory has uncovered the masculine assumptions of the liberal ideal of the autonomous individual. Many feminists argue that idealizing autonomy devalues not just women's but also men's human experiences of dependency and relationship. The most famous illustration of the bias in our evaluations of morality came from the social psychologist Carol Gilligan, whose pathbreaking book *In a Different Voice* suggested that an ethic of care, expressed more often by women, might be just as important or healthy as the kind of moral reasoning based on ideals of autonomy that is generally viewed as superior.

There are good reasons to be cautious about associating love and sex so closely with freedom and individual rights, and both with the modern West. Historians, political theorists, philosophers, and feminist scholars have questioned these dogmas. Michel Foucault, for one, has shown us how modern discourses of sexual liberation came with new forms of discipline, medicalization, and a language of perversion. An older Marxist tradition held that the subordination of women emerged with the development of private property and the nuclear family. Many feminists have documented the ways women are objectified and turned into commodities in our late capitalist consumer society, whether to sell cars or pornography.

But even if one ignores this kind of theorizing and research, shouldn't one at least ask for a more nuanced understanding of the place of love in the sorts of societies that Khouri and others disparage? In the literature on honor crimes, there is a striking absence of any mention of Arab literary culture, which is renowned for its artistic elaboration on the themes of love. Love has been a special theme since pre-Islamic Arabic poetry and on to the romantic storytelling that formed the basis for European chivalric genres. Certainly for the Awlad 'Ali Bedouin I lived with, love and desire were the stuff of the poetry, songs, and stories they cherished. These were their creative reflections on love and life, which is why I wrote about them in *Veiled Sentiments*.

Things *can* go wrong for people everywhere. Some fathers are violent, some brothers commit incest, there are men who kill their wives and lovers on suspicion, and there are families and marriages that are dysfunctional and abusive. "Honor cultures" do not have a monopoly on violence against women. American and European newspapers, judges, lawyers, psychiatrists, and prisons testify to this. And not all families in communities where sexual modesty is a key element of young women's morality react the same way to suspicions or sexual infractions. The problem is that when violence occurs in some communities, culture is blamed; in others, only the individuals involved are accused or faulted. As Leti Volpp has shown in her classic article called "Blaming Culture," violent or abusive behavior gets attributed to culture only when it occurs in minority or alien cultural, racial, or national groups.

The honor crime seems to function as a comforting phantasm that empowers the West and those who identify with it. Not only does it shift attention to an abjected stage where caricatured people are victims of their own violent culture but it also encourages self-righteous commitment to change those backward or dysfunctional cultures. As Appiah prescribes, we should persuade Muslim men to shift their sense of honor so that killing their women feels shameful; as others recommend, we should save the women from their cultures. Rather than enabling us to understand social lives that, like ours, are unfortunately too often marred by violence, the legal/cultural category of the honor crime produces strong distinctions. It distracts our gaze from violence within, and establishes the superiority of a dense concatenation of cultural values associated with liberalism—autonomy, individualism, and sexual freedom. In some settings, it enables Westernized elites in Muslim communities to distinguish themselves from their local backward compatriots and to gain new opportunities and alliances, mounting campaigns against honor crimes. The political alignments of a bright, articulate young Jordanian engineer who ran a web campaign against honor crimes are illustrative. Mohammad Al-Azraq had answered the call of a Swiss-educated Bahraini friend to take on the issue. I contacted him shortly after the website called "There is No Honor in Honor Killing" (nohonor.org) went live in 2007. He identified his motives: "From the most obscure days of Arab tribalism till the 21st century, many crimes have been committed against women in the name of 'honour'. People kill their own flesh and blood to satisfy backward tribal values and traditions that are by no means related to religion. We—in 'No Honor'—are trying to raise awareness among young people from the region, and encourage young males to respect their sisters'/daughters'/wives'/cousins' . . . etc. choices in life."[22] When I interviewed him on March 29, 2009, he elaborated, "The core thing I believe in is that men and women are absolutely equal. My sister, my mother, my wife, my son—as long as eighteen or over, have the right to make their own decisions. That's the thing that we're trying to preach." Attractive as they are, these views must be put in the context of the wider liberal politics of dialogue and tolerance represented by cosmopolitan youth like him.

In short, the popular concern with the honor crime solidifies certain violences as timeless cultural practices associated with particular kinds of communities defined by their alien difference from us, rather than treating them as the perverse and diverse acts of individuals in different circumstances who sometimes work with a complex of concepts linked to honor. In assuming the uniformity of such practices, popular narratives affix values of individualism, freedom, humanity, tolerance, and liberalism neatly onto the West while denying them to others, despite the actual distribution of acts of inhumanity, intolerance, and illiberalism across many societies.

Erasing Governance

The sober forms of knowledge production we find in human rights or women's rights reports by and for grassroots and international organizations work differently and do a different kind of political work. Here we come to the third problem with the way the category of the honor crime is used. Human rights reports on honor crimes arise from and at the same time hide the ways in which governments and transnational organizations now penetrate the lives of most people and communities. Unlike the sensationalist romance novel/memoir, such reports have all the neutral features of scientific objectivity. In such reports, one typically finds a mix of telegraphic case studies and confusing statistics. For example, Human Rights Watch's 2006 report on violence against women in Palestine begins its section on "Murder of Women under the Guise of 'Honor' " in a predictable way—with a clinical quote from an autopsy report: "An 18-year-old female died as a result of manual strangulation and smothering, which were carried out by her family members."[23] The lists and numbers in these reports convince us that there is something out there. The multiplication of cases lends credibility and objective weight to the existence and specificity of the phenomenon. The accumulation makes it appear that all the cases are variations on each other. These incidents are not to be considered as individual aberrations or pathologies but as patterned forms.

Feminist activists contribute to these reports. Genuinely motivated by concern for the victims and committed to working on behalf of women, these feminists work in grassroots organizations led by courageous individuals. Some offer good services; most carry out research as part of advocacy. Yet when even the most careful scholar-activists attempt to compile statistics, the results are utterly confusing. These anecdotes and noncomparative or unreliable statistics reveal little about contexts, incidences, and individual situations. They are unable, in the end, to draw either distinctions among or commonalities across forms of violence against women.

Even so, these are not the most important lessons I want to draw from the genre of the human rights report. Instead, as the late Turkish sociologist Dicle Koğacioğlu alerted us, we need to pay attention to the infrastructure that enables the manufacture of this statistical and case information. We need to pay attention to the production and circulation of such reports. Looking at the way honor crimes became such a hot topic in Turkey in the wake of Turkey's bid for inclusion in the European Union, she showed how the honor crime was defined and managed in party programs, legal arguments, and newspaper articles. The crimes, she concluded, are produced in relationship to these institutions. Her most important argument was that if we care about women's rights and well-being, we need to reverse the invisibility that modern institutions, national and international, manufacture about their own roles in perpetuating such practices.[24]

This infrastructure and these institutions are not traditional, tribal, or rural; they are the infrastructure of modern government such as social service organizations that are alerted to and follow up on complaints about abuses.[25] They are often run by middle-class, educated women committed to justice, versed in contemporary feminist politics, and connected to wider networks that are willing to work with state agencies and even international organizations. In Europe and the United States, they serve immigrant women; in other countries, they focus on the poor and the rural. In addition, there are the police who go to the crime scenes, arrest killers, and investigate violent incidents. Almost every report of an incident by the Jordanian journalist Rana Husseini mentions that the brother or father either turned himself in to the police immediately or waited for the police to come and arrest him. The extensiveness of the Swedish police records actually allowed Wikan to write her book about Fadime.

Then there are the medical institutions, from hospitals to morgues. Rana Husseini's acknowledgments include special mention of the pathologists at the Jordanian National Institute of Forensic Medicine. Forensic medical teams determine cause of death, conduct autopsies, and even routinely administer virginity tests. Nearly every reported incident concludes with a finding about the virginity of the victim, the result of an invasive medical practice that even nineteenth-century court records in Egypt document as part of the institutionalization of modern medicine.[26]

There are the prisons that house remorseful or stoic killers. Those in Jordan, Pakistan, and Afghanistan also house women who are kept there for their "protection," whether they are the victims of rape, pregnant out of wedlock, or otherwise in danger. It was such women who provided much of the interview material for the 2004 Human Rights Watch report on honor crimes in Jordan. Associated with the prisons are the judicial and legal systems with their laws, judges, trials, and records, and the political systems that ratify international conventions or entertain debates about relevant articles from legal codes.

It turns out that honor crimes, whether "over there" or "in our midst," are almost always implicated in the social institutions of policing, surveillance, and intervention. As research by Palestinian women activists and scholars has shown, for example, it is the failure of those very institutions to respond properly to women's pleas—whether because of racism or sexism—that is responsible for the victimization of so many women. Proposed legislation that promises to punish men for killing women in the name of honor does little to help the women victims, for whom it comes too late. Shalhoub-Kevorkian and Daher-Nashif document how Palestinian women in danger regularly face hostile Israeli police who humiliate them, hand them back to elders who are favored collaborators, and fail to follow up on threats or the willingness of family members to testify against murderers.[27] A discriminatory legal system compounds the problems for women and girls.

Moreover, honor crimes are taken up in national and international political debates and activities, with the media usually fanning the flames. Concrete examples of how honor crimes are implicated in political institutions appear in human rights reports, even when these reports ignore it by introducing matters in clichéd ways. The Human Rights Watch's report on Palestine that I discuss in Chapter 5 repeats Amnesty International's earlier diagnosis almost word for word: "These murders are the most tragic consequence and graphic illustration of deeply embedded, society-wide gender discrimination."[28] Yet when the report comes to discuss the case of a sixteen-year-old Ramallah girl, it notes: "The Palestinian police were held by Israeli soldiers for hours at an Israeli military checkpoint between the city of Ramallah and the village of Abu Qash, where the family lived. The staff of the Women's Center for Legal Aid and Counseling said they were not able to reach her house in time to try to save her life due to movement restrictions between Jerusalem and the West Bank." Here, we see honor crimes caught within checkpoints, curfews, the Israeli occupation, and women's nongovernmental organizations (NGOs), at a minimum.

And finally there is the media—newspapers, magazines, television, film, and now websites through which honor crimes are filtered, whether in exposés or cyber campaigns. Fadime turned to the press for protection and then was hounded by it. Local, national, and international media—honor crimes are everywhere, in the *Jordan Times, Sydney Morning Herald,* and *Der Spiegel;* on CNN, the BBC, and *The O'Reilly Factor* on FOX News.

The role media play cannot be underestimated. An example from Germany shows how this works. Katherine Ewing, an anthropologist who wrote a book called *Stolen Honor,* traces how a key incident in Berlin gradually came to be classified as an honor crime and how, in its wake, a set of previous murders of women was reclassified, inducing a national panic about the crisis of the barbaric immigrants within the national fold, a panic that she considers the eruption of a national fantasy.[29] In early February 2005, Hatun Sürücü, a young woman of Turkish background, was murdered in Berlin, allegedly by her brother(s). Journalists at first called the shooting a head scarf killing (since she wasn't wearing one), playing on fears about Islamism. Two weeks into the media frenzy, they had confidently come to call this the sixth honor killing in Berlin in the previous five months. Ewing argues that this "spate of honor killings in Berlin was not likely even a statistical anomaly," but an artifact of classification. A range of murders under various circumstances "retrospectively came to be labeled honor killings."[30] Most involved husbands killing wives, which does not fit the definition.

A young, single mother estranged from her family, living a more "German" life, complete with dancing at clubs, barhopping, and boyfriends, Sürücü's story could easily become about honor. Confusing details like hints that she had a diverse sexual life or that she might have been the victim of incest dropped quickly out of the news. However, Ewing urges us to focus on the institutional and historical context in which she was murdered and became a symbol. In the neighboring Netherlands, the filmmaker Theo van Gogh had just been killed by a Moroccan immigrant for his role in producing *Submission,* Ayaan Hirsi Ali's anti-Muslim "hard core" Orientalist film that I discuss in Chapter 3. Although the Islamic Council condemned German-Turkish youth for "self-administered justice" and deplored cultural traditions, the Right in Germany took advantage of this incident to tar the Muslim community—and multiculturalism.

The context was one, Ewing argues, in which immigrants could serve as "a focal point for the country's ills and a threat to the democratic principles that are the foundation of the German state."[31] In contrast, people who knew the social scene well attributed the murder to the gender politics of boys in gangs created in response to neo-Nazi racism and post-9/11 anti-Islamic sentiment. Honor crimes by then had become a signifier for both the machismo and the cultural authenticity of youths of Turkish origin. They had also come to stand in for Germans' fears of an untamed parallel society in their midst. Turkish women's rights activists, for their part, seized on Sürücü's murder to campaign against honor crimes. In the end, this frenzy incited a good deal of speculation on Sürücü's lifestyle, at the center of which again were the erotics of sexual freedom and the fetish of personal choice.

In Europe, honor crimes are also closely connected to border control and what Miriam Ticktin, the anthropologist whose work on illegal immigrants and humanitarianism in France I quote in Chapter 3, calls the policing of immigration and immigrants. These are matters of national and international administration, not culture.[32] Nacira Guénif-Souilamas, a French scholar who has written about the stigmatization of North African immigrant men for their "sexual deviance," links this phenomenon to efforts "to mask the new forms of social and economic domination experienced by working-class young people of non-European origin" and to the "precarious lives" into which they are being forced, as sons of the formerly colonized.[33] In the United Kingdom, the major study of honor crimes was conducted by the Centre for Social Cohesion, a conservative think tank devoted to the study of religious (Islamic) extremism. Asylum cases, the extension of welfare benefits, and most interestingly, the issue of visas (an issue we saw lurking in Leila's memoir of "forced marriage";

honor crimes are often said to be committed because girls refuse marriages that are related to acquiring visas for their spouses) also confirm how embedded honor crimes are in European immigration politics.

Jacqueline Rose provides more support for these arguments with her eloquent decoding of the role of obsessive discussions of the honor crime in the European politics of immigration, her criticism of its branding as "archaic" or "tribal" when it is so thoroughly connected to modernity and nationalism, and her praise for those who insist that we must refuse to generalize but instead enter the complexity of lives.[34] In a comprehensive comparative study of the relationship between media and political debates on "honour-related" violence in Britain, Germany, Canada, and the Netherlands, Anna Korteweg and Gökçe Yurdakul too have shown how unhelpful the common stigmatizing discourses are. They insist that policy must be built on a recognition of the way that such violence is actually shaped by immigration experiences. They show that targeting this form of violence will be more effective if it is framed as a variant of domestic violence. They recommend that women's groups be made full partners and the emphasis be shifted toward empowering women as citizens rather than calling for restrictions on immigration.[35]

In addition to nation-states worried about immigrants, honor crimes involve international organizations, UN bodies, donor communities, and local grassroots NGOs. If you look at them closely, in fact, you see that honor crimes do not occur *outside* of these modern state institutions or those of the international community. Honor crimes cannot be analyzed as if they were free-floating or rooted in ancient codes and tradition-bound cultures. The honor crime gives legitimacy and resilience not just to all the mechanisms of regulation, surveillance, and mass mediation intrinsic to modern state power but also to the specific forms and

forums of contemporary transnational governance, whether
neoliberal economic institutions or humanitarian intervention of
the feminist or military sort.

The Winds of Change

This brings us to the fourth problem with the way the category
of the honor crime works. Blaming culture means not just flat-
tening cultures, stripping moral systems of their complexity, and
hiding the most modern political and social interventions that
no community escapes; it means erasing history. In all the discussion of honor crimes, where is the recognition of the dynamic
historical transformations that are affecting women, families,
and everyday life in all communities, including those associated
with "honor killings"?

A constant refrain in the alarmist literature on the honor crime
is that it is on the increase, even if virtually every article or book
published in the past decade cites the inexplicably unchanging
figure attributed vaguely to the UN of 5,000 honor killings per
year, worldwide. Even Dalia's mother, in the fictional *Honor Lost,*
seems to have known the figure. There is, of course, no proof of
this, since we have no reliable evidence of prevalence in the past
and there are, as everyone concerned has noted, formidable
problems of reporting and classification in the present. It would
not be surprising, however, to find that familial violence against
women might indeed be increasing in some social contexts. The
question is where one would look for explanations.

Studies from Europe, Turkey, and Palestine/Israel have noted
some relevant factors. They have described the retrenchment of
family under insecure conditions among Kurds; reactions to racism in Britain, Germany, and France; and deliberate policies of
strengthening traditional patriarchal authority among Palestinians in Israel. In many settings, we see contact with alternative

moral systems and competing forms of authority; differential incorporation into the state and its institutions, including schools and labor markets; and clashing forms of control, just to mention a few of the circumstances that might affect family violence.

Even more crucial to observe is the way the past three decades have brought not just changes in state institutions, migration patterns, ethnic politics, and the spread of global media, but piety movements across the Muslim world. Alongside the Islamic revival come arguments for the Islamization of law and society that are taking different forms. How is this trend of more self-conscious affiliation with what is presented as correct and complete Islamic practice playing out in the sphere of gender? What effects is the Islamic revival having on women's rights or gender violence? The answers, not surprisingly, are complicated. These effects vary tremendously across countries and communities. Surely, such effects should be part of any discussion of honor crimes. But they rarely are.

A look across the Muslim world shows that the "winds of change" that are moving non-elite women—and many elite women—in Egypt, Lebanon, Pakistan, Malaysia, and even Norma Khouri's Jordan are not the ones Khouri celebrated in her imaginary friend Dalia, which took her to restaurants in four-star hotels, dance clubs, or to liberated sexuality. Instead, these winds are moving them toward what they perceive as a higher Muslim morality. Sexual desires outside of marriage are no less problematic for Islamic piety and Islamic legal codes than for "traditional" moral codes based on family honor. Some Bedouin women in Egypt contrast new restrictions imposed on them by an Islamist turn by young men to an older set of freedoms they felt their tribal ways gave them, even while they are endorsing piety.

This channeling of sexuality through religious language and law is leading to three trends in gender politics, at least in the regions I know. First, young pious women and men want to live up to the morality of the religious code and this guides them away from a celebration of liberal freedom from sexual restrictions. Many women say they want to be close to God, with all the moral entailments from shyness to sexual propriety and a sort of formidable untouchability that this sometimes involves.[36] Across the Muslim world now, women who mark their piety by wearing the new Islamic dress, or the hijab, have gained autonomy from family and the domestic sphere. Their self-monitoring is at least as powerful a form of conformity to moral standards regarding sexual freedom as that of the kinds of girls I knew among the Awlad ʿAli Bedouin in the 1980s, for whom it had been a matter of family standing. Women and men must figure out how to negotiate their relations given these terms. They are doing so in all sorts of creative ways. Not insulated from pop music, television, coeducational institutions, and leisure activities and consumption, they have made use of institutions like temporary or ʿurfi (secret) marriages. They also struggle with themselves and society.[37] Many attribute women's embrace of the hijab as a public assertion of morality, not just religiosity, for those who are massively present now in schools, the workforce, and public space.[38]

Second, with the Islamization of states and legal systems in the last quarter of the twentieth century in countries like Pakistan and Iran, radically new modes of regulation and enforcement of moral standards tied to sexuality, new vocabularies and conceptions, and new forms of authority (and resistance) have developed. Some incidents have even been described as state-sponsored honor crimes. This means that morality is being given religious grounding and is mediated through channels that claim the authority of Islam. The voluntary embraces of morality described earlier are taking place alongside more official interventions in moral discourses, including their manipulation. A new language is coming into play: one of sin and *zina* (the crime of sex outside marriage). This dominates state efforts at Islamization in places like Iran and Pakistan, as well as the lively internal legal and social challenges to such efforts wherever they are being imposed.

Third, a consequence of this situation is that tensions have emerged between Islamic religious institutions and community regulation. In recent years, major religious leaders in Syria, Lebanon, and elsewhere have issued legal opinions *(fatwas)* condemning honor crimes as unlawful. As Lynn Welchman, a legal scholar based in London, has shown in her analysis of the sudden public intervention that the Islamic Chief Justice of the Palestinian Authority made in 2005 on the subject of murder in defense of honor, Islam and Islamic law (the Shari'a) are coming to be invoked more and more against honor crimes. This has new jurisprudential, legislative, and social consequences that have yet to unfold.

At the same time, the honor crime (and women) have become pawns in political battles. In Jordan, we have good documentation on how the honor crime was manipulated by politicians from the Islamic Party in their resistance to the efforts of feminist campaigners backed by the Jordanian royal family to reform penal law. These populist Islamist politicians stymied the efforts by linking these reforms to a Western plot to undermine Jordanian society and morality. This is ironic given that the laws on which the honor defense relies came into Jordanian law from the Napoleonic Code, Ottoman law, and British common law.[39]

These changing responses to sexuality and honor signal important transformations not just in the discourses but also in the institutions through which the honor crime now travels. Any diagnosis of gender violence that attributes it to culture—backward,

traditional, or barbaric—distracts us from these kinds of historical dynamics that are essential to an analysis of violence and to
responsible efforts to mobilize against it. It is time to stop talking about "deep-seated cultural beliefs," "ancient codes from the
desert," and efforts to "understand" how people in certain alien
cultures could want to kill their daughters. Even feminists from
the Muslim world need to be more careful. Although they tend
to be vigilant about racism and wary of the dangers of civilizational discourse, they sometimes let their fears of Islamic fundamentalism distort their understandings. The Women Living under Muslim Laws (WLUML) campaign called "Stop Stoning and
Killing Women!" that I discuss in Chapter 5 conflates a bewildering range of practices and puts into service the fascination
with horror and sex that attach to the timeless honor crime for
their antifundamentalist agenda.

Dilemmas for Concerned Activists

The seductive power of the honor crime, with its unique mix of
sexual titillation and moral horror and its capacity to subsume
and consume diverse acts, has allowed it to emerge as a robust
category that does significant political and cultural work. My
intention in challenging the usefulness and accuracy of the category is not to defend or excuse the violence it tries to name; nor
do I wish to undermine the value of much of the reparative work
carried out in its name. Instead, I have sought first to redirect our
attention to the historical conditions and precise political configurations that lead certain figurations of suffering to become
objects of earnest and widespread concern while so many others
go unremarked or unlabeled. Second, I wanted to trace the varied impacts of this structured concern, nowadays framed in the
hegemonic language of our times as violations of women's rights.

I would not want to say, as some might, that familial violence is not a serious problem, pointing out, for example, that more women die in traffic accidents. I am not even saying that we should look at how many (more) women fall victim to structural and military violence, whether through the malnourishment of poverty or the burning flesh of aerial bombardment. There is no excuse for brushing under the rug the harms of interpersonal violence and ignoring its gendered or sexed forms. It is the achievement of feminism to have made violence against women and sexual violence public moral and legal issues, not hidden or taken-for-granted matters of private life.

However, it is a problem when we consistently fail to compare murder and assault rates by intimates between societies in which women are allegedly victims of honor crimes and those in which honor is not invoked as a motive, justification, or legal excuse. The specifics are important, and as an anthropologist, I am committed to going deeply into different systems of gender, power, and morality. But as part of the attention to specifics, we also need to look systematically at all the political and legal institutions through which everyday life, including violence, proceeds in various places.

My main concern has been with the determinants of the cultural construction of the honor crime and the effects of its deployment.[40] We have seen the articulating domains in which the category works. We have examined the work of the honor crime in distinct projects and scales of power and have begun to untangle its effects in different spheres and locales. These have included policing and exclusions of immigrants; the disciplinary penetration of rural and urban subaltern communities by state and social service organizations; particular attempts at domination by national, class, or ethnic groups; defenses of liberalism that fuel a divisive separation of West and non-West; attraction of funding for feminist projects and research; international militarism; and new forms of transnational governance carried out in the name of rights or humanitarianism.

Looking ahead, there are signs that other cultural categories might be moving into the limelight. We should watch out for these, and be equally wary. Polygamy is a likely candidate for a new campaign, following along the lines of "forced marriage," that theme of so much pulp nonfiction and political work by governance feminists.[41] Such categories will draw strength from new political-cultural configurations that include religious debates about gay marriage, controversies about competing legal systems and religious arbitration in Europe, the emergence of a number of international Islamic feminist reform organizations, the dynamics of Islamist identity politics, and the justification of continuing military intervention in Muslim lands in the name of introducing "rule of law." These two figurations of women's suffering—polygamy and forced marriage—are both redolent of sex (harems and rape). They work slightly differently from the honor crime and have different political and social effects. Dealing with real abuses and women's suffering in many cases, they also will provide new opportunities for rights work, scholarship, and intervention. They will present feminists and human rights advocates with ethical and political conundrums, as has the honor crime.

CHAPTER 5

The Social Life of Muslim Women's Rights

Fayruz had some big news to share. When I arrived in the village after a year's absence, I went to visit her. She had been in the midst of a cancer scare the last time we'd seen each other. They had removed a tumor that doctors assured her was benign. She told me about the pain she had suffered and the long nights when she wept thinking about what would happen to her children if she died. She was now back to her bold, beautiful self, full of energy and determination.

Fayruz wanted to show me something. We set off on foot, her long, flowing dress complemented by the black head covering all women in the village wear. She had her daughter and her new daughter-in-law in tow. Down some rutted dirt roads, we found ourselves in the midst of the open agricultural land that surrounded the village. She proudly pointed to a monstrous three-story house under construction in the midst of the fields of wheat. Fayruz showed me around, struggling up the great spiral staircase, stepping over the construction rubble. Then she took me to see the side door, which someone had blocked up with mud. She explained that her younger brother had gone to war with her.

Her father had been the largest landowner in this village and an intriguing figure of whom I had been fond. Since he had passed away a couple of years earlier, she and her sisters had been fighting for their share of the inheritance. They had worked through the local village head and had been to court. She paid fine after fine because her brother reported her for illegally building on agricultural land, for putting in electricity, and then for getting piped water. He still refused to give her the few feet she needed for an easement to this side entrance. It would have had to be taken from a field he owned.

As we stood on the roof, surveying the lovely fields that abutted the house while she let her chickens out of their coop to get some sunshine, she told me about the conflict. By Islamic inheritance law, she and her three sisters were entitled to half of the land. The other half should be split between the two brothers. As she put it, the four sisters are like two men. She was furious that her brother didn't want to give them their share. He was making life difficult for her. He had finally agreed to give her the few feet she wanted—but only in exchange for an acre of the fields she had inherited somewhere else.

I was sad to see this family feud. This brother of hers had been a genial soccer player in his youth, content to let his father manage the estate, reluctant to take on responsibility. He was the baby of the family, and she had always been the loving older sister. Now he wouldn't even talk to her, she said, except to curse her. Her older brother would greet her politely if he bumped into her on the road. He would call her "daughter of my father," but he no longer invited her to the family home. Yet Fayruz was defiant. She accused her brothers of being greedy. "Why shouldn't I get it? In this place, the men always try to keep the land."

She confided that she wanted something of her own. She pointed to her brother-in-law, whose wife had built a house on some land she got from her parents. They had always been competitive. Fayruz explained, "This house is for me. For my sons." She explained that the main house (where she lives with her husband) is her husband's family home. She doesn't have any rights in it.

Is this an example of the war on women for which popular writers seek to enlist us? Fayruz actually accused her brother of making war on her. But a moment's reflection leads us to realize that this is not a simple struggle against Muslim patriarchy. And what about the problem of Muslim women's rights that so exercises those who are leading the moral crusade against Islam and Muslim culture? The rights Fayruz is fighting for are hers through Islamic inheritance law. The community elders and the state courts both uphold them. Her brother, even though he has become more religious than in his soccer-playing days, ignores them. The violations that she is being fined for involve state law, which forbids building on agricultural land; this law is not gendered. And the reason she is having some success is not just because of her persistence but because other men are supporting her. Her husband is himself a wealthy merchant. From his complaints about the exorbitant cost of the construction, I got the impression that he was bankrolling the building project. Fayruz defends her fight for her inheritance rights on the basis that she wants something for herself and her sons. But, of course, these are her husband's sons too. Each has a floor of the house. Now Fayruz's children will inherit from both sides of the family.

I tell this story about Fayruz to remind us that Muslim women's rights are pursued in particular places through a variety of institutions and instruments, including state and religious law. We need to recognize that Muslim women's rights—something to fight for, debate, consider historically, see cross-culturally, make happen, organize around, fund, and examine in action—have very active social lives in our contemporary world.

The new common sense about global women's rights and saving Muslim women in particular is built on a variety of texts that inform the Western imagination of women's plights in the Muslim world. These range from United Nations (UN) documents and "pulp nonfiction" to political speeches about nail polish in Afghanistan. But as the concept of "Muslim women's rights" circulates across continents—traveling in and out of airport bookstores, classrooms, and government policy offices; UN forums in New York and Geneva, and local women's organizations in Pakistan and Malaysia; television soap operas in Syria and Egypt; model marriage contracts developed in Morocco and Algeria; and mosque study groups in North America—we are confronted with the question of how to make sense of its travels and its translations across these forms and forums. Muslim women's rights produce everything from websites and battered women shelters to inheritance disputes in rural villages.

Given this proliferation of sites and forms, how should we frame the question of rights? If we do not presume that there are such things as rights to be found and measured on a scale of 1 to 10 using some kind of universal standard, and ask questions on that basis about whether Muslim women do or don't have rights, have enough rights or too few, we may better understand the international and national politics of rights. I would like to set aside the standard questions of whether Muslim women do or do not want rights, gain or lose more rights through secular versus Islamic law, or need advocates to deliver them their rights. Instead, I want to track Muslim women's rights into the multiple social worlds in which they operate. Who uses the concept and how? How is this changing?

What can we learn by stepping back from the usual terms of debate and the common sense that Muslim women are abused and have no (or precious few) rights and instead follow Muslim women's rights as they travel through various worlds and projects? We have seen how this concept circulates through debates and documents in the United States and Europe, including in legislation against "honor crimes" and outcries about "forced marriage." But we haven't yet considered how the concept organizes women's activism on the ground. We haven't looked at how it mediates the lives of women like Fayruz or Amal or Zaynab in various places in the Muslim world. Turning to the many institutions organized around rights, we can ask: What work do the practices organized in the name of Muslim women's rights do in various places, and for various women?

It might sound odd to describe rights as having a social life. I use this term to suggest that Muslim women's rights are to be found only in their social play. By this, I mean not just that "rights" circulate in social interactions or get transplanted and appropriated in various local settings but also that the concept takes different forms as it moves through social networks and technical instruments. The kinds of instruments that are crucial here might be anything from television soap operas to focus groups to beadwork cooperatives to gender awareness training sessions.[1]

I use the term "Muslim women's rights" not because there is something that unites all Muslim women or makes their lives and access to rights unique, but because, as I said from the outset, the notion that there is such a thing and the work and debates framed in terms of this concept have become commonsensical. I could have picked any number of locations where organizations work for women's rights or where women are fighting for their rights. I focus on Egypt and Palestine here because these are regions in which I have studied feminist activism.[2]

Egypt: In Shifting Fields

Egypt is a good place to examine the social life of women's rights. Its rich history of women's activism has been well documented and it boasts a very significant number of educated women involved in organizations that promote women's rights and offer women services. Many of these organizations are part of what might be thought of as the development industry, with women's empowerment as a goal. Women's rights (not framed, for the most part, as "Muslim women's rights" for good political reasons, given the history of nationalism and the mixed Coptic and Muslim population) have had an especially long and busy social life there. The formation of the Egyptian Feminist Union in the 1920s is one indication. The leaders of this organization went to international conventions and interacted with suffragettes and other feminists, whether from France, the United States, or India. Women's rights had been debated even earlier in Egypt, in the context of the colonial feminism I describe in Chapter 1 when talking about Afghanistan. The most significant early moment was when the modernizing nationalist Qasim Amin published an influential book in 1899 called *The Liberation of Women*. This book was read all over the Arab world and beyond.[3]

After the critical period of what scholars call state feminism under Gamal Abdel Nasser in the 1950s and 1960s, when independent women's organizations were shut down but sweeping legislation was put in place guaranteeing women education, jobs, labor rights, maternity leave, and various forms of state welfare, a new phase began under President Sadat and continued under Hosni Mubarak, who was deposed dramatically in 2011.[4] Neoliberal economic reform and the opening to the United States starting in the 1970s led to the retraction of important protective legislation. This paved the way for various civil society organizations—from the Islamists to women activists, many working through the paradigm and projects of development—to play a more active part in society while picking up some of the pieces of social welfare now abandoned by the privatizing state under structural adjustment.[5]

A wave of new women's nongovernmental organizations (NGOs) were formed in the 1980s and 1990s, enhanced by the full reentry of international foundations such as the Ford Foundation, the Population Council, and the United Nations International Children's Emergency Fund (UNICEF), and massive aid from European governments and the United States as part of the dividend from Egypt's peace with Israel. The traffic in women's rights was intensified with Egypt's participation in international conferences in the mid-1990s, most notably hosting the International Conference on Population and Development and sending delegates to the Fourth World Conference on Women in Beijing.[6]

Significant international funds ensured that women's rights and service organizations became a growth industry. During the Mubarak period, there were tens of thousands of NGOs operating in Egypt, despite dire restrictions on civil society organizations and periodic government crackdowns. Women's NGOs reflected perfectly the transformation of the political and economic terrain in Egypt and confirmed how critical such factors as transnational political organizing, economic exchange, class relations, and national historical shifts have been to the social life of women's rights.[7]

A study of women activists in the 1990s had already pointed out the link between women's organizations and the wider context. Nadje Al-Ali, an anthropologist now based in Britain, suggested that the debates and conflicts among these women's organizations were "a mirror of Egyptian political culture."[8] Debates about foreign funding were fierce as activists sought political independence and worried about American influence. This was true even though a later study based on a survey of sixty Egyptian NGOs showed that local organizations tried hard to get foreign funding even while complaining about the ways this funding constrained their choice of projects and forced local organizations "to tailor their objectives to suit the priorities of these agencies."[9]

The political-economic context affected women's rights most forcefully by setting down the channels through which they operated and setting up the technologies that mediated them. The three most significant shifts in the social life of rights in Egypt in the decade before the revolution were (1) their takeover by the government, (2) their entanglement with Islamic institutions and religious discourse, and (3) their commercialization or corporatization. Beginning in the 1990s, not only did government organizations like the National Council for Women or foreign NGOs come to mediate women's rights differently, but the politics, projects, and self-presentations of groups working for women's rights shifted to reflect the transnational appeal of human rights and to respond to the local situation in which religiosity has gained tremendous legitimacy.

The dramatic uprisings in Egypt in 2011 that toppled the regime reconfigured the political landscape, with women's rights issues attracting media attention and mobilizing many groups in relation to the elections and the new constitution. It is too early to tell how the electoral victory of the Muslim Brotherhood in 2012 will affect the social life of women's rights in Egypt over the next decade.[10] What is certain is that the issues have electrified the international sphere and media, and sparked local debate from the first moments of the demonstration in Tahrir Square.[11]

The Governmentalization of Rights

The way women's rights had been taken over by governmental organizations in the decade before the uprisings can best be seen in the establishment in 2000 of the National Council for Women (NCW) by presidential decree. As one observer noted, "under the auspices of Suzanne Mubarak, wife of the [then] Egyptian president, the Council was set up to advise the presidency and the government on the effect of public policies on women."[12] Some of the leaders of the NCW were respected individuals—like the leaders of its predecessor, the National Council for Childhood and Motherhood (set up by Suzanne Mubarak in 1988)—even though they worked with this governmental organization, something that often detracted from trust and respect, given the reputation of the regime. Yet there was initial suspicion by many in the NGO world just after the NCW's formation.

Rather than judging the NCW, let us ask what role it played in the field of women's rights in Egypt. The NCW tried to be inclusive, inviting the participation of many women previously active in women's issues in Egypt. They were invited as individuals, not as representatives of their organizations. This weakened the NGOs.[13] The NCW, run by the wife of the president, not surprisingly received significant funding from the Egyptian government, the United Nations Development Program, and many foreign sources including the United States Agency for International Development (USAID). Many of the smaller, more radical feminist NGOs would not accept this kind of funding. The significant number of projects conducted under its auspices suggests that the NCW became the major institution through which women's rights gained both visibility and practical existence in Egypt.

The NCW channeled funds along particular social and political lines. The funds for women's rights that the NCW could make use of were not negligible: the estimated cost to the UN system for one project outlined in the 2006 United Nations Development Assistance Framework was to have been $340 million over the five years, which did not include the amount to be contributed by the World Bank.[14] In taking a lion's share of development assistance available for women's projects, the NCW could determine who could be active in the business of promoting women's rights.[15]

State organizations' involvement in defining and producing women's rights was not the only change in the social field of "Muslim women's rights" in Egypt in that period. There was a decided shift in the kinds of projects and languages that defined work on behalf of women in Egypt due to the internationalization of women's rights in the NGO world. In a sense, the NGOs themselves are part of what Janet Halley and her colleagues have called "governance feminism," in which elites speak for women and use their gender expertise in influential institutions.[16] Human rights language came to dominate women's rights advocacy in Egypt.

International support for women's rights organizations also merged the interests of educated professional women in Egypt with the international hyperconcern about Middle Eastern and Muslim women's rights discussed in previous chapters. This led to the proliferation of organizations and projects and the sort of transnational governance structures found in many countries of the global South. This is well illustrated by the Association for the Development and Enhancement of Women (ADEW), an organization founded in 1987 to provide microcredit to women heads of household.[17] With a hugely impressive list of international donors, ADEW eventually came to boast literacy programs, health services, legal awareness seminars, and a shelter. It operated from fifteen offices in five different areas of Egypt with a staff of 200.[18]

Accommodating Islamic Institutions and Religious Discourse

A second characteristic of the social life of women's rights in Egypt in the past decade was the new accommodation with religious institutions and ideology. Although most of those involved in the official world of women's rights work in Egypt, like elsewhere, believed that women's rights are under threat by rising conservative Islamist elements (and are now wondering how to respond to leadership by the Muslim Brotherhood), there had been various ways to respond, especially in a world of close social and personal ties.

The more explicit engagement with Islam could be seen clearly in the NGO world, as well as in governmental organizations. The Center for Egyptian Women's Legal Assistance (CEWLA) offers a good case for analysis. It was founded in 1995, and is located in a poor and crowded informal neighborhood in Cairo. It had been set up there to help just this sort of population; even after it was better funded, it refused to leave the area because of its commitment to serving the community. CEWLA had started small, with just a couple of rooms and file boxes for furniture.[19] Headed by a female attorney, Azza Sleiman, many of the staff are also women lawyers. They are graduates of the Egyptian universities where women constitute more than half the students, as they do in higher-education institutions in most countries of the Arab world. Given financial support initially by such organizations as the Canadian International Development Agency and Dutch Oxfam, and later by many others including the Now or Never Fund of the Global Fund for Women, the Ford Foundation, and the Sawiris Foundation,[20] CEWLA expanded its mission from legal aid to raising awareness about violence and children's rights, lobbying at the national level, conducting studies and publishing research, and providing direct services including adult literacy education, democracy training for children, and sexual and reproductive health education for teenagers.

CEWLA's initiative in 2008 took the organization in a relatively new direction that represented a shift in the social life and institutional mediations of Muslim women's rights. The particular dynamics were Egyptian but, as I argue in Chapter 6, what CEWLA was funded to do reflected a global trend. The trend has been toward highlighting the religious identities of women, even though the NGOs are not faith-based or linked to a particular religious organization.[21]

CEWLA was dedicated to demonstrating the compatibility of the UN Convention on the Elimination of All Forms of Discrimination against Women (CEDAW) and Shari'a, or, more correctly, Islamic family law. CEWLA took up this project in response to both the larger cultural-political context—in which religiosity has been increasingly respected—and the concerns brought to them by the ordinary poor women, men, and youths they serve. Seham Ali, the lawyer who spoke to me about CEWLA, explained that people in Egypt tend to be suspicious of anything that comes from the West. Some have accused CEDAW of seeking to destroy the family and undermine religion. This new project was intended to counter that ignorance. For this, CEWLA was going to route itself through new institutional networks, enlisting experts in Islamic law, and particularly a respected and "noncontroversial" professor of Islamic philosophy at Al-Azhar University, the great religious establishment in Egypt.[22]

CEWLA was not the only NGO to be dealing with Al-Azhar. In the UN Development Assistance Framework for Egypt 2007–2011, Al-Azhar is listed as a partner of the National Council for Women and several ministries, including that of Religious

Endowments, in the pursuit of two goals: changing perceptions of women's rights and combating gender violence.[23]

Commercializing Rights

In one of the more dramatic shifts since around 2000 and symptomatic of a tilt toward a neoliberal model for civil society, Dr. Iman Bibars, the feminist cofounder of ADEW, became the coordinator of the Middle East North Africa fellows program of Ashoka. Ashoka describes itself as the global association of the world's leading social entrepreneurs. In a television interview, Bibars explained, "We are the venture capitalists of the social sector." Ashoka accepts no government funding, but instead looks for partnerships between corporations and foundations.[24] The business language of Ashoka's creed is on its website: "We believe that the growth of a global citizen sector begins with the work of individual social entrepreneurs. These entrepreneurs drive the sector forward, responding to new challenges and changing needs. They are rooted in local communities but think and act globally. They are the ultimate role models and the pillars of Ashoka's [trademarked] vision of Everyone a Changemaker."[25]

This is the third path that was being taken in the evolving social life of Muslim women's rights in Egypt, at least before the revolution. Women's rights talk began to operate in a commercial world. The dramatic change could be seen most clearly in the work of the Egyptian Center for Women's Rights (ECWR), founded in 1996, only a year after CEWLA. The ECWR's website announces its liberal ideology: "CWR's work is based on the belief that women's rights are an integral part of human rights and are key to any substantive progress towards building a democratic culture and development in Egypt and the Middle East region."[26] But the

ECWR makes a novel appeal—to socially responsible corporate sponsorship.

One of the ECWR's high-profile campaigns was against sexual harassment on the streets.[27] Without denying that harassment of women occurs on the streets of Cairo and other cities, I want to draw attention to one aspect of their campaign that is crucial for thinking about the social life of rights. The ECWR mobilized innovative technologies for this depoliticizing issue that has no structural analysis of gender inequality and no target other than men with bad cultural attitudes. One attempt to raise money consisted in a proposal to develop a system for mapping harassment through Short Message Service (SMS) text messages. The proposal was submitted for the 2008 USAID Development 2.0 Challenge through NetSquared; the winner was to be determined by a jury after a popular vote narrowed the contestants down to fifteen finalists (à la Star Academy and American Idol, which are both popular TV genres in the Arab world now).[28] The ECWR thanked its corporate "volunteers"—Nile and Nugoom FM, Masrawy.com, Filbalad.com, Egyptsoft.org, Goethe Institute, and Netsmart Egypt—for having "given a life and professionalism to the campaign that was unmatched in NGO work in Egypt." The bid for mobile phone technology development, corporate cooperation, and popular voting fit perfectly in contemporary Cairo, where shopping malls, satellite television, ads for vying cell phone companies, and consumerism had come to dominate the landscape.[29]

This campaign also marked the transplantation or implantation in Egypt of the transnational trend to focus on violence against women, supported through various UN organizations, particularly the United Nations Development Fund for Women (UNIFEM) and the CEDAW Commission.[30] It is interesting to observe how much fund-raising and career building takes place around this issue that circulates well beyond the halls of the UN and CEDAW hearings. The One in Three Women Global Campaign to raise awareness about violence against women, for example, encourages you to buy their cards, charms, and dog tags;[31] Peacekeeper Cause-metics asks you to support women's causes by purchasing their lipstick and nail polish.[32] Peacekeeper Cause-metics gives a fraction of its proceeds to fight honor crimes and other forms of cultural violence against women associated with the Muslim world. Ayaan Hirsi Ali's foundation is only the most recent to pick up this commercialization of women's rights, inviting us to get our own high-quality "Honour" tote bag, for a donation.

Palestine: Inescapable Politics

Thinking about violence against women takes us to another case and space of rights work. The Global Campaign to Stop Killing and Stoning Women is a global project orchestrated in the name of Muslim women's rights. Launched in 2007, it is coordinated by the network Women Living under Muslim Laws (WLUML), founded on a shoestring in 1984 by the antifundamentalist French Algerian feminist Marieme Hélie-Lucas.[33] The WLUML has grown to be a major international player in defending Muslim women's rights, producing alerts, research, and conferences cast in terms of endangered or abused Muslim women.[34]

The campaign isolates, targets, and publicizes culturally specific forms of violence against women: violations of Muslim women's rights by Muslim regimes, Muslim fundamentalists, and local (Muslim) families. In its press announcement, the new campaign justified itself by the need "to address the intensifying trend of cultural and religious legitimization of lethal violence against women."[35] Individual cases of stoning or threatened stoning, whipping, and honor crimes merge together on the campaign website as if they were instances of the same phenomenon, despite radical differences among individual cases, countries of origin, reliability of information, and legitimacy in the eyes of Muslim thinkers, state legal systems, and ordinary people.

Violence against women is a serious problem worldwide. But to begin to see what is peculiar about its deployment in the service of work on Muslim women's rights, I have to draw attention to the context in which this campaign is being mounted. First, we can't ignore the fact that this campaign emerged in the midst of a dense terrain of similar sensationalizing projects to save Muslim women from their cultures, whether imagined as backward rural cultures by educated youths, as I show in Chapter 4 for honor crimes, or as the result of an oppressive Islamic law or religion, as Ayaan Hirsi Ali, right-wing Americans and Europeans, and even other feminists, argue as part of the new common sense.[36]

The second aspect of the context is that the campaign was launched in a period of great violence against (Muslim) women inflicted in war. Military conflict still gripped Afghanistan and Iraq. Soon after the campaign was launched, just before Christmas, the Israeli Defense Forces attacked Gaza. In twenty-three days, more than 1,300 Palestinians were killed—buried alive in houses bombed by F16s, shot at close range in their beds, machinegunned from the sea, shelled by tanks using flechettes, and burned by white phosphorus, which acts like napalm.[37] How many were women? I asked myself then: Where was the "global feminist campaign" against killing or hurting such significant numbers of Muslim women? Women and civilians in conflict zones suffer and die in great numbers because of the violence.[38]

Palestinian women activists have had to negotiate this situation for years, balancing their commitment to women's rights, as well as contact with feminists from other countries and regions, with an awareness of the specific political context within which they and the women for whom they advocate live and work. Despite widespread self-criticism about the depoliticizing effects of the "NGOization" of the Palestinian women's movement that has brought on professionalization, hierarchies based on expertise, diversion of energies to funders' desires for gender training and research reports, and deflection of women from political mobilization to grant writing, Palestinian women's rights advocates have remained consistent in their national commitments and constant awareness of the larger political situation.[39] Palestinian NGOs and projects, whether in the Occupied Territories or within the 1948 borders, may be funded by the Scandinavians, the Germans, the Ford Foundation, the Open Society, the World Health Organization (WHO), and UNIFEM, just like Egyptian NGOs, but at the core of their efforts are the inescapable realities of occupation and militarization, and in the case of the Palestinian citizens of Israel, marginalization and discrimination.[40]

One of the most moving studies from this region is the report on some "action-research" on women and loss that was conducted during the second intifada, which began in 2000. The report illustrates several features of women's rights work in Palestine that make it different, perhaps, from the social life of rights in Egypt. The study was designed to help produce effective psychological and social therapies for women while at the same time giving voice to women's experiences of political conflict. As Nadera Shalhoub-Kevorkian, the initiator of the study, argues in her chapter in *Women, Armed Conflict and Loss: The Mental Health of Palestinian Women in the Occupied Territories,* the project was to stand "at the crossroads between human rights violations, mental health and research."[41] The study produced stories of individual women—wrenching accounts of trauma and coping in response to political violence (like watching your son's brain spill on the ground as Israeli soldiers trample his body), house raids and demolition (seeing your house blown up when you've hidden your sons in the well at the center of the house), terror and sexual harassment (soldiers molesting your daughters), gender-related violence (surveillance of martyrs' wives, births at checkpoints, unemployed and frustrated husbands at home), and continuous fear and insecurity.[42]

Many committed feminists in Palestine cooperate with international and governmental organizations to work for women's rights or empowerment. Human rights claims, in particular, are recognized as a powerful tool for Palestinians, claims they cannot forfeit even though they know and understand the academic and political critiques of human rights.[43] Palestinian women's NGOs point to the larger structural features that affect Palestinian women's lives, even as they participate in women's rights institutions and networks that are transnational and that are often silent on such political features of everyday life. This was not often the case in Egypt, where the regime could barely be criticized, and where the devastating consequences of neoliberal reform policies for women's and men's lives seemed to lie outside the frame, at least until the revolution.

The problem Palestinian rights workers face, according to Penny Johnson, a researcher at Birzeit University, is that those scholar-activists like Shalhoub-Kevorkian who assist international organizations such as Human Rights Watch (HRW) are sometimes dismayed to find "that none of their analysis of violence of the occupation and siege and its effects on women and families" is included in the final reports.[44] Johnson complains that *A Question of Security,* one such HRW report, "isolates domestic violence and implicitly gender relations and Palestinian families from all the contexts in which they function." She charges that such reports ignore the effects of occupation and siege on the Palestinian Authority's ability to enforce law and do not take into consideration the effects of pervasive violence and economic strangulation on Palestinian family relations.[45]

If Halley's "governance feminism" nicely characterizes much of Egyptian women's rights work, Islah Jad and others have similarly shown how the establishment of the Palestine National Authority in the West Bank and Gaza, and particularly its patronage of "femocrats" alongside the proliferation since the 1990s of foreign-funded NGOs, led to what they call the demobilization of the Palestinian women's movement, which used to be political.[46] Paying careful attention to the types of work, forms of organization, hierarchies, and social networks the new means of pursuing women's rights have entailed—the social life of rights—reveals that there has been a gradual disempowerment of women activists. Jad is most concerned about how this has left the field of grassroots women wide open for Islamist mobilization (about which she has been uniquely open-minded),[47] but I think she underestimates the distinctive way that even the depoliticized NGO technologies of gender training courses might still, in the highly charged Palestinian national context, intersect with and enhance other sorts of women's rights work carried out in more activist veins.

A hint of this can be gleaned from the story another researcher, Sama Aweidah, tells about her first encounter on a trip to the Jenin refugee camp that also formed the subject of the study of women's loss by Shalhoub-Kevorkian.[48] The multinational delegation she accompanied in order to get into the devastated refugee camp was organized by the Union of Palestinian Medical Relief Committees. When they arrived, they were greeted by some young men doing medical relief. When these young men found out there were two Palestinians who had managed to come with the international delegation, they were excited to hear that they came from women's centers because, it turned out, these young men had previously had some gender training by the Jerusalem Women's Studies Centre. They even recognized her name from their training course materials. Such crossovers from gender training to therapeutic and political work characterize the field of women's rights work in Palestine because of the peculiarities of this national context.

Hybrid Circuits in Everyday Life

If we now understand more about the shifting fields of women's rights work in Egypt and the tight nexus of women's rights and national politics in Palestine, we still need to think about how Muslim women's rights are mediated outside of the direct reach of these local advocates and defenders of women's rights. For all of these professionals, sometimes held up as brave heroines for fighting for women's rights in their own societies, there are women (other than themselves) who are imagined as the targets of their protective efforts. How do Muslim women's rights circulate in the lives of these grassroots beneficiaries?

I want to return to the village I know in Upper Egypt to look at how the social instruments of rights mediate women's lives there. We need to understand how the circuits of rights within such villages intersect with—and diverge from—those we have been following in elite urban and international sites. What happens when we turn to communities of women who seem to lie outside the catchment areas and social networks of Egyptian women's rights groups? I turn to these women not to discredit or disparage the professionals and activists who plow the social fields of Muslim women's rights, but to give a sense of both the reach and the shapes of discourses of Muslim women's and girls' rights far away from the metropolitan centers where they are so vivid, variegated, and well funded.[49]

I have traced some nodes in the international circulation of rights—going in and out of the various women's organizations that promote them, the donor foundations that fund these organizations, and the states that entangle with a rights agenda in two particular countries, Egypt and Palestine. As an anthropologist who works in rural communities, I also want to ask how Muslim women's rights run, if they do, through ordinary women's lives.

When I was doing research in Egypt on women's rights organizations in 2008, I took a break and went back to some of my friends in the village to talk about this new project. Many had something to say (just as Zaynab would three years later, when she criticized the government). A couple of young women I'd known since they were girls immediately launched into an animated discussion of a popular television serial that they had just finished watching during Ramadan. It featured Egypt's biggest film star, Yusra. They told me the plot: A group of youths kidnap a female doctor and some nurses on their way home late at night and rape one of them. The show, they said, was about bringing these rapists to justice. They wanted me to know that rape is punishable by death.

That they had paid attention to the message of the television serial and were part of a national conversation is significant, but nothing new. Egyptian television dramas often take up important social issues, as I explored in my book, *Dramas of Nationhood*. This serial, *A Matter of Public Opinion*, had launched public debates on violence against women. After it was broadcast, the serial was discussed and the main actor praised at a celebration in Amman of UNIFEM's global campaign, "Sixteen Days of Activism to End Violence against Women."

Another young woman showed that national television had mediated women's understandings of women's rights in this

Upper Egyptian village. When I asked her what she knew about
women's rights, she said, "It's something Suzanne Mubarak is
working on. It's about female circumcision." Indeed, one of the
key projects of the National Council for Childhood and Motherhood that addressed violence against girl children was the push
for circumcision-free model villages.

Village women were tied into national discourses of rights.
When I asked another woman and her teenage daughter if they
knew of any local organizations for women's rights, they had no
idea. They agreed that perhaps such organizations existed in
Cairo, but they didn't know of any in their region. But then we
got onto the subject of what happened if a woman was having
troubles with her husband. The mother explained that their families would come together to try to sort things out and make
peace. When I asked about inheritance (the subject that would
several years later be at the heart of Fayruz's struggles), at first she
said that a woman could go to court. But, she added, it was more
likely that people would come to talk to her brother if he was
resisting. They would try to persuade him to give the sister her
fair share.

When I explained to her that the reason I was working on the
topic of women's rights was that some Westerners consider
Egyptian women oppressed, she laughed. "No, no. They *used* to
be," she said. "That was in the past. Now there's progress. All
the girls are getting educated now." Her generation had been required to help their mothers in the household, she explained.
Now, they all wanted their kids educated. She and her husband
were working very hard so that their kids could do well in
school. He was encouraging his daughter to study French, in the
hope that it would help her get into college. So though the word
"rights" did not come up in this woman's response, she certainly
shared the developmentalist discourse of girls' education as the

quintessential sign of progress, even a right. She knew full well that she had to work harder in the house and with the animals because her husband wanted more for his daughters.[50] This equation had been established and publicized by the state in schools and media since the dreams of national development in the 1950s became the stuff of mass consumption.

Discussions with other women revealed the multiple mediations and registers of women's rights in this village. 'Aysha, a woman in her forties whom I had met in a literacy class in the mid-1990s, gave me the best evidence of the hybridity of the concept of "Muslim women's rights" in this rural village and a sense of the multiple institutional circuits through which rights are produced and pursued. The literacy classes where I met her were themselves part of the national machinery of women's rights: sponsored by Suzanne Mubarak for a couple of years with local women graduates hired to teach, then discontinued for no reason.

When I told 'Aysha that my new project was on women's rights in Egypt, she exclaimed, "Let me tell you, the woman in Egypt enjoys the highest level of rights. Truly . . . Do you know, Lila, that we have women ministers in the cabinet? Ministers! The minister of social affairs. The head of the Finance Ministry. All of them are women. Here in Egypt, the government has given women their rights, 100 percent."

But then she went on to qualify this: "But people, a woman's family, they are the ones who undermine her rights. Say it happens that my father leaves me three acres of land. Her brother comes along and says, 'No, she shouldn't take it. The girl shouldn't take the land.' Here, the government gives her her rights." Picking up on the shifting pronouns—my father, her brother—I asked if this happened to her. She laughed. "This is just a for instance. Praise be to God," she added (so as not to be complaining about her fate), "my family doesn't have any land!"

Then she continued, "So the brother takes his sister's land. It happens. In some families. Not all, because some families give to the daughters . . . He says, 'I want the land. I'm a man, I should take the land.'"

Her response to this imagined brother was, "But God, Glory be to Him, gives women an inheritance."[51] She then quoted the Qur'anic passage that mandates that women inherit. She concluded, "So if God sent down in the Qur'an word that a woman is entitled, that the woman should get her inheritance, how dare you fight this?"

When I asked what a woman would do in these circumstances, she responded, "She goes to the government." Only a few seconds later, she modified this. "Well, first she goes to complain to the family. To the elders." Immediately after that, however, she gave a different example that related to their specific village. She reminded me that they had an important religious figure in the next village, a respected man whose father and grandfather had also been religious leaders. She said, "We go to him with any problem like this. Women do." Just then, her older brother walked into the room and she confirmed with him, "Isn't it true that a girl goes to the shaykh if she has a problem with her uncle or her brother? Yes, she complains to him. It's normal. And he listens to her." Her brother nodded and then went on to tell a story of a major problem that the shaykh had resolved, interestingly, not between a girl and her family, but between a Christian and some Muslim families in a dispute over land. This showed the shaykh's enormous grace, generosity, and wisdom, and suggested why he had the respect of all in mediating arguments.[52]

During this one conversation, 'Aysha talked about rights in multiple registers: she invoked national legal rights for women; she assessed women's rights in terms of political representation;

she talked about local conflicts within and among families; and then, finally, she described the God-given rights granted to women in the Qur'an. In another conversation we had a year later, she defended Islam in general. She insisted that Islam says women are free to work and free to go to school. She then gave examples of important women in the Prophet Muhammad's time: Nafisa, who was a teacher, and 'Aysha who transmitted *hadith*s, the sayings of the Prophet. But, she added, some women had decided that freedom meant wearing short dresses with short sleeves and walking around the streets naked. There is too much freedom now, she concluded. Mixing yet again several registers of rights, she explained that this kind of freedom was not what Qasim Amin had meant. Here she invoked Amin, that classic turn-of-the-twentieth-century Egyptian modernist reformer and author of the tract *The Liberation of Women,* who supported women's limited education and unveiling.

In her discussion, 'Aysha also referenced the multiple institutions that mediate rights in Egypt. These are the forums through which individual women might seek justice: the courts with their lawyers, legalities, and papers; local family arbitration with its pull of emotions, hierarchies, and cross-cutting ties; and the institution of the local religious figure who would intervene in the name of Islamic rights and morality if a woman was wronged by her family. She did not mention NGOs, even though in a nearby region an extremely well-funded transnational humanitarian project was under way, dedicated to uplifting and educating village girls about their "natural claims to rights, including the right to learn, play, and be physically mobile."[53] Like the other women and girls whose conversations about women's rights I have quoted, 'Aysha has learned these multiple ways of framing lives and asserting rights from television, from school, from religious study, and from the everyday lives of those around her. Community members tend to have few secrets, so their knowledge of the possible is rich and intimate.

When I returned to visit 'Aysha in 2012, a year after the uprisings and in the immediate aftermath of the parliamentary elections, I was struck even more that everywhere I went, women and girls wanted to talk.[54] They were talking politics. At the national level, they were stunned by the unfolding revelations about just how corrupt the regime had been from top to bottom, and just how vast the scale of wealth appropriation and theft by the elites had been. They were especially scandalized by the discovery (or rumor) that Suzanne Mubarak had taken for her personal property the jewels of Queen Nazli, the mother of the former monarch, King Farouk. These belonged to the nation, they insisted. They were furious that the former president's yearlong trial was probably not going to deliver justice. They expressed a special empathy for the families of the young people killed in the streets by security forces during the first weeks of the uprisings—the martyrs. They deserved justice.

At the local level, they were excited about the parliamentary elections that had just taken place. They were eager to talk about the campaign platforms—their concerns about the Muslim Brotherhood had been eased by the reassurances that they would not ban tourism, but only ask that tourists respect local morality. They liked that idea. But some also joked about aspects of the process. The Muslim Brotherhood had arranged for transportation to take girls and women to vote, but the young women shrewdly noted that the expectation was that they would support the party's candidates for parliament. As one girl said mischievously, "But how would they know who we voted for?"

Everyone commented on how before, people had not been able to talk. Now there was a strong sense that they could. They would not go back to silence and despair. Too much had been revealed about just how much and exactly how the system had wronged them—as citizens, not as women.

In an ethnographic study of the interaction between a Scandinavian feminist NGO and the village women's organization it supported on an island off the coast of Tanzania, Christine Walley has argued that a universalizing term like "rights" accumulates meanings from multiple sources.[55] She shows that for the Muslim women in the community in which she worked, the Kiswahili term translated as rights *(haki)* could refer to prerogatives and obligations found in Islamic law, as well as suggest customary justice. But she also found that in the independence and socialist periods, *haki* had accumulated other meanings that were tied to ideas of citizenship. More recently, the term had come to be used in the context of international human and women's rights frameworks that the leaders of this organization encountered when they were sent to conferences by their Scandinavian funders. As a consequence, when a woman asserted or claimed her "rights," one simply could not know what register she was using, which meaning(s) of rights she was referencing, or whether in fact these all inflected each other, producing a dense sense of rights.

Walley's challenging presentation of the way conceptions of rights are layered in one grassroots situation is intriguing, and seems to describe women's mobilizations of "rights" in Egyptian villages well, too. Walley did not pursue what I attempt to showcase here: the need to do a more sociological tracking of the networks, institutions, and technologies that mediate such rights. In the Egyptian village from which I have been drawing my examples, it is clear that even though there are no women's rights organizations, comments like 'Aysha's reveal the ways national and international enterprises of women's rights have shaped local conceptualizations of rights and made certain institutions, from schools to state courts, central to their pursuit. At the same time, her comments also reveal something worth noting: how many social institutions and imaginative frameworks outside of the dominant work of NGOs and government are part of local women's active pursuit of justice and their imagination of rights. The religious idiom of Islamic law—only now becoming a track for rights in urban centers, as we see in the case of the legal rights organization, CEWLA—and the local moral force of popular religious authorities, alongside the extended family that remains the most significant social form, exceed the frames and social institutions of more official women's rights work in Egypt.

We need to find new ways of thinking about Muslim women's rights—that sensationalized international issue that is so entangled with military intervention and transnational feminism, progressive foundations and right-wing think tanks, elite careers and welfare administration, literary commerce and marginal lives. An ethnographic approach that tracks the social lives in which the concept partakes may be more useful for understanding this subject and the moment we are living than moral posturing that judges women's rights to be either collusion with imperialism (to be denounced) or a hopeful sign of universal emancipation and progress (to be celebrated).

I have offered an alternative: approaching Muslim women's rights as something that makes and remakes the world. How, when, and where is the concept deployed? What transformations of social and individual lives are produced in its name? Who enables that work and is in turn enabled by it? What new paths of power and channels of capital—financial and cultural— does it open up?

Anthropologists have urged us to study the "social practice of rights" and to closely observe rights talk and implementation.[56]

I argue here for something more: to trace carefully, across multiple terrains, the way both practices and talk of rights organize
social and political fields, producing organizations, projects, and
forms of governing as much as being produced by them. If we
take this approach, there is no alternative but to go into the details of Muslim women's rights as they move in and out of particular locations and communities. In Cairo, the women's rights
industry creates careers, channels funds, inspires commitments,
gives credibility to new actors, creates and disrupts social networks, and legitimizes intellectual and political frameworks and
ideals. Women's rights provide a conduit for foreign intervention
and government involvement in ordering the daily lives of both
the middle classes and those at the margins. Women's rights are
subjects of corporate sponsorship and adopted as a symbol of
modernity, but they are also, and increasingly so now, the objects
of struggle among religious institutions and organizations, especially Islamic parties and movements, and have been taken up by
new forms of feminism that some call Islamic feminism, as I explore in Chapter 6.

Juxtaposing the Egyptian case to the Palestinian reveals how
dependent the operation of Muslim women's rights is on the
larger political situation. We need to look at the organization
and resources of countries and the configuration of international interest. Palestine may have women's NGOs that are just
as well funded as Egypt, but the nature of the work they do, the
social networks they forge, their links to international and national institutions, and even the class relations and solidarities
among the women and their beneficiaries differ dramatically
from the Egyptian case.[57]

Anyone seriously interested in Muslim women's rights must
follow them as they move. The village in which I've been fortunate to work over so many years houses the kinds of marginal

women often imagined to be the beneficiaries of rights work: "traditional" women in need of rights and empowerment. The women and girls in this village are not members of any women's rights organizations or recipients of their funds. They have not been the objects of rights, except through a short-lived government literacy program for women in the 1990s (in which Fayruz learned to write her name), and a few equally fleeting initiatives by individual Europeans for handicraft production.

The fragments of conversation on the subject of women's rights I have reported from this village demonstrate that no one is unaffected by the circulation of discourses on Muslim women's rights and the practical ways their pursuit is being negotiated. At the same time, these fragments indicate that the framework and the projects of Muslim women's rights do not begin to exhaust women's conceptions of rights or their experiences of trying to assert them.

CHAPTER 6

An Anthropologist in the Territory of Rights

All of us who are concerned about women's suffering and well-being find ourselves in a world saturated with talk about rights and the institutions—small and large, local and transnational—that have arisen to defend them. I entered the territory of rights because of my consternation about the ways Muslim women's rights were being put to political use for intervention in Afghanistan. Then, during the past decade, I began exploring other regions and tributaries of this rights system. The advances of feminists into the international and local organizations for women's rights led me to understand that rights activists, as discussed in Chapter 5, were not outside of power, even if their sense of solidarity with other women and feeling of common subordination might distinguish women's rights work from some other forms of international rights work or humanitarian sentiment.

Perhaps because I was such a latecomer to this territory—someone whose anthropological research over thirty years had *not* been organized around rights, human or otherwise—I continue to struggle with the framework.[1] I experience some uncomfortable problems of fit when I think about rights because of the ethnographic research I have done, some "thick" and some "thin."[2] The thick ethnography is of everyday life in the village in rural Egypt. The thin is some modest research on organizations that promote women's rights and empowerment in and across the Muslim world. Muslim women's rights work is taking new creative forms. Rather than talk about the more secular nongovernmental organizations (NGOs) that have dominated the scene since the 1970s and that I discuss in Chapter 5, I focus here on the newer initiatives of Islamic feminists.

Taking both conceptual and practical rights as objects of study, other anthropologists have shown that rights can be performative—they make things happen and they mobilize people—and that the rights framework can be transplanted and translated into other languages, what Sally Merry has called vernaculars.[3] They have traced how rights instruments and language are produced through a social machinery that operates in many sites, from United Nations (UN) and government offices to NGOs around the world.[4]

Some anthropologists have stood by indigenous people and other disadvantaged groups to defend their rights; others have been more wary of engagement.[5] Even when they have supported marginal groups, they have been conscious of the double binds and paradoxes. In Australia, for example, the demands of liberal multiculturalism have placed aboriginal Australians trying to make land claims in the odd position of having to prove cultural authenticity and continuity when the very same settlers who took their land had devastated their culture too.[6] Anthropologists working in Africa have shown how human rights work has ended up promoting new social distinctions, opening career paths for some, and depoliticizing neoliberal reform and transnational governance.[7] Many anthropologists have realized that human rights claims depend on treating human suffering at the natural level of bodies, displacing other sorts of more political claims, such as those based on people's citizenship.[8]

When they challenge the innocent morality of the rights regime, anthropologists join a number of political and legal theorists who have asked whether humanitarianism is the new face of colonialism. Some have pointed out the paradoxes of rights-based arguments: that they allow people to make claims, but lock them into fixed identities defined by their injuries rather than freeing them from these identities into a world of equals; or they absolve the perpetrators of past violence by making them the defenders of rights.[9] Transnational feminist theorists have worried about the implications of linking women's rights to human rights. Ratna Kapur's influential analysis of the way rights discourses construct third world women as "victim-subjects" and Inderpal Grewal's charge that human rights is "a regime of truth" linked both to welfare and forms of power are both exemplary.[10]

My own discomfort with the framework and practices of rights for those who want to address suffering and promote social justice stems from something additional that I clarify by looking not at conventional secular human or women's rights, but at some new initiatives that seek to establish women's rights through Islam. They do so by seeking to reform Islamic law, particularly family law, or by offering nonpatriarchal interpretations of the Qur'an. My ambivalence about these activist projects— diverse, innovative, and potentially transformative as they may be—arises from thinking about them in light of what I know about women's lives in rural communities in Egypt. Women like Zaynab, 'Aysha, Amal, and others I introduce in this book are the imagined beneficiaries of these Muslim feminists' efforts to guarantee women's rights through a more indigenous framework.[11]

These are the same "oppressed Muslim women" that, as we have seen, other moral crusaders seek to save.

My argument is in two parts. In a sociological sense, I ask whether initiatives like these can be understood outside the frames of global governance that are tied to class privilege and education, even though the participants work with a shared sense of religious community and admirable religious knowledge. Second, I ask whether any legalistic framework of rights or gender equality can do justice to the complexity of women's lives and suffering. An intimate look into the troubles women face in one Egyptian village leads me to conclude that there is always a certain incommensurability between everyday lives and the social imagination of rights, whether by outsiders, by veterans of women's activism in the region, or by these new cosmopolitan Islamic feminists.

I use the situation of one young woman, Khadija, to articulate my discomfort with a rights frame. She is a victim of domestic violence. Violence is considered a classic violation of women's rights and has been the focus of transnational feminism for years. It is also the focus of at least one of these new Muslim feminist initiatives.[12] My concern here is that the selective rendering of women's lives in the Muslim world in terms of rights risks reinforcing existing (and sometimes malicious) simplifications of their complicated lives and experiences. This is the case even though most of those working to improve women's rights in these communities do not share these negative or simplistic views, and even though women across the world now—even in villages such as this one in rural Egypt, as we see with 'Aysha in Chapter 5—use various hybrid and sometimes contradictory languages of rights to assert claims.

Women's Rights and Islamic Reform

A couple of recent initiatives suggest that a new social configuration and playing field for advocacy of Muslim women's rights is emerging. Building on many local initiatives in Iran, Afghanistan, Turkey, Indonesia, Lebanon, and Egypt, and responding in complex ways to the Islamic revival and the growing appeal of Muslim politics, many educated cosmopolitan Muslim women are no longer defensive about exploring what Americans would call "faith-based" feminism.[13] These serious and thoughtful projects are quite distinct from the highly publicized efforts of some individual Muslim women in the West who claim to be criticizing Islam from within but are playing a different game.[14] They are also distinct from the political engagements of many women across the Muslim world who have joined Islamist political parties and movements—women who, without appealing to a rights language, have challenged gender norms in their communities through their political activism and public service.[15] I would like to look closely at two initiatives before asking how they might relate to the everyday lives of some women in one village.

The first group to consider is Musawah (which means equality). Launched in Kuala Lumpur in February 2009, it calls itself "a global movement for equality and justice in the Muslim family." It was spearheaded by a leading organization of what many call Islamic feminism, a Malaysian-based feminist organization called Sisters in Islam.[16] Registered as an NGO in 1993, Sisters in Islam has been active since the late 1980s in advocacy around Muslim women's rights and discriminatory family law.[17]

Three features of the way Musawah's mission statement begins are significant: "We, as Muslims and as citizens, declare that equality and justice in the family are both necessary and possible. The time for realising these values in our laws and practices is now."[18] First, note the "we" as an entitlement to speak from within. Second, note the mixed religious and political identities that define the rights claims: "We, as Muslims and as citizens." Third, consider the hybrid sources of rights they invoke in what follows: "Musawah declares that equality in the family is possible through a framework that is consistent with Islamic teachings, universal human rights principles, fundamental rights guarantees, and the lived realities of women and men." Musawah's reasoning follows two principles: they prioritize the objectives of Shari'a rather than the legal schools (as they have developed historically); and they insist that there must be a fit with the contemporary world. Here is the way they put it: "Muslim laws and practices must reflect justice, which is the indisputable objective of the Shari'ah. They must also uphold equality, which is an essential part of today's understanding of justice."[19]

The generic models for Musawah are drawn as much from the ideational world of liberal international organizations as Islamic legal or moral discourse. Musawah's Framework for Action is deliberately structured along the lines of documents such as the *Universal Declaration of Human Rights:* It has a preamble that declares principles and states the conditions, followed by a delineation of principles using the form of numbered articles. What distinguishes it from its models and marks it as a hybrid form is its religious opening line: "We hold the principles of Islam to be a source of justice, equality, fairness and dignity for all human beings."[20]

The reformist projects of these Muslim feminists who have established organizations like Musawah share qualities of thought and argumentation with earlier reformist projects in the Muslim world that emerged from the colonial encounter. The explicit focus of Musawah is Muslim family law. It does not engage in debates about how best to interpret the Qur'an; instead, it begins with the more modest and sound observation that family laws are man-made, the result of interpretations shaped by the social conditions of the periods in which Islam's sacred texts were turned into law by jurists.[21] However, it also follows the standard modernist reformist arguments of the last century that one must seek an ethical Islam, true to its spirit and guided by the objectives of Shari'a, and thus to make Islam appropriate for contemporary realities. The targets of Musawah's critiques are the Muslim jurists and the claims to expertise and authority of those conservatives who follow them. To support its stance, Musawah reminds people of the importance of diversity of opinion in the Islamic tradition, points to specific verses of the Qur'an that promote equality, exposes the way human interpretation has corrupted understanding, and highlights concepts within the tradition that could support human rights.[22]

The vocabulary of democratic liberalism saturates Musawah's arguments. Holism is a key concept in Zainah Anwar's introduction to their resource book, *Wanted: Equality and Justice in the Muslim Family*.[23] She points out that women's groups in various Muslim countries "have begun to explore a broader, more holistic framework that argues for reform from multiple perspectives— religious, international human rights, constitutional and fundamental rights guarantees, and women's lived realities."[24] One aspect of holism for Anwar is therefore to limit the role of religion: she advocates treating religion as *only one source* for policy and legal reform.[25] The first major research project Musawah undertook was a study of the common ground between the UN Convention on the Elimination of All Forms of Discrimination against Women (CEDAW) and Muslim family laws.[26]

Some have celebrated Sisters in Islam, Women Living under Muslim Laws (WLUML), and now Musawah as heralding a new "enlightenment" in the Muslim world. This suggests that at least some people associate these reform initiatives with the tradition of secular liberalism. The clever title of one legal scholar's blog about the Musawah launch even played on, and therefore reinforced in a ghostly way, one key text in the "oppressed Muslim women" literary genre that has been promoted so hard by neoconservative hawks in the United States. Mahdavi Sunder's "Reading the Quran in Kuala Lumpur" inflects Azar Nafisi's best-selling *Reading Lolita in Tehran*.[27] Sunder's representation of Muslim women's rights groups like Musawah in this way reproduces the standard liberal views, both within and outside the Muslim world, that contrast religious backwardness and conservatism to enlightened modernism.[28]

Some of those involved would dispute this framing. Ziba Mir-Hosseini, one of the founders of Musawah, considers Islamic feminism (a term she finds confusing) to be the unwanted child of political Islam.[29] Yet she defends the new efforts of Muslim feminists this way:

> Faced by an apparent choice between the devil of those who want to impose patriarchal interpretations of Islam's sacred texts, and the deep blue sea of those who pursue a neo-colonialist hegemonic global project in the name of enlightenment and feminism, those of us committed to achieving justice for women and a just world have no other option than to bring Islamic and feminist perspectives together. Otherwise, Muslim women's quest for equality will remain hostage to different political forces and tendencies, as it was in the twentieth century and continues to be in the new century that began with the politics of the 'war on terror.'[30]

Not as far along in its institutionalization is another initiative that dovetails with Musawah. It treads some of the same pathways and has some overlapping membership. With a very different kind of institutional base, a more cosmopolitan and deterritorialized outlook, and a more explicitly religiospiritual cast, the Women's Islamic Initiative in Spirituality and Equality (WISE) had its first public event in 2006 in New York.[31] Out of this conference came the decision to form a Global Muslim Women's Shura Council (consultative body) to address the perceived lack of women's participation in the discourses on Islamic law. WISE is directed by Daisy Khan as part of the American Society of Muslim Advancement (ASMA; formerly the American Sufi Muslim Association, though nowhere in their current materials is this acknowledged). Founded in 1997 in New York by her husband, Imam Feisal Abdel Raouf, ASMA is closely connected to an initiative he directs: the Cordoba Initiative dedicated to Muslim-West understanding and "bringing back the atmosphere of interfaith tolerance and respect that we have longed for since Muslims, Christians and Jews lived together in harmony and prosperity eight hundred years ago."[32] Moderation, pluralism, toleration—these are the key liberal terms that he believes are crucial in a polarized world.[33]

In 2008, I was invited to participate in and observe one of WISE's preparatory meetings. This is the kind of fieldwork that anthropologists of human rights do when they work with lawyers and commissions, or observe the social processes of the bureaucracies that establish and negotiate human rights issues. What struck me most about the daylong deliberations was the creativity and unpredictability of the process by which they made collective decisions. No sweeping critiques about rights regimes or humanitarianism as the new colonialism can capture this quality. The women who gathered for this meeting brought to the table a cultural imagination formed by modernist and liberal Sufi ideals, United Nations (UN) and human and women's rights documents, models of transnational feminist organizing and activism, and academic conferencing. They brought tools of knowledge drawn from everything from Qur'anic exegesis to feminist historiography and quantitative social science.[34]

In a survey sent out to members just before this meeting, the steering committee had proposed five potential issues to research and then use as the testing ground for its first fatwa, or statement as they began to call it, to draw away from the negative cast of fatwa in the West and perhaps not to antagonize official sources of fatwas in different countries. The statement was to constitute the focus of the official launch of the Women's Shura Council in July 2009 in Kuala Lumpur, the same place where Musawah had just had its launch. The membership overwhelmingly voted for two issues: domestic violence and women's religious authority. Yet in the give-and-take of the meeting, a consensus emerged around a slightly different focus for the Shura Council's first pronouncement. A few strong personalities led them to an ambitious project: they would deal with domestic violence in tandem with violent extremism. Over the course of the day and with thoughtful objections being raised by different participants to aspects of what was being proposed (How was extremist violence a gendered issue? Weren't there formidable analytical challenges in linking domestic and military violence? Weren't the religious textual sources that would have to be brought into conversation quite diverse? Wasn't it dangerous to invoke the term jihad?), a general enthusiasm developed for *Jihad against Violence* as the Shura Council's first campaign.[35] Although the staff communicated their criteria for choosing an issue (its importance to women, its likely support by women, its feasibility in terms of research, its ability to draw media attention, and the level of resistance it might provoke from traditional institutions), the outspoken women at this meeting—mostly academics, journalists, and lawyers—went their own way.

My ethnography, thin as it was, revealed that the outcome emerged from a lively social process, not a conspiracy or any sort of engineering. Those with strong convictions, good analyses, and experience shaped the result. Diverse in outlook and background (with family origins in South Asia, the Arab Middle East, Turkey, Iran, and the United States), some of the participants were experts on Islamic law and practice, while some were experts on the Qur'an and the history of Islam. Some seemed to be using the vocabulary and tools of Islam strategically because of their imagined persuasive power for others; others were secure in and vocal about their convictions that they were doing this to be good Muslims. Some were devout followers of Sufi shaykhs, learned and philosophical students of the faith and veterans of interfaith dialogue. Some covered their hair, some didn't. Notably, some were sharply critical of Western imperialism, while others were more supportive of the U.S. government's War on Terror.[36] The discussion was heated at times, but the women remained civil and respectful. The democratic, inclusive, and positive tone set by the director helped the women work hard toward the common goal of determining what the Shura Council might best do.

WISE had already achieved a good deal in its two years of existence. It had a structure, a talented staff, a strategic plan and vision, and a major conference and several planning meetings under its belt. It had hammered out a compact that like Musawah's drew on Shari'a by grounding its commitment to women's rights in the six objectives of Shari'a—the protection and preservation of religion, life, the intellect, the family, property, and dignity. These, the accompanying letter sent to the membership explained, had a long history in the Muslim tradition and are rooted in the Qur'an.[37]

WISE had also been successful in fund-raising. It had just won a 1 million euro grant from the Dutch Foreign Ministry's MG3 Fund, an initiative related to the third Millennium Development Goal of Gender Equality and the Empowerment of Women.[38] As Daisy Khan stressed at the meeting, WISE planned to facilitate and enhance the work of others, not to compete. And indeed, several years later, in June 2011, they launched the inclusive Muslim Women's Web Portal and have supported numerous initiatives.

The meeting I attended was followed four months later by a two-day retreat at which certain principles were agreed upon. Again, there was an unanticipated outcome in terms of content and rhetorical strategy. The major breakthrough of the brain-storming meeting was finding a way to link domestic and extremist violence. Drawing on the Islamic tradition, the two were linked by the question of good and bad leadership.[39] The Queen of Sheba story was used as the organizing parable.

At this retreat, the worldly participants brought into play multiple models and genres of representation and argumentation. The women shared deep Islamic knowledge and the skills and vision of the cosmopolitan professional women who get heard in transnational women's rights initiatives: they are fluent in the languages of English, rights, and bureaucratic UN-speak.[40] The document they produced, like that of Musawah, had a preamble. WISE also used the social science–based instruments of democracy—surveys and polls. Even more prominently than in the case of Musawah, WISE's commitment to religious exegesis and Qur'anic quotation blends with the conventions of culturally secular international rights work.

Initiatives like Musawah and WISE's Global Women's Shura Council seem to be the wave of the future. Although they build on a decades-long tradition of Muslim women's activism, some of which has been explicitly grounded in religious identity and conviction, they are finding surprisingly strong support now from Western foundations and governments.[41] Their efforts are commendable, particularly in light of the recent forms of Western hysteria around Shari'a and head scarves represented in controversies discussed in previous chapters, such as the British and Canadian outcries about religious family arbitration councils and the European bans on burqas (not to mention absurd proposals such as the Jihad Prevention Act introduced by a Republican member of the U.S. House of Representatives in 2008; the bill would require aliens to attest that they will not advocate installing a "Sharia law system" in the United States as a condition for entry visas and even naturalization!).[42]

As with the crude criticisms of NGOs in places like Egypt, where facts of outside funding could be—and often have been—blown out of proportion and used to discredit rights initiatives in the service of either the religious Right or a government anxious to limit independent political activity, one must be cautious about making too much of foreign funding of Muslim feminist projects of internal reform.[43] Yet as time goes by, the causes that the Global Women's Shura Council has adopted have aligned surprisingly well with the clichéd causes familiar to us through our study of sensational media and pulp nonfiction. Prominent are the usual cultural violations such as female genital cutting, stoning, honor killings, and forced marriage.[44]

It is worth examining the new consensus in the international rights community and among many Muslim feminist activists and scholars that Islam and women's human rights must be reconciled and that internal reform is necessary. A human rights lawyer and scholar published an important article in 2006 about the crisis facing international NGOs like Human Rights Watch (HRW) and Amnesty International that have been working in the Middle East and Muslim world. Uncomfortable about how the human rights movement's rhetoric echoed that of the Bush administration, she noted that the dilemma facing the practitioners was "how the human rights movement should deal with Islamic law."[45] Current practice, Naz Modirzadeh argued, was to evade the issue by beginning every report with a caveat that the organization would take no position on Islamic law (to appear neutral and nonimperialist) but then proceeding in the body of the report to list violations linked to "rules of Islamic law" without admitting it explicitly.[46] She offered three ways out of the dilemma. Two years later, she was surprised at the outcome of her assessment of the way international NGOs dealt with Shari'a. HRW decided to create a position for an in-house Shari'a expert, a position that still has not been filled.[47]

Twenty years ago, no one would have predicted that Muslim women's rights would be traveling so regularly in and out of Islamic law, Islamist parties, and now the discourses and practices of moderation and Islamic reform among an educated and cosmopolitan professional elite.[48] This is not to question the authenticity or integrity of such projects. As an ethnographer, I want only to note the circuits in which they are participating— social, political, and economic. And I want to point out the multiple cultural resources they draw on to formulate their Islamic rights projects.

Incommensurate Lives

One of the most important questions an anthropologist like me with experience in rural areas and among non-elite women feels compelled to ask, though, is how organizations conceived and run by educated urban elites who spend a good deal of energy studying, thinking, drafting position statements, applying for funds, and presenting Islam to the West (and the East) as something not incompatible with gender equality, might relate to those in whose name and on whose behalf they work. These new feminist groups operating within the framework of Islam hope to ameliorate the lives of grassroots Muslim women by finding locally and personally meaningful resources. They also hope to avoid accusations that they are importing foreign ideologies or devaluing women's commitments to being good Muslims, even while most of them insist that religion, on the liberal model, is a matter of private faith. How do these new reformist projects, with their constructions of women's rights in terms of Islamic law and tradition and the Muslim spirit—yet arising from these women's own social locations in global fields of feminist governance in which elites from the South have a very visible and prominent place—fit with the everyday lives of some ordinary Muslim women in particular communities?

No one can represent or speak for "ordinary women," but I think it is fair to use the life stories of women in one Upper Egyptian village that I know to clarify the conundrums we all face when we try to think about the complex terrain of women's rights in the Muslim world today. These women's experiences can help us reflect on the existing frameworks for addressing Muslim women's problems, whether those that organize initiatives like WISE or Musawah, or those of any other international and local projects of empowerment and rights advocacy. There is a profound incommensurability between the lives of these particular "grassroots" women I know and the terms in which they are being imagined in the field of rights, including Islamic feminist versions.

One way to see this incommensurability is to consider dimensions of what religiosity or piety means to women these days in this village. The varieties and tensions among everyday forms of the religious life are obvious, as is the way Islamic thought and practice have changed in this village over the past fifty years. This makes clear the particular cast and the class politics of some of these projects of Islamic reform that go under the name Islamic feminism. When we juxtapose village lives and international projects, we are forced to ask how far visions of a modern enlightened interpretation of the Qur'an or legal reforms guided by the objectives of Shari'a take into account the variety of meanings of Muslim religious experience for women like the ones I know. A more urgent question that presents itself is: What authority and channels might such projects find in order to compete with existing authorities and institutions on the ground? In this particular Egyptian village, these range from teachers in the Azhar school system or the local Qur'anic afterschool programs to popular televangelists; from Sufi brotherhoods to new Islamic studies institutes for girls.

Islam in village life is variegated and constantly evolving. There are generational differences related to the political, social, economic, and cultural transformations in Egypt over the past decades. Older women think of themselves as good Muslims and wear modest, loose clothing and cover their hair. The oldest generation also still wears the traditional black wool cloak over their clothes for formal occasions, but this has been replaced by the more fashionable abaya, or tailored overcoat, for women in their forties. Although the national trend to become more strictly observant had already reached the village when I arrived in 1993, older women's regular prayers were nothing new.

For the younger generation, the key factors have been the simultaneous spread of the influence of education and television and the Islamic revival. Young women and men increasingly express their faith in other ways and dress differently. Some young women wear jeans with various forms of long-sleeved fashion tops or tunics. Some wear sweaters and long skirts. These are urban forms of dress that link them to Luxor, across the river, and Cairo, the distant capital. No one would think of leaving the house without a hijab or head scarf; the more fashionable wear colorful hijabs that change with the current styles. But not all the young women are like this; those who attend the Azhar schools, a parallel system that follows the national curriculum but includes more rigorous Islamic studies, pull their hijabs more fully over their hair and wear long shapeless dresses (which can be of pretty fabric, however). These are the girls whose families prefer schooling that is not coeducational, where the fees are lower and the opportunities to pursue a higher education more plentiful.

Multiple religious activities engage girls in the village. Most girls and boys are sent from a young age to the traditional *kuttab* to learn Qur'an as an after-school and summer holiday activity. More recently, a modern Islamic institute for girls has opened in the next village. Young women are eagerly taking up training in religious studies both for its own sake and because it is meant to prepare them to teach in the Azhar schools where there is a shortage of women teachers.

For one young woman I knew, working toward the certificate was her salvation from boredom. Having finished her vocational business degree, she found herself stuck at home. It was hard to go from dressing up and heading off to Luxor every day—to study, take exams, mix with other girls, and endure the pleasant annoyance of the boys who hung around the school—to sitting at home. An avid soccer fan, she came alive cheering her teams on TV. But most of her time was taken up with lonely housework that she did to relieve her mother, who was busy herself with the cows and sheep that helped supplement her husband's income from farming and a low-paying but skilled job. Only a marriage proposal would give her a different life because there is precious little employment in the area, especially for a girl from a poor family with no connections.

While she waited for someone to ask for her hand—and perhaps mindful of the increasing number of young women in the village who never got asked—the religious institute gave her an intellectual challenge, an unimpeachable moral claim to be out and about (after four years in the house), and possibly, later, a respectable way to make some kind of living. She could go for up to eight years; she would get a certificate after two years, then another after two more. She said she liked knowing more about her religion and she absolutely loved studying, though she was finding the different interpretations of the four schools of Islamic law terribly confusing.

All those in the Azhar schools, the kuttabs, the university courses in religious studies, and this new kind of institute are becoming knowledgeable about Islam in ways their mothers, and even fathers, are not. They are literate and they study Islamic history, Qur'anic exegesis, and law. They are being empowered by this knowledge, and others—even their families—respect them for it. They have confidence and know more about their rights. They are also empowered in practice, as they have good reasons to be out and about, independent. But the kind of religious education they are receiving is, I think, conservative. So, although the students might be equipped to understand the grounds on which Musawah or the WISE Shura Council are making their arguments (insofar as they draw on Islamic concepts and sources), it is unlikely that they will ever hear such arguments as the compatibility of CEDAW and Shari'a. And the interpretations of women's roles in Islamic society they are hearing in such institutes are probably far from revolutionary or egalitarian. This is the case even though some key principles, such as the importance of consent to a marriage, have now become widely established among this group of young women, as I describe in the conclusion.

This new generation is participating in forms of religious life that are in tension with the more "popular" local traditions of religious experience and practice, some associated with the Sufi brotherhoods that are still quite strong in Upper Egypt. It is women and girls like these in one village in Egypt that the cosmopolitan professional women of Musawah and the Shura Council project as the beneficiaries of their efforts to reinterpret Islam and introduce reforms in the laws governing family and marriage. These are the sorts of marginalized women and girls the grant proposals promise to train in knowing their rights. Yet the distance is vast between the reformers and these girls and women embedded in the particular socioreligious institutions of one village in Egypt and similar ones elsewhere. What social or political mechanisms will bridge this?

Violence in the Domestic Sphere

A different gap exists between the framework used by reform organizations and these village women's imaginations of social responsibility and individual desire. To explore this, I want to unpack one case of "domestic violence" in the village. Domestic violence is a cornerstone of women's rights work around the world and in international forums; in recent years, it is the most publicized issue the United Nations Development Fund for Women (UNIFEM), succeeded by the United Nations Entity for Gender Equality and the Empowerment of Women (UN Women), is promoting. It is also a central element in the WISE Shura Council's first campaign, *Jihad against Violence*. Musawah would treat domestic violence as a key dysfunction in marriage and family. Reforms in Islamic family law and educating people about more just interpretations of Islam should address this problem. For this part of the world, as with honor crimes, such violence—now labeled a violation of women's human rights—is generally represented as the result of "tradition" or patriarchal culture. If many outsiders blame Islam for this culture of violence, the Muslim feminists of Musawah or WISE are quick to argue that the fault lies in cultures that, contrary to such arguments or those of Muslim conservatives, are actually based on *insufficient* knowledge of or *incomplete* adherence to Islam. Islam, they insist, enshrines justice, equality, human dignity, and love and compassion among humans and in the family. They can find plenty of textual evidence for this.

Village women's lives confound for me this key subject of advocacy for women's rights. With these women in mind, I stumble when trying to apply the standard feminist framing of and solutions to domestic violence. The standard idea is that patriarchy is the problem. The solutions are shelters, police training, anger management training, media campaigns to increase awareness, the development of women's rights consciousness, holding governments accountable for not protecting women, and becoming modern. Nowadays, the tactic of Islamic feminists is to look for bases in Islam for care, love, and peace within families.[49]

The situation of one young woman whose traumas have troubled me ever since I met her suggests the inadequacy of these frameworks and solutions. I sketch the contours of Khadija's situation to show why I am reluctant to mediate such an unhappy story through the language of women's rights, either Islamic or human.[50] Resisting the women's rights frame and exposing the poverty of the categories set by the Violence against Women (VAW) discourses, including on domestic violence, her personal life needs to be understood in terms of both global forces that deform her life and local bonds of attachment and dependency that go without saying.[51] In the conclusion, I will also introduce a difficult personal circumstance that complicates her marriage, a special remainder. I insist throughout this book that there are always particulars that confound our easy attempts to generalize or to find quick fixes. Khadija's life need not be typical to teach us something general about the relationship between everyday life and rights frames.

When I saw her mother in the spring of 2009, I learned that Khadija had just returned to her husband after a month or so of living back home. This had become a pattern in her six-year marriage. Khadija was unhappy and her husband was sometimes violent. I knew Khadija complained that her husband did not like her to leave the house or go to visit her mother, even though she lived nearby. Khadija had said that he stayed at home most of the time. He would start drinking early in the morning; first he'd drink coffee (most villagers drink tea), then beer, then whiskey. During this latest escape to her mother's home, Khadija was taken by her brother to Cairo (which neither had ever visited) to consult a psychiatrist recommended to them by a European expatriate neighbor. According to Khadija's mother, the psychiatrist had talked with her daughter at length and told her there was nothing wrong with her except that she was unhappy. He told her to come and talk to him every three days—and to leave her husband.

As Khadija's mother explained, neither was possible. There was no way her family could afford to stay in Cairo for long or pay the psychiatrist's fees. Even the medicine he had prescribed was expensive and they could not afford to refill the prescription. But why couldn't Khadija leave her husband? Her mother put it starkly: She has two children already and one on the way. Who would support them? How could she bring them with her to stay in their crowded house? Khadija's mother and father were long divorced. He had little work and a new family to support anyway. Khadija's mother lived with and was supported by her brother, along with her son, her parents, and her widowed sister-in-law with her three children. This maternal uncle of Khadija's was the only one in the family with a job, and since he was a schoolteacher, it paid a pittance.

The vectors of oppression that consign Khadija to remaining in this conflictual and violent marriage can be traced here not so much to culture or traditional forms of gender inequality as to poverty. Their poverty is a result of local family history, on the one hand, and broad political economic transformations on the other, which for at least a century have concentrated wealth in the capital and the north of Egypt, and that now, thanks to neoliberal reform, organize the distribution of property and welfare in even more unequal ways. Even beyond that, global inequalities that have their own colonial and contemporary histories have positioned places like Egypt in certain ways too—condemned, it seems, to endemic poverty.

These global, national, and local dynamics of inequality that have placed the poor under such pressure also have had a peculiar impact on Khadija's marriage because of how they have shaped her husband's life. Why does he drink in a community where most people do not and where their religion specifically proscribes it? In a region of Egypt where Pharaonic sites have long attracted Western tourists and archaeologists, he and his brothers were among the first men in the village to get involved in tourism in the period after feminism, women's employment, and other transformations in Europe and the United States made independent women active participants in the global tourist industry.[52] As a youth, he mixed with tourists, drank with the foreigners, and took up with European women. Like many of the young men in the area who have done this in the last twenty-five years or so, he became involved with an older European divorcée.[53] These men have found a new way to make a living without having to migrate to Cairo or the Gulf. The European women build them houses, buy them taxis, partner with them to run hotels and music festivals, and occasionally take them home with them.

Everyone knows that Khadija's husband has had a European friend for twenty years. But like most men, he also wanted to start a family. When he had saved up enough, he married this local girl. It was not surprising that Khadija's husband had chosen her, much younger, to start his own family. His mother seems to have been involved in arranging the match because she is always the one who intervenes to persuade Khadija to return. He built a house for Khadija in 2001, but didn't tell his European friend. These kinds of situations can be difficult for all concerned. The tricky time for everyone seems to be when the European woman comes to visit. Some people say that at first she didn't know the truth. Now that she knows, others say she is jealous.

Six years into the marriage, though, Khadija's mother insists that his European "wife" adores his children and walks proudly around the village hand in hand with his little boy. I could understand why when I met this bright boy. Dressed neatly in a pink button-down shirt and chatting merrily and showing off the French he was learning in his private school, he was irresistible. Everyone in the village notes with a certain respect that this woman, unlike many of those duped, had made sure that the house she built to rent out to tourists was legally in only her own name. Her relative wealth and European status confound norms of gendered power. Khadija's husband, everyone comments, is docile around this woman. Did he feel he was compromising his masculine standing in the village? I wondered if he might be compensating in his marriage to the much younger and more vulnerable Khadija by being so harsh. One can only speculate.

What is apparent and significant, though, is that domestic violence in this case is anything but "traditional." It is produced at
the nexus of the global field of European tourism in the Third
World and the inequalities between rich foreigners and local villagers that fuel it. The alcohol that is so taken for granted in the
European circles in which men like Khadija's husband travel
also surely plays a part.

Having known Khadija for many years, I understand that she
cannot leave the marriage for other reasons beyond these com-
pulsions of poverty and the fallout of global inequalities. There
is also kinship: Khadija and her husband are distant cousins;
he is thus a precariously well-off relative whose marriage to a
troubled cousin from a broken home may also have been a way
to help out these poor relations. Khadija is attractive, but this
marriage may have been something of a protection and a gift to
her and her desperate family.

In this aspect of her life, there seems to be something of a repetition of Khadija's family history (with a more unfortunate
outcome). Khadija's grandparents, who were cousins, had married
for the same reason—as a way to make sure her grandmother was
cared for. People told me that she had been possessed by spirits at
the age of twelve or thirteen. She was a volatile young woman
who ran off to saints' tombs and caused her parents tremendous
worries. Although many young men had wanted to marry this
beautiful girl, their mothers and families would forbid them. She
was not considered normal, always running off to religious sanc-
tuaries and chanting God's name. So finally it was arranged that
her cousin marry her, taking on the lifelong responsibility to care
for her out of family concern. He got her treated and she was
much better for a while. Her daughter told me that she was stable
for about ten years, but then reverted to her religious practices,
periodically running off and leaving her family, including her

three children. Khadija's father was her son. He too has had a troubled history of abusive behavior that was much worse when he was married to Khadija's mother, hence the divorce. The difference in the two stories is that Khadija's grandfather was kind to his wife and his daughters. Khadija is not so fortunate in her husband. Still, her relationship with him cannot be disentangled from the family bonds of attachment and dependency that help keep her in the marriage.

This last piece of the story suggests that we must see Khadija's difficult marriage as something that the language of violations of women's rights in traditional patriarchal culture cannot begin to describe because it cannot be isolated from the dynamics of globalization or the intimacies of family ties. Given the layers of this story, we need to ask ourselves whether the framework of rights—even if expressed in the new, more indigenous initiatives to reform Muslim family law or to promote and publicize gender egalitarian interpretations of the Qur'an—can capture the complexity of Khadija's life situation. Would any approach that talks in terms of freeing her from patriarchal culture or saving her from Muslim men enable us to see the tangled strands of her suffering?

Women in the village used other frameworks for judging and analyzing Khadija's unhappy situation. They had a variety of opinions about and degrees of empathy with Khadija. When I would ask them why she didn't leave her husband when he was violent with her, some would explain that she didn't want to end up like her mother, divorced and raising two kids on her own, or that she didn't want her children to grow up, as she had, without the love of a father. Others mentioned that she had wanted to marry this particular man, knowing full well his situation and his drinking problem. It was her choice and therefore she had some responsibility to make the marriage work. Some women blamed her for being too touchy and hypersensitive. They contrasted Khadija's flighty mother, who had provoked her ex-husband's violence, to Khadija's father's calm second wife who had managed just fine for eighteen years to get along with her husband. And, indeed, he was good to her and his three children from this new family.

The frameworks they used were drawn from local ways of understanding the many sorts of difficult situations in which women find themselves. Some frameworks were religious, based on the ideals of patience (*sabr*) or accepting one's fate and God's will. Others were based on intimate knowledge of what women value most and a fuller recognition of how messy life can be. They were quick to point out to me that Khadija had actively sought a third pregnancy, giving up contraception. Did this suggest to them a (perfectly understandable) desire, even a will, to stay in the marriage so that she could have a full family life? This is a value that remains largely unquestioned in their social world, even if its realization is so often fraught. I don't think any of us would scoff at this wish.

Six months after Khadija's crisis and her trip to Cairo, she safely delivered a lovely baby girl. Khadija's mother confided happily to me on my next visit that from the moment of the birth of this child, Khadija's husband had stopped drinking completely. He had become pious, observing Ramadan for the first time in decades. Others told me that actually he had been very ill and the doctor had warned him that if he did not quit drinking, he would have complete liver failure. Either way, there was marital harmony for the moment. Everyone, including Khadija, was hoping it would last.

Selective Intervention

I have set side by side one set of social and moral relations in one Egyptian village to another set of relations that constitute new and interesting forms of rights activism by Muslim women working explicitly within an Islamic framework. Through this, I have shown why, from my experience, it seems that none of the kinds of global rights discourses at work in the world now are adequate for assessing or judging the lives to be redeemed. The single case of domestic violence I began to unravel was meant to shake our confidence that frameworks of women's rights or campaigns for gender equality capture or solve the kinds of vexing problems that women face.

Activists working in the name of rights tend to come from certain social locations, work within political situations, and use particular cultural resources. It is not my intention to denigrate individual efforts on behalf of women or to dismiss any of the forms of activism organized in the name of improving women's (human or Islamic) rights. I see these new projects of Islamic feminism, for example, like the more secular women's rights projects that came before them as having mobilized concerned, hardworking, creative, committed, and, in this case, impressively learned individuals.

I do not deny that those who speak out for rights and gender equality may contribute to improving lives by making certain critiques of social inequality and social injustice possible. Some have provided legal and moral remedies for intractable problems. The political or strategic uses of dialects of rights have enabled political and moral gains and may offer future benefits for disenfranchised groups and individuals, including women, who learn to use this powerful language or who come to translate their grievances into its terms. In Chapter 5, I describe the ways some Egyptian village women now deploy multiple vocabularies of rights to make claims when they feel wronged, drawing from national political and legal spheres, local familial norms, and from knowledge of Islamic law and texts.

However, we need to recognize the limits of this language. We need to see what it excludes and to recognize its links with institutions and political configurations. We also want to be aware of the violence that translating into this language might entail for people, even those for whom it feels like a "mother tongue." In short, we have to be more realistic about the limits and locations of the vocabularies and imagination of rights. We need to be attentive to the intersection of rights work with a range of global and class inequalities. We must look closely at what various forms of rights work and women's advocacy actually produce in the world by way of careers, social distinctions, public discourse, new social and financial circuits, documents, legal debates, travel opportunities, intellectual excitement, and even hope. Some of these effects are unintended. Some may even harm the women they intend to help, especially when caught up in international politics. The intellectual tools of the rights frames that are common sense now turn out to be inextricable from the socially located political projects of the people and groups who put them to use. They are also not adequate for appreciating the complexities of women's experiences.

Conclusion
Registers of Humanity

This book is a long answer to the question of whether Muslim women have rights or need saving. I have examined the work and the frameworks of the many who want to do something about violations of women's rights globally, especially Muslim women's rights. There are the moral crusaders who view Muslim women as distant and different and want to save them. There are writers who have capitalized on the international political situation and individual women's traumas by selling sordid memoirs of sensational abuse and escape. There are hardworking activists leading organizations dedicated to fighting forms of gender inequality, including violence. Most speak a dialect of universal rights; others use dialects specific to the Muslim discursive tradition. Some work at the international level, some work locally. Sometimes it is hard to disentangle the two. The vibrancy of this entanglement is clearest in the case of a new type of feminist who has emerged on the scene. She quotes fluently from the Qur'an, is familiar with Islamic law, invokes precedents from early Muslim history, writes sophisticated articles on the UN Convention on the Elimination of All Forms of

Discrimination against Women (CEDAW), arranges conferences on Google Calendar, conducts online surveys, and draws from a wide range of experiences of organizing for change.

In concluding, I want to return to rural Egypt one last time to consider the experiences of some women who are not part of these efforts, though they would qualify as suitable objects of intervention in the world that all these activists imagine. Just as Zaynab was shocked to hear that anyone would blame Islam for what she and other women in Egypt were suffering, so would these women be puzzled, even offended, by some of the ways they are being viewed and judged. I want to use their lives to open up a way we might think differently about Muslim women and their rights—and about our responsibilities.

In this book, I argue that rather than clicking on a website to donate $10 or flying to distant lands to bring school supplies to girls, and certainly before calling in military troops, we should take time to listen. I have shown how hard it is to hear through the noise of the familiar stories. These stories have been made authoritative through their association with the purity of the language of universal rights. Popular (porno)graphic memoirs and media have made them believable. Gendered Orientalism has taken on a new life and new forms in our feminist twenty-first century.

If we were to listen more closely, I believe we would discover that matters are not so simple. If we were to listen and look, we might be forced to take account of contexts that are not as disconnected from our worlds and our own lives as we think. These contexts are shaped by global politics, international capital, and modern state institutions, with their changing impacts on family and community. Above all, these examples of women's situations might shake our moral certainty about some cherished values of liberalism that have diffused so widely in this era when human rights ideals have become hegemonic. Along with Talal Asad, I would argue that we should not dismiss these values as mere instruments of new imperial interventions. We have to take this language of justice seriously. It frames the new common sense about saving Muslim women because it has, as Asad put it, produced political subjects around the world who share these values and speak this language.[1]

Choice, consent, and freedom are the grammar. So let us look at what this grammar allows and what it does not.

Taking into Account . . .

Shortly after saying good-bye to Zaynab in Upper Egypt, I made a quick trip to another part of the country. I went back to the northwest coast to visit the Bedouin families I had lived with in the late 1970s and 1980s. It was two years since I had been there to mourn the passing of the extraordinary man who had been my host, and who had become like a father to me.

A lot had happened. The family had been adjusting to the loss of this charismatic figure who had held together not just his family but also the wider community. I noticed two new houses that had been built nearby. I knew these houses had been in the works for years; they were part of the family's attempt to stake their claims to land that the government was trying to seize from them to build public housing. Each time they built a wall around the plots of barren land, bulldozers would come and knock them down. For as long as anyone could remember, these Bedouin families had lived on this open land surrounded by no one but relatives and friends. They did not want this taken, but government policy was to move people out of the crowded Nile Valley into the desert.

I was pleased to find Gateefa still in the house in which I had lived with her and the family. Serious and intelligent, she was the woman I most looked up to and appreciated. I was grateful for the warm generosity with which she had taken me into their household and was indebted to her for the wealth of knowledge, stories, poetry, and wise insights into her community she had shared. It was sad to see her living alone in the section of the house she had shared with her husband and children for the thirty-some years that I had known her. We sat close, catching up on the news. Our shared memories and people gave us a lot to talk about, even if time had made my return awkward and my long research in another part of Egypt had compromised my dialect.

As we reminisced about her husband, she suddenly said, "You need a man who knows how to rule." I was jolted by the comment. She said it with some force. I knew that she and her husband had been close. She had married him when she was only thirteen and she'd had nine children with him. It had not always been easy. He had imposed co-wives on her. But she had understood why and had always been at his side. In his final illness, she had organized his care. She knew the most intimate details of his illnesses, and then his death.[2] She had been philosophical and strong after he died, her faith enabling her to reassure all those who burst into tears around her that we should accept what God wanted. We all pass on. She cherished her husband's last gift to her: arranging for her to go with her son on the pilgrimage to Mecca.

So what had provoked this outburst? Did she unthinkingly accept male domination? Was she getting her ideas from the Qur'an? As we talked, I came to realize that this was an angry comment directed—indirectly—at her eldest son. He had recently moved out of the large family home, taking his wife and children to live in one of these new houses. I remembered her critical remarks on previous visits about her daughters-in-law. She was

annoyed when one daughter-in-law left her infant with an aunt
while she went off to get her eyebrows plucked. She considered
it frivolous. The baby was crying for its mother. She disapproved
of the other daughter-in-law for going shopping with her mother
to buy special clothes just for her own children. The new generation was selfish.

In this comment, Gateefa was expressing her disapproval of the
way her son had, as she interpreted it, succumbed to the power
and desires of his wife. She blamed her daughter-in-law for ma-
neuvering the breakup of the family that she and her husband had
built together. Each woman now gets her husband to go off and
buy special things for his own children, she complained. Each
woman wants her own household, not all the work of the joint
household. She then appealed to my knowledge of the way
things had been in the past, when her husband was alive. No one
would have dared to buy special things for their own children. In
the old days, she reminded me, her husband was in charge. He
made sure that everyone in the household got whatever they
needed. But they all got the same things. If he bought food, it
was for everyone. If he bought new clothes, everyone got the
equivalent item—bolts of cloth for dresses, gallabiyas (the robes
that boys and men wore), shawls, and even socks. The family fi-
nances were still joint—her husband had wanted it that way and
it was the respected norm for prominent families.

Gateefa thought that "the man" should rule because her first
commitment was to keeping the family together. This is what her
husband had done. She could not let herself think that her son
might want his own household too. He should be committed
above all to the integrity of the family and the honor of the kin
group. She presumed that her son's wife was selfishly trying to
break this up. She could not see that this was a normal generational transition, much like ones she had seen so often in her

lifetime (and that anthropologists have written so much about
under the name "the domestic cycle"). It was perhaps hard for
her to accept that she was entering a new phase in the life of the
family, set in motion by the passing of her husband. She responded to her own sense of personal loss through this moralis-
tic formulation. As perhaps everywhere, there was an unresolv-
able tension between her desires as a mother and those of her
daughter-in-law as a wife. Their choices clashed. This had nothing to do with the Qur'an or anything Islam might have to say
about men's rights over women. I had often seen her fiercely defend her Islamic rights to equal treatment in her marriage.

   That specific personal situations like this give meaning to
what appear to be such clear signs of the cultural oppression of
Muslim women can also be seen in the developments in Khadija's marital life. In Chapter 6, we see how she was subjected to
violence by her alcoholic husband. I describe how regional poverty, international tourism, and feminist gains in Europe (as well
as high divorce rates) affected her marriage. But there is a further complication I do not mention there—a kind of remainder
that introduces some doubt about whether her husband's violence and the circumstances that prevent her from walking away
from the marriage are the only or even the main sources of her
wretchedness.

   Long before she was married, Khadija had been subject to
crises. Her relatives regularly covered them up in the face of village gossip. I will never forget the day many years ago that I
stopped in to see her family. It was just a week before the first of
what would become a succession of postponed wedding dates. I
found a terrible situation. Khadija was lying on the couch, dazed
and in pain. Her tongue was swollen and she couldn't speak.
Her mother, worried sick about her again, had this time taken
her to a specialist, an expensive neurosurgeon who flew in from

Alexandria once a week to see patients. He had barely spoken with Khadija before prescribing some medications. He administered an injection that knocked her out. Enmeshed, as all Egyptians are now, in a flawed medical system driven by the politics of expertise, profit, and the pharmaceutical industry, this was not the first or last time medical intervention failed to help Khadija. The forms of religious healing her mother had pursued earlier had not helped either. The Cairo psychiatrist had been just the most recent, and perhaps the most harmless, of these attempts to make her feel better.

A careful look at Khadija's situation forces us to see that we don't quite know what to make of her problem of domestic violence. The complex bonds of protection and constraint that kinship introduced to her marriage, her husband's oddly international circumstances, the various aspects of globally regulated poverty that foreclosed her options, the uneven reach of an inadequate medical system, and the demons she lives with—whether they are the result of childhood trauma (her father was violent), inherited mental illness (her grandmother was possessed by spirits), or parasites and anemia (as the various interpretations circulating in and out of the family suggest)—make us realize that there is no simple story here. Would getting out of the marriage help? It is hard to say. All her life, she has struggled with headaches, felt she was being strangled, and periodically withdrawn into herself.

Khadija's saga continues. Her future remains unclear. Despite the fervent hopes for a happy ending that her husband's sudden decision to stop drinking and fast Ramadan seemed to presage, she was back at home with her mother when I last visited the village. Her aunt quietly took my hand and walked me across the road to see the house they were building for her on a field that had salted up and where nothing would grow. Did I know of any charity that could help them build this house for Khadija and her children? This time, she told me soberly, Khadija has sworn she will never go back.

Consent and the Right to Freely Choose

As an anthropologist whose business it is to understand how individuals are formed within the contours of their cultures and social worlds, I have always been wary of concepts like choice. The legal category of consent that goes with it poses similar problems for anyone who stops to think about how we go through life and what intimate relationships mean for us. Especially in societies that value relationality and mutual concern above individualism, and where gender is closely tied to familial power, liberal dreams like those found in CEDAW's Article 16 about the equality that men and women should enjoy in marriage and family relations strike me as aspirational but troubling fictions. Musawah's *Framework for Action* to reform Muslim family law reiterates this goal; it proposes that women and men should have "the same right freely to choose a spouse and to enter into marriage only with their free and full consent."[3]

The complexity of human lives formed in social worlds challenges such fictions. What does it mean to freely choose, or to consent? These are difficult questions for marriage. A look at what has been happening in rural Egypt in the past twenty years or so shows one aspect of the difficulty. An intriguing phenomenon has emerged: girls in different rural communities have been developing knowledge of their rights under Islamic law. They have been using this knowledge to challenge the customary arrangement of marriages by families by pointing to the requirement of consent.

Parallel efforts have been under way across the Muslim world by feminist reformers of various sorts, from secular to Islamic, to make choice, consent, and contract the instruments for guaranteeing women's rights in marriage. In North Africa, for example, feminist reformers developed a model marriage contract that would build in requirements of consent for a husband's decision to take a second wife. In India and Egypt, there have been campaigns for legal reform of Islamic family law that would establish women's rights to initiate divorce.[4]

But one of the most striking changes I noted in the late 1980s in the Bedouin community in Egypt's Western Desert where I had first done fieldwork a decade earlier was the impact of the Islamic revival on young men and women. In an essay a young woman wrote for me on the theme of what she believed deserved to be preserved and what traditions should change in her community, she returned again and again to marriage.[5] She was the first girl in her family to graduate from high school. Her commentary bore the traces of the mixture of modernization and Islamization ideologies that were the stuff of Egyptian state education.[6] Of the Bedouin girl in the past, she wrote: "She had no right to an opinion in any matter, however much the matter might concern her personally. She had no say even in the choice of a husband . . . what she had to do was carry out her family's orders even if she didn't want him. It was not right for her to refuse." She commented to me, "And to this day, no matter how educated she's become, very seldom does she have a say . . . Even if he was older than she was, for example, or very different from her, she had to agree to what the family wanted. For example, if they said I had to marry someone and I didn't want him—I hated him—if my kinsmen had agreed to the match and told me I had to marry him, what I would have to do, despite my wishes, was marry him." I found this statement surprising. Why did she depict girls as powerless in decisions about marriage? She had heard all the same stories I had—vivid accounts, like her grandmother's, of ways they had resisted marriages arranged for them by their families.[7] She also knew plenty of young women like the one who, in love with someone else, had married her cousin. She understood her strategy perfectly. She kept storming off to her father's household at the slightest provocation. Eventually, her husband divorced her, which was what she wanted.

This depiction of a simple story of past powerlessness allowed her to foreground the new standards that were coming into play. Her religious training at school had given her moral ammunition against arranged marriage. The Prophet, she reported authoritatively, says that it is wrong to marry someone you have never seen. A girl must be asked her opinion and she must give her consent.[8]

In this period of her life, marriage was on her mind. As her mother teased, "Now that she has her diploma, we're going to get her the other diploma!" She was frank about her feelings about someone rumored to have been selected for her. She told her aunts and her mother how she felt. She insisted to her grandmother and anyone who would listen that she wanted to marry someone educated, an Egyptian, not a Bedouin. She wanted someone with his own house. She wanted someone who wanted a small family. She wanted someone who would not take a second wife. When her grandmother retorted, "Your father won't agree to it!" she had hugged her grandmother affectionately, reassuring her, "We're just talking with you to see what you'll say. Is there anything in our hands? Or in my father's? Only God knows what will happen."[9]

More and more girls are invoking Islam to argue against customary ideas about the propriety of arranged marriages. Twenty years later and hundreds of kilometers south, I heard the same confident insistence on the Islamic principle of the necessity of a girl's consent to marriage, thanks to the power of education and of the growing legitimacy of the Islamic revival. Women's rights activists, whether working on state law or the reform of Muslim family law, have drawn on the existence of guarantees intrinsic to the Islamic tradition such as the requirement of consent to marriage. Musawah, the most significant reform initiative to have emerged in the past few years, lays out the principle in its *Framework for Action*. Arguing that "in the twenty-first century, the provisions of the Convention on the Elimination of All Forms of Discrimination against Women (CEDAW)—which stands for justice and equality for women in the family and society—are more in line with the *Shari'ah* than family law provisions in many Muslim countries and communities," it proposes that such laws must change to ensure such rights.

Having the principle of consent in place, though, does not resolve the quandaries of young women as they try to decide whether to marry a particular person. In the village in Upper Egypt from which so many of my examples have come, families were still closely involved in marriage arrangements. There was no institution of dating, even though young men and women might get to know each other if their families were related or if they had been at school together. When a man or his parents went to a girl's parents to ask for her hand, the girl was always asked her opinion. But how do these girls form an opinion? Marriage everywhere is no small matter and it is hard to know what the future holds.

I was intrigued to hear the way people talked about how someone might decide whether to refuse or consent to a marriage. The broken engagement of Zaynab's oldest daughter provided the occasion for many such discussions. She had refused several suitors during the past decade. Then one day, she agreed and got engaged. A close friend of her mother's made sense of her consent this time as a matter of fate *(nasib)*. As she explained to me, "That's when it works. You can say no, and I don't like this one or that one. But when it is meant to be (there's *nasib*), you say okay."

Another young woman affirmed that nowadays they always ask a girl if she accepts. In the old days, they didn't; if her family agreed to the match, she agreed. But again, on what basis? Girls now expect to sit and talk with the prospective groom and to get to know him a little, if they didn't before. But this can hardly tell either of them much about the person with whom they plan to spend their lives. Something else has developed to help girls decide. As this young woman who was studying at a new Islamic studies institute for girls explained, when a girl doesn't know whether to consent or not, she should perform a certain prayer. During the prayer, it will become clear whether you should or should not accept the man. That is when you're so close to God, she confided, that He reveals it to you. If you feel during this prayer that he's not right for you, you say no.

Both invoked a higher force, not inner feeling; fate is, after all, God's will, and the special prayer to ask God for guidance in making one's individual choice is even more direct. Given how hard it is for anyone to decide whether a future intimacy will be fulfilling or miserable or whether something as long-term as a marriage might work, this reference to some guiding force to replace the formerly trusted parents makes sense. This is not the free choice idealized in CEDAW or Islamic feminist documents, but it is very much about consent and choice.

In this case, though, the factors that shaped Zaynab's daughter's decision about the marriage were more mundane. Her fiancé was the son of a friend of her mother's. Like many young men from this region, he was working in Europe. Lack of opportunity means that when young men can get out to find work, they do. He was fairly young and not unattractive. I recalled her positive words about him. She said she had asked him a lot of questions and found him easy to talk to.

I was happy for her when I learned she was engaged. She had always been open with me and I enjoyed her company. She deserved to have a family of her own. A teenager when I first met her, she had worked hard in high school and done well. She was smart, sensible, and warm. She had always been a great support to her mother, who was raising a big family on her own. Keenly feeling her mother's hardships, she gradually took over all the household work and even the care of her younger sisters. She took her responsibilities seriously, but she was less needed now that they had the business and her brother had the café. So finally it seemed that she would be getting a life of her own.

Yet eight months later, she suddenly decided to break off the engagement. She returned the gold jewelry that had made her feel special. She created bad feeling between her mother and this friend. When I asked her what had gone wrong, she said he'd had very old-fashioned demands. He told her that he would be away a year at a time, working in Europe, and that during that time, she wouldn't be allowed to leave their apartment in his family's building, which was the next hamlet over. He told her that she could not go to stay with her own family while he was away. He said she shouldn't even go downstairs to hang out with his extended family. When I asked how she had discovered all this, she explained that they'd been talking a lot on the phone. When I expressed surprise that he was being so rigid, having lived in Europe for years, she agreed: "I thought he would be more open-minded after living in Europe. In fact, no one here would ever impose those kinds of conditions on a woman."

From her mother, I discovered something else. He planned to stick with his European wife/girlfriend, the one who had obtained the work permit for him. He wanted to keep this new marriage to her daughter secret for a while. This was too much. Perhaps Zaynab said this to save face. But her daughter seemed to be refusing this insult to her dignity. This was not the kind of marriage she wanted. These were not conditions she would accept, even though it would have meant finally having a husband and starting a family. This is what most people want in this community, as in many.[10]

As she gets older, though, it becomes increasingly less likely that she will ever marry. She had already refused marriage proposals from men she said were too old or not as educated as she was, or from men who seemed boorish. Her parents respected her decisions, though they were sad that this engagement hadn't worked out. Secretly they worried, as I did, that no more marriage offers would be forthcoming. No one said this. She was now well over thirty in a community where girls marry as early as seventeen and most brides are in their early twenties. This was also a community that had its share of women who never married, passed by and left taking responsibility for the care of aging parents. As in so many places, there are a lot of women in the village who remain single. In the Arab Middle East, they are part of what alarmists call the "marriage crisis."[11]

Two years later, Zaynab's daughter confided her regret that she had not married. She said she had misjudged life. She felt so needed, so responsible for helping her mother with the heavy household load, especially after her mother broke her ankle and was no longer able to farm or even keep a water buffalo to milk. She said she couldn't imagine abandoning her mother and the household that needed her so much. She added that she had been so attached to her little sisters (including the one with diabetes) that "I felt like I was their mother."

The trouble was that circumstances had changed. Her father had retired from his job in Cairo and returned home to live with his family. Her sisters were growing up fast—too fast, she thought. The twenty-two-year-old, who had graduated from college in religious studies, was engaged. The seventeen-year-old had just accepted a marriage proposal. One of her brothers had married and his wife now shared the household work. She confessed that she probably should have looked out for herself more. Her sacrifice had not even been appreciated; her parents had thought she was just being picky when she refused those marriage offers. It wasn't that she hadn't wanted to marry; it was that she had felt a sense of responsibility, but did not want them to feel this as a burden.

The unexpressed fear now was that it might now be permanent. How else to explain her anxiety attacks and fits of uncontrollable crying? She now was going from doctor to doctor. Among the pills she had been prescribed, piled into a plastic bag she opened for me to inspect, I noticed an antidepressant.

Consumed by Love: An Alternative Bondage

This description of the way one young woman weighed responsibilities and desires, wanted to be part of what she knew and loved and at the same time wanted to choose something new not knowing if it was right for her or not, whether it would bring her happiness or misery, should remind us of what we all know: choices are not easy and what we want is not always clear. The guarantee of consent, whether backed by CEDAW, Shari'a, respect and family love, or rational calculation, could do little to help Zaynab's daughter make this important decision. Wherever we turn in the world, we find people caught in similar binds. These binds have to be factored into any discussion of what it means to freely choose, or to consent.

So let us return briefly to the pulp nonfiction discussed in previous chapters to amplify these reservations about consent: that it is not easy in people's lives to distinguish freedom and duty, consent and bondage. Embedded in these tales of force, as I have shown for Ayaan Hirsi Ali's autobiography, *Infidel,* we can detect traces of alternative understandings and of contradictions that are never given prominence because they do not fit the popular narrative. These throw light on the complexities of women's situations and feelings.

Without wanting to minimize the hardship, betrayal, and abuse suffered by the two Yemeni-British teenagers Zana and Nadia, one would, for example, still want to ask in the cases of these girls whose stories are told in *Sold* and *Without Mercy* if their reactions would have been different had the marriages been arranged to wealthy or middle-class, educated young men living in comfort in Taiz, the city to which they are eventually taken by the Yemeni authorities as a refuge. Leaving the rough Birmingham neighborhood in which they lived, the council housing, the long hours working at a sandwich shop, an abusive and alcoholic father, limited futures, and run-ins with the racist law (all described in these books), would these girls or their mother have complained of force?

Zana's outrage seems to be directed mostly at the harshness and desolation of their mountaintop hovel, the excruciatingly hard work of simple farming, the torture of milling corn by hand, and carrying water buckets up cliffs while pregnant. Her complaints are about insufficient food and a sickly husband. These merge imperceptibly into a condemnation of forced marriage and violent patriarchy. Yet if one reads her account carefully, one sees that the men who support these girls are up against the same harsh conditions. They too missed out on the normal joy of being the centers of attention at weddings celebrated by the community. There was no wedding, no marriage gift—a requirement of Muslim family law. In short, this was a pathological situation for all involved, though for people used to living in this harsh region, the tough conditions of livelihood are normal.

But I noted something more poignant and complicated in my reflections on the younger sister Nadia's ambivalent refusal to take her mother's ticket to freedom and "home." Her mother does not seem to be able to hear her daughter's confusion as she reconciles her anger at having been tricked into this situation to which she did not consent, and her sense that she has now built a meaningful life in Yemen. She is bound by love for her children, and even perhaps her husband. She cannot choose "freedom."

Nadia's all-too-human dilemma, like the dilemmas faced by so many of us at the other end of the life cycle who find their "freedom" compromised by caring for elderly parents or ill loved ones, opens up new ways of thinking about Muslim women and their rights and wrongs. In a profound essay on sexual consent, Judith Butler goes beyond the usual critiques of legal consent by noting how consent might not be simply a core liberal value, but part of a strong fantasy of autonomy; hence, our intense attachment to the idea. She reminds us that, as Antonio Gramsci put it, consent is always manufactured, at both the personal and the political levels. We need to recognize the importance of power in determining "choices." But most originally, Butler asks us to reflect on how, in matters of personal desire or intimacy, consent might not have much meaning. In the end, we can never know what we are consenting to when we say yes. How will it go? What will it mean to consent to a relationship? A deep unknowability characterizes all human desires, acts, and futures.

A century of anthropological thought about humanity has established that our everyday understandings of the individual are culturally and historically specific and that the dominant modern Western understanding of the self contrasts with many other conceptions of self that have valued autonomy differently and have worked with more grounded perceptions of the inter-relationship between self and other.[12] Anthropologists also agree with Clifford Geertz that the best way to understand human nature is to recognize it as thoroughly cultural. To be viable as humans, we need a drastically long period of socialization within families and communities.[13]

Yet, anthropologists have rarely gone the next step to see how, in certain circumstances, the values of consent and choice might be fetishized and defended in order to uphold for individuals the fantasy of being autonomous subjects. This is a dynamic I found at work in pulp nonfiction about forced marriage and honor crimes. Nor have they articulated so well how foundational for our humanity it is to be related to each other, even if so many of us who have written about people in other places have commented on the deep meaning that family ties hold for men and women. I certainly have done this in my studies of the Arab Muslim communities in which I have had a chance to live and do research.[14]

In the final paragraph of her essay on sexual consent in law and psychoanalysis, Butler offers a poignant truth about the limits we all face as individuals and as people in our time and place who assert the value of freely choosing. The most basic fact of our existence, she reminds us, is that we are born into and depend on families we did not choose. "There are form of proximity, of living with, of adjacency and co-habitation that are radically unchosen," she writes. "And these constitute a basic form of sociality that no one enters contractually, that constitute the social conditions of life to which we never consented, and which are finally indifferent to our consent. These are conditions we are nevertheless obligated to protect and defend, even though we never agreed to them, and they do not emerge from our will."

As a philosopher, she can then make a general statement about how this situation shapes all of us: "Those lives which exceed me and are not a matter of my choosing are a condition of who I am, and so there is no life that is exclusively my own . . . We are finally creatures of life, including creatures of passion, who need what we cannot fully understand or choose, and whose sexual and emotional lives are marked from the start from this being bound up with one another with unknowing and necessity."[15]

These words give us a different way to think about Muslim women's rights. Here are some universals that are not normative and do not pretend to be abstract, carefully hiding their parochialism and politics.[16] Here are some universals that begin from the premise that we all share something as humans. These universals join us together instead of dividing us artificially into those who freely choose and those who don't, those who champion rights and those who do not have any, or don't have enough or the right kinds. This position has implications for how we think about rights, what we should do about women's rights, and whether or how we should we go to war for distant women.

Invoking this kind of common humanity is not the same as fantasizing about the universalism of human rights. One might be reminded here of the famous photography exhibit "The Family of Man," which was imagined as part of the wishful declaration of a common humanity in the postwar period.[17] That it was called a family of "man" is only one index of its historical specificity, of course. And that the preamble of the UN's Universal Declaration of Human Rights should define members of the "human family" by their "equal and inalienable rights" is very peculiar, given our experiences of actual families we know. Families are by nature contingent and ever-changing, their dynamics volatile, and their membership flexible. Anthropologists used to study kinship. They studied the bewildering array of ways that humans have imagined their social and emotional relations, as well as the logics by which they have organized themselves. They taught us about the different meaning people have given to their differences and affinities and they have studied the various inclusions and exclusions of kinship, configured by the workings of memory and amnesia. Like novelists, they have marveled at the intense emotions and sharp interactions that shape individual experience and personhood within diverse families. In recent years, feminist anthropologists have become fascinated with the forms of kinship that new reproductive technologies and organ transplantation have spawned, just as earlier they critiqued the heteronormative constructions that made us imagine families only one way, or as biologically given.[18] On the ground, every "family" is different, even the happy ones, contrary to Leo Tolstoy's famous pronouncement in the opening of *Anna Karenina*.

Families harbor distance and closeness, violence and love, indifference and passion. Does this make them a better model of the relatedness of people in the world than an abstract humanity marked by uniformity, or the agonistic oppositions of backward versus modern cultures or civilizations? Family is about living together, across individual differences, in ever-changing relations not just of affiliation or affection but of dependency, struggles over authority, and ambivalence.[19] As Roland Barthes said, commenting on the pietistic presentation of the magical natural unity of the "family of man," what get lost are the differences, whose other names are history and injustice.[20]

Justice, Not a Click Away

I have shown that we can best understand "rights" as projects imagined and pursued by people in particular social settings, whether in their families or in court, in international organizations created to realize them or grassroots ones that use them as tools. Rather than asking, therefore, if Muslim women have rights, I suggest that we ask instead what the concepts of "Muslim women's rights" or "the oppressed Muslim woman" are doing in the world and who is making use of these concepts. I have uncovered some ways that a commitment to going to war for women's rights in distant lands participates in divisive and sometimes devastating political projects. But I have also called into question the capacity of any rights framework to capture the complexity of actual people's lives. I recognize that this language of justice has become a part of many women's and men's lives around the world. We do not have a monopoly on it, even if the sources and outlines of rights vary. We see this in 'Aysha's appeal to a mixture of rights drawn from state law, customary practice, and the Qur'an.

By offering some glimpses into women's lives and dilemmas in some communities that lie on the other divide of the imaginative geography that fuels the "clash of civilizations," I make four arguments in this book. First, like other women, the kinds of suffering that Muslim women undergo are of many sorts and have various causes, only some of which might be traced to religious traditions or cultural formations. These formations need to be understood in their fullness, not caricatured.

Second, the violations of what might be widely agreed upon as rights to equality, safety, dignity, or even choice may indeed be patterned along gender lines in ways that are crucial to analyze. Yet we must realize that these patterns are configured differently in relation to opportunities and possibilities available to people in different communities and historical eras. So we want to be attentive to the ways gender structures violence as well as status, well-being, and options in each particular context.

Third, none of us is immune to suffering or difficulties, or to the potential of violations of the most horrible sort. Our newspapers give daily evidence of terrible inhumanity in our own world. Yet we distract ourselves by focusing our gaze on spectacular wrongs elsewhere, led by those who are often well-meaning and sometimes self-righteous, and fed by sensational accounts, including mass-mediated memoirs. I often think of the short stories of Alice Munro, the Canadian writer, when I am confronted with sanctimonious talk about women's suffering elsewhere in the world. These stories about the everyday lives of women model the opposite of what a rights discourse does when it glosses the lives of women. Munro exquisitely captures their desperate searches for meaning or happiness in and out of marriage. She writes hauntingly about the compromises they make in life, the ambivalences they can't escape, the desires and dreams that die. She quietly draws out the sudden strength of character or the impulsive transgression, the misunderstandings between those who love, the ties that strangle, the lies that poison, and the judgments and solaces of social convention and religion. We usually fail to balance the universalizing discourse of rights, like the distancing forms of social scientific description, with this more human perspective when it comes to those we don't know well or those who seem culturally distant.[21]

The failure to look for similarities is dangerous. Through such failures, we disavow not just our common humanity but also our complicity in the forms of suffering that people, including women, experience elsewhere in the world. As we see from Kandiyoti's analysis of the impact of insecurity and war-imposed poverty on families in Afghanistan who now find themselves pressed to "sell" young daughters, or Hirschkind and Mahmood's analysis of the long-term impact of CIA Cold War funding of Afghani mujahideen, warlords with disturbing views and practices toward women, poverty produces debilitating limits on women's choices and cultures of militarism make respect for women elusive. Khadija, with her alcoholic husband and his European "friend," strangled by her poverty in a region deliberately disadvantaged not just by transnational capitalism but also by state policy, is as much part of the modern global economy and social system as we are, sitting in the United States or France or Britain. When a coalition decides to go to war for women, it brings in its train unforeseen consequences for all.

Fourth, we need to always think about power. This is not to place blame, but to ask some basic questions about who has the power to reduce other women, and particularly Muslim women, to subjects known only by deficits in their rights, with the remedies—in development, empowerment, Christianity, women's rights, human rights, or Islamic reform—known in advance by others. What social capital enables projects of bringing rights to Muslim women? This is not a matter for moral judgment but careful analysis. To insist on our innocence and our separation from those whose lives cause us so much concern is to deceive ourselves and make it hard to know what to do. For me, as an anthropologist, reducing the poignant and complex lives of Muslim women to a question of rights or equality—whether women's or human—is not satisfying. This is partly because their lives and the sources of their suffering are so complicated.[22] But it is also because the lives of the unschooled, the poor, or the rural seem to be more regularly rendered legible through talk about their rights and the violations of their rights than the lives of the rest of us. Don't Khadija and Amal and others in their village have complex feelings, tangled relations, and dreams? Don't they do their best to maneuver within their circumstances and constraints? Don't they explore the creative possibilities open to them in this hamlet in Upper Egypt, just as we all do in the settings in which we find ourselves?

I don't have "four steps you can take in the next ten minutes," as offered by other comforting books on global women's suffering. The stories I've told and the analyses I've developed here suggest that there are no quick fixes or easy answers. If pressed for an alternative formula, I would probably give the following advice: look and listen carefully, think hard about the big picture, and take responsibility.

What can looking and listening teach us? This book has introduced you to some women in particular places who are trying to lead good lives. They are making choices that are sometimes hard, limited by the constraints of the present and the uncertainties of the future. I have known all of them for many years as people living in families, in communities, and in nation-states that are part of this world. How do they see the problems they are facing? What do they say they want? How do they invite us to think differently about that mythical place where Muslim women, undifferentiated by locality or personal circumstance, live lives that are totally separate and distinct from our own? Looking carefully at these women's circumstances can teach us much about loaded values like choice and freedom and how they actually work in the context of human lives.

To think about the big picture means remembering that no person is an island. People are involved with others—with their families, their friends, their villages or neighborhoods, and their countries—whether these are hopeful with political uprisings, succumbing to drone attacks, or fielding elections in which politicians run on racist anti-immigrant platforms. All of us are shaped by forces that engage wide groups and that go well beyond us. We all live in real time, our worlds marked by change, argument, and social contestation. What occurs in places that (are made to) appear timeless or backward is always a product of a long history. Ignoring the past or the dynamic contexts of the present may lull us into believing that we can transcend the messiness of actual lives with their fractured and contradictory practices, but there is no escape from politics or history. We should be suspicious of anyone who asks us to gaze on the sufferings of "other" kinds of women, as if they are not connected to us and what we do, including our governments and our financial institutions, and as if these women do not share our humanity.

Finally, honest self-reflection about how the privileges of elites or middle-class people might be connected to the persistence of devastating inequalities—whether on distant shores or in our backyards—is essential to any ethical stance toward women's human rights. Can we trace the lineaments of the particular formations of power and inequality that bind us together? The consistently disappointing results of well-intended interventions— whether military, humanitarian, or developmentalist—are sufficient evidence that we have failed to grasp the character of the connections.

What responsibilities should flow from awareness of women's suffering or of the persistence of gender inequality in other parts of the world? It is not enough to click on a woman-to-woman website to donate a few dollars to support African women learning beadwork or Afghani women sewing bags (with the hope that the sponsoring organization can arrange to sell these wares in New York department stores, meanwhile earning nice salaries for their efforts). Websites of international organizations that urge "technology-savvy" teenage girls "to 'reach out' to impoverished girls in the developing world by feeling 'compassion' for their plight and by donating five U.S. dollars to the organization on their behalf," only reinforce, as Rana Sweis explains, the schism between donors and their objects of compassion.[23] Clucking about ancient tribal honor codes will not get us to the heart of problems in Karachi or Bradford, or be met with sympathy even by women there. Asking women like Zaynab or 'Aysha in Egypt, or my Palestinian aunt in Jordan to renounce their faith, their identities as Muslims, or their deep sense of belonging to their families or communities shows a lack of respect. Advising Muslim girls to run away from home is simply irresponsible.

This book is about what lies behind such deceptively simple responses to problems we think we already understand or believe that we should act on even before we understand.[24] I have uncovered some of the ways that representations of Muslim women's suffering and arguments about their lack of rights work today, both politically and practically. I have followed "Muslim women's rights" as they travel through debates and documents; organize feminist organizations and women's activism; ignite public passions; structure sexually violent memoirs; and mediate lives in villages, refugee camps, slums, and the halls of the United Nations. I have outlined what this framework—which seeks to capture distant women's lives only in terms of rights, present or absent—hides from us about everyday violence and forms of love. We need to ask what this framework, which evaluates lives in terms of rights versus culture (or religion), does for (and against) different kinds of women. I have shown how the key symbols of an alien "Muslim culture"—from the veil to the honor crime—have been deployed in current political projects of destructive warfare, chilling xenophobia, and lucrative humanitarianism.

I am all too aware of the ironies of a privileged scholar in North America invoking the lives of poor rural women in distant lands to comment on the gap between such lives and the visions put forth by other privileged cosmopolitans. My excuse is that a devotion to observation rather than intervention in village lives has made me sensitive to the complexity of these lives, and even to their amazing richness. A commitment to studying the long histories of projects to "remake women" across the

Muslim world has humbled me.[25] I cannot put out of my mind the global inequalities that make women such as those I have written about so much more vulnerable than we are to interventions, imagined or actual, by outsiders.

The world in which I feel a moral pull to intervene is the world of the privileged in which I participate as an equal, not the world of village women elsewhere. In light of the global reach of rights work and rights talk, and their implication in forceful projects to remold human lives, I would rather use my knowledge and experience to intervene into the worlds of power that authorize and naturalize rights work and the sometimes dangerous understandings of human social life to which they are made to give rise. I would rather recognize that societies everywhere debate justice, struggle over power and right, and seek change. Others may choose differently. But I hope that it will be on the basis of careful analysis, critical self-reflection, and constant recognition of our common humanity, a humanity subjected to different forces and expressed in different registers.

NOTES

INTRODUCTION: RIGHTS AND LIVES

1. Zaynab is a pseudonym, as are all the names of the women in Egypt whose lives I describe.

2. She was even hauled off to the police station once for arguing with her envious neighbor. This was shocking for a middle-aged, respected woman from the community who had lived in this house for most of her life.

3. Zaynab depended on her mother for help in the years when her children were young. She shared her knowledge generously with folklorists and anthropologists. For more on Zaynab, see Elizabeth Wickett, *For the Living and the Dead: The Funerary Laments of Upper Egypt, Ancient and Modern* (London: I.B. Tauris, 2010); and Lila Abu-Lughod, *Dramas of Nationhood: The Politics of Television in Egypt*, Lewis Henry Morgan Lectures 2001 (Chicago: University of Chicago Press, 2005).

4. Lila Abu-Lughod, *Veiled Sentiments: Honor and Poetry in a Bedouin Society* (Berkeley: University of California Press, 1986).

5. Paul Riesman, *Freedom in Fulani Social Life: An Introspective Ethnography* (Chicago: University of Chicago Press, 1977).

6. For more on this subject, see the preface to Lila Abu-Lughod, *Writing Women's Worlds: Bedouin Stories*, 15th anniv. ed. (Berkeley: University of California Press, 2008).

7. Scholars have called this "gendered Orientalism." Taking off from Edward Said's book, *Orientalism,* many have analyzed the representation of women and the role of gender in Orientalist discourse. For a few

examples, see Dohra Ahmad, "Not Yet beyond the Veil: Muslim Women in American Popular Literature," *Social Text* 27, no. 99 (2009): 105; Rana Kabbani, *Europe's Myths of Orient* (Bloomington: Indiana University Press, 1986); and Meyda Yegenoglu, *Colonial Fantasies: Towards a Feminist Reading of Orientalism* (Cambridge: Cambridge University Press, 1998).

8. Suad Joseph, "Elite Strategies for State Building," in *Women, Islam, and the State*, ed. Deniz Kandiyoti (Philadelphia: Temple University Press, 1991); Nadje Sadig Al-Ali, *Iraqi Women: Untold Stories from 1948 to the Present* (London: Zed Books, 2007); Nadje Al-Ali and Nicola Pratt, *What Kind of Liberation? Women and the Occupation of Iraq* (Berkeley: University of California Press, 2009).

9. Christina Hoff Sommers, "The Subjection of Islamic Women and the Fecklessness of American Feminism," *Weekly Standard*, May 21, 2007, weeklystandard.com/Content/Public/Articles/000/000/013/641szkys .asp. She cites Phyllis Chesler, notorious for her support of a tawdry campaign against "Islamofascism" that targeted women's studies programs, initiated by the right-wing Zionist David Horowitz. Chesler has coauthored a pamphlet on women and Islamic law that collates Qur'anic quotes out of context to argue that Islam is to blame for violence and all the other wrongs suffered by Muslim women everywhere.

10. Amy Farrell and Patrice McDermott, "Claiming Afghan Women: The Challenge of Human Rights Discourse for Transnational Feminism," in *Just Advocacy? Women's Human Rights, Transnational Feminisms, and the Politics of Representation*, ed. Wendy S. Hesford and Wendy Kozol (New Brunswick, N.J.: Rutgers University Press, 2005).

11. Clifford Geertz once quoted a line from William Blake to capture how it is that anthropologists go about knowing, and why they spend years in small or obscure places attending to the minutia of daily life in order to grasp the human condition. Anthropologists, like poets, he suggested, "see a world in a grain of sand."

12. Fatemeh Fakhraie, "Just . . . Ugh," *Muslimah Media Watch*, April 13, 2011, muslimahmediawatch.org/2011/04/just-ugh/.

13. Maya Dusenbery, "Agency Is Easily Overlooked if You Actively Erase It," *Feministing*, April 14, 2011, feministing.com/2011/04/14/ agency-is-easily-overlooked-if-you-actively-erase-it/. I am grateful to Laura Ciolkowski for bringing this article to my attention.

14. Nussbaum corrects the term, noting that what is being legislated against is not the burqa but the niqab, or face veil. Martha Nussbaum, "Veiled Threats?," *New York Times: Opinionator*, July 11, 2010, opinionator.blogs.nytimes.com/2010/07/11/veiled-threats/. As I describe in

Chapter 1, there are many forms of covering that Muslim women wear. The words for these different types, from Arabic or Persian, are used in English with some fuzziness about the reference. The hijab or head scarf simply covers the hair. The niqab and some forms called the burqa cover the face except for the eyes. The chador, in Iran, is enveloping, but only covers the head and body, not the face. Interestingly, I discovered that the leather mask used by Qatari Bedouins to cover their hunting falcons' eyes is also called a burqa. Hans Christian Korsholm Nielsen, *The Danish Expedition to Qatar, 1959: Photos by Jette Bang and Klaus Ferdinand,* English-Arabic version (Moesgård Museum, 2009).

    15. Martha Nussbaum, "Beyond the Veil: A Response," *New York Times: Opinionator,* July 15, 2010, opinionator.blogs.nytimes.com/2010 /07/15/beyond-the-veil-a-response/.

    16. Martha Nussbaum, "Veiled Threats?," *New York Times: Opinionator,* July 11, 2010, opinionator.blogs.nytimes.com/2010/07/11/veiled -threats/; and Martha C. Nussbaum, *The New Religious Intolerance: Overcoming the Politics of Fear in an Anxious Age* (Cambridge, Mass.: Harvard University Press, 2012).

    17. For a clear summary of this position, see Martha Nussbaum's latest iteration for a general audience: Martha C. Nussbaum, *Creating Capabilities: The Human Development Approach* (Cambridge, Mass.: Harvard University Press, 2011).

    18. For the best analysis of the workings of the UN Convention on the Elimination of All Forms of Discrimination against Women (CEDAW), see Sally Engle Merry, *Human Rights and Gender Violence: Translating International Law into Local Justice* (Chicago: University of Chicago Press, 2006).The timing of CEDAW was important for what was about to happen to the relationship between Islamic and human rights law, and the centrality of "the Muslim woman" to this relationship. Ziba Mir-Hosseini, a feminist legal anthropologist originally from Iran, has pointed out that the Iranian Revolution took place in the same year that CEDAW was passed at the UN. It was a shock to find that people chose an Islamic government. It was ironic that after years of secularization in Iran, Islamic law became valued. Women became the flash point. Forced to cover themselves in public, women also gave birth to a new kind of feminism. Islamic feminism has taken many forms since 1979, but the women involved must be taken seriously as examples of what happens when you see feminism transnationally. Ziba Mir-Hosseni, "Beyond 'Islam' vs. 'Feminism,' " *IDS Bulletin* 42, no. 1 (2011): 67–77.

    19. These debates are taken up later, focusing on such key figures as Nussbaum, Susan Moller Okin, and Catherine MacKinnon, and using

the work of Wendy Brown, *Regulating Aversion: Tolerance in the Age of Identity and Empire* (Princeton, N.J.: Princeton University Press, 2006); Inderpal Grewal, "On the New Global Feminism and the Family of Nations: Dilemmas of Transnational Feminist Practice," in *Talking Visions: Multicultural Feminism in a Transnational Age*, ed. Ella Shohat, Documentary Sources in Contemporary Art (Cambridge, Mass.: MIT Press, 1998); Inderpal Grewal, *Transnational America: Feminisms, Diasporas, Neoliberalisms (Next Wave: New Directions in Women's Studies)* (Durham, N.C.: Duke University Press, 2005); Chandra Talpade Mohanty, *Feminism without Borders: Decolonizing Theory, Practicing Solidarity* (Durham, N.C.: Duke University Press, 2003); Gayatri Chakravorty Spivak, "Can the Subaltern Speak?," in *Marxism and the Interpretation of Culture*, ed. Cary Nelson and Lawrence Grossberg (Urbana: University of Illinois Press, 1988); Rajeswari Sunder Rajan, *Real and Imagined Women: Gender, Culture, and Postcolonialism* (London: Routledge, 1993); Leti Volpp, "Blaming Culture for Bad Behavior," *Yale Journal of Law & the Humanities* 12 (2000): 89–116; and Leti Volpp, "Feminism versus Multiculturalism," *Columbia Law Review* 101, no. 5 (2001): 1181–1218, among others.

20. Zakia Pathak and Rajeswari Sunder Rajan, "Shahbano," *Signs* 14, no. 3 (1989): 558–582; For a good analysis, see Flavia Agnes, "Interrogating 'Consent' and 'Agency' across the Complex Terrain of Family Laws in India," *Social Difference Online* 1 (2011): 1–16, socialdifference.columbia.edu/files/socialdiff/publications/SocDifOnline-Vol 12012.pdf.

21. Elora Halim Chowdhury, *Transnationalism Reversed: Women Organizing against Gendered Violence in Bangladesh*, SUNY Series, Praxis: Theory in Action (Albany: State University of New York Press, 2011), 4.

22. Makau W. Mutua, "Savages, Victims, and Saviors: The Metaphor of Human Rights," *Harvard International Law Journal* 42, no. 1 (2001): 201–245.

23. Dina M. Siddiqi, "Crime and Punishment: Laws of Seduction, Consent, and Rape in Bangladesh," *Social Difference Online* 1 (2011): 46–53, socialdifference.columbia.edu/files/socialdiff/publications/SocDif Online-Vol12012.pdf.

24. The most famous international case was that of Amina Lewal in Nigeria.

25. Jacqueline Aquino Siapno, "Shari'a Moral Policing and the Politics of Consent in Aceh," *Social Difference Online* 1 (2011): 17–29,

socialdifference.columbia.edu/files/socialdiff/publications/SocDifOnline
-Vol12012.pdf.

26. I discuss Musawah's work in Chapter 6.

27. Elora Shehabuddin, "Gender and the Figure of the 'Moderate Muslim': Feminism in the Twenty-First Century," in *The Question of Gender: Joan W. Scott's Critical Feminism*, ed. Judith Butler and Elizabeth Weed (Bloomington: Indiana University Press, 2011), 107.

28. Leila Ahmed, *A Quiet Revolution: The Veil's Resurgence, from the Middle East to America* (New Haven, Conn.: Yale University Press, 2011).

29. Virginia Woolf, *A Room of One's Own* (London: Hogarth Press, 1929).

30. Wendy Brown, "Civilizational Delusions: Secularism, Tolerance, Equality," *Theory and Event* 15, no. 2 (2012). For a good critique of French secularism and its treatment of the veil, see Joan W. Scott, *The Politics of the Veil* (Princeton, N.J.: Princeton University Press, 2007).

31. Saba Mahmood, *Politics of Piety* (Princeton, N.J.: Princeton University Press, 2006).

32. Ayaan Hirsi Ali has resisted "the closing of the Muslim mind" by reading Voltaire. Ayaan Hirsi Ali, *The Caged Virgin: An Emancipation Proclamation for Women and Islam* (New York: Free Press, 2006): 129–140.

33. Ayaan Hirsi Ali, "Ten Tips for Muslim Women Who Want to Leave," in ibid., 111–122.

34. Maya Angelou, *I Know Why the Caged Bird Sings* (New York: Bantam Books, 1993). The full poem can be found in Maya Angelou, *The Complete Collected Poems of Maya Angelou* (New York: Random House, 1994), 194–195.

35. For a powerful analysis of the post–Cold War triumph of a new "ethical" human rights discourse that justifies intervention of any sort by the "world community" to rescue others from atrocities committed by their "neighbors," see Robert Meister, *After Evil: A Politics of Human Rights* (New York: Columbia University Press, 2011). The summary of the principles of this discourse on p. 6 shows just how much the concern for Muslim women's rights fits within the new humanitarian human rights. In a more sarcastic vein, Laura A. Agostín refers to the "Rescue Industry" in which journalist heroes like Nicholas Kristof (see Chapter 2) "get a free pass to act out fun imperialist interventions masked as humanitarianism." Agostín, "The Soft Side of Imperialism," *Counterpunch*, January 25, 2012, counterpunch.org/2012/01/25/the -soft-side-of-imperialism/.

1. DO MUSLIM WOMEN (STILL) NEED SAVING?

1. Derrick Crowe, "*Time*'s Epic Distortion of the Plight of Women in Afghanistan," myFDL (FireDogLake), August 2, 2010, my.firedoglake.com/derrickcrowe/2010/08/02/time's-epic-distortion-of-the-plight-of-women-in-afghanistan/.

2. See "Jodi Bieber Speaking about Her Bibi Aisha Photograph," audio clip, n.d., audioboo.fm/boos/350494-jodi-bieber-speaking-about-her-bibi-aisha-photograph.

3. Richard Stengel, "The Plight of Afghan Women: A Disturbing Picture," *Time*, July 29, 2010, time.com/time/magazine/article/0,9171,2007415,00.html.

4. Esther Hyneman, "Staying Honest about Afghanistan," *HuffPostWorld*, September 20, 2010, huffingtonpost.com/esther-hyneman/staying-honest-about-afgh_b_732185.html; Ann Jones, "Afghan Women Have Already Been Abandoned," *Nation*, August 12, 2010, thenation.com/article/154020/afghan-women-have-already-been-abandoned. For an informed and empirically grounded study of the current work of women's organizations in Afghanistan, see Torunn Wimpelmann, "The Price of Protection: Gender, Violence and Power in Afghanistan" (Ph.D. diss., Department of Development Studies, School of Oriental and African Studies, University of London, 2013).

5. This chapter draws heavily on Lila Abu-Lughod, "Do Muslim Women Really Need Saving? Anthropological Reflections on Cultural Relativism and Its Others," *American Anthropologist* 104, no. 3 (2002): 783–790. For an excellent early analysis of the politics of this move against the Taliban in the name of women, see Charles Hirschkind and Saba Mahmood, "Feminism, the Taliban, and the Politics of Counter-Insurgency," *Anthropological Quarterly* 75, no. 2 (2002): 339–354. Wendy Hesford shows the visual potency of the Afghan woman for humanitarian publicity in her analysis of an Amnesty International campaign, *Spectacular Rhetorics: Human Rights Visions, Recognitions, Feminisms* (Durham, N.C.: Duke University Press, 2011).

6. Jasbir K. Puar and Amit Rai, "Monster, Terrorist, Fag: The War on Terrorism and the Production of Docile Patriots," *Social Text* 20, no. 3 (2002): 117–148.

7. Laura Bush, "Radio Address by Mrs. Bush," *The American Presidency Project*, November 17, 2001, www.presidency.ucsb.edu/ws/index.php?pid=24992#axzz1Zh0bpVSX.

8. Gayatri Chakravorty Spivak, "Can the Subaltern Speak?," in *Marxism and the Interpretation of Culture*, ed. Cary Nelson and Lawrence

Grossberg (Urbana: University of Illinois Press, 1988), 271–313. Antoinette Burton, "The White Woman's Burden," in *Western Women and Imperialism*, ed. Nupur Chaudhuri and Margaret Strobel (Bloomington: Indiana University Press, 1992), 145; Lata Mani, "Contentious Traditions: The Debate on Sati in Colonial India," *Cultural Critique* 7, The Nature and Context of Minority Discourse II (1987): 119–156.

9. Leila Ahmed, *Women and Gender in Islam: Historical Roots of a Modern Debate* (New Haven, CT: Yale University Press, 1992). Elora Shehabuddin has laid out the problems of colonial and missionary feminism in fine detail in "Gender and the Figure of the 'Moderate Muslim,' " in *The Question of Gender: Joan W. Scott's Critical Feminism*, ed. Judith Butler and Elizabeth Weed (Bloomington: Indiana University Press, 2011), 102–142.

10. Marnia Lazreg, *The Eloquence of Silence: Algerian Women in Question* (New York: Routledge, 1994), 135.

11. Ibid., 68–69.

12. Saba Mahmood, "Feminism, Democracy, and Empire: Islam and the War of Terror," in *Women's Studies on the Edge*, ed. Joan Wallach Scott (Durham, N.C.: Duke University Press, 2008), 81–82. This normative secularism has implications for the kinds of Muslim women who get celebrated in the West now. Hirsi Ali declares herself an atheist. For an excellent discussion of missionary views and the role of Christianity even today, see Shehabuddin, "Gender and the Figure of the 'Moderate Muslim.' "

13. Hannah Papanek, "Purdah in Pakistan: Seclusion and Modern Occupations for Women," in *Separate Worlds: Studies of Purdah in South Asia*, ed. Hannah Papanek and Gail Minault (Delhi: Chanakya Publications, 1982), 190–216.

14. Ruth Fremson, "Allure Must Be Covered: Individuality Peeks Through," *New York Times,* November 4, 2001, 12.

15. Ibid.

16. Suzanne Goldenberg, "The Woman Who Stood up to the Taliban," *Guardian,* January 23, 2002, guardian.co.uk/world/2002/jan/24/gender.uk1.

17. I am grateful to Tonunn Wimpelmann for this update on the shifting meaning and use of the burqa in Afghanistan.

18. Lila Abu-Lughod, *Veiled Sentiments: Honor and Poetry in a Bedouin Society* (Berkeley: University of California Press, 1986).

19. For examples, see Lila Abu-Lughod, ed., *Remaking Women: Feminism and Modernity in the Middle East*, Princeton Studies in Culture/Power/History (Princeton, N.J.: Princeton University Press, 1998); Lila

236   NOTES TO PAGES 39-44

Abu-Lughod, *Dramas of Nationhood: The Politics of Television in Egypt*, The Lewis Henry Morgan Lectures 2001 (Chicago: University of Chicago Press, 2005); Suzanne April Brenner, "Reconstructing Self and Society: Javanese Muslim Women and 'the Veil,' " *American Ethnologist* 23, no. 4 (1996): 673–697; Arlene Elowe Macleod, *Accommodating Protest: Working Women, the New Veiling, and Change in Cairo* (New York: Columbia University Press, 1991); Aihwa Ong, "State versus Islam: Malay Families, Women's Bodies and the Body Politic in Malaysia," *American Ethnologist* 17, no. 2 (1990): 258–276.

20. Saba Mahmood, *Politics of Piety: The Islamic Revival and the Feminist Subject* (Princeton, N.J.: Princeton University Press, 2005).

21. Lara Deeb, *An Enchanted Modern* (Princeton, N.J.: Princeton University Press, 2006).

22. In Iran, the name for pushing the boundaries of obligatory covering is "bad hijab," alternately tolerated and cracked down on by the regime.

23. For a glimpse into some of the controversies about veiling in Europe, see Annelies Moors, "The Affective Power of the Face Veil: Between Disgust and Fascination," in *Things: Material Religion and the Topography of Divine Spaces*, ed. Birgit Meyer and Dick Houtman (New York: Fordham University Press, 2012), 282–295; Joan Wallach Scott, *The Politics of the Veil* (Princeton, N.J.: Princeton University Press, 2007).

24. The special problems of feminist anthropologists in that awkward relationship were articulated by Marilyn Strathern, "An Awkward Relationship: The Case of Feminism and Anthropology," *Signs* 12, no. 2 (1987): 276–292.

25. See Charles Hirschkind and Saba Mahmood, "Feminism, the Taliban, and the Politics of Counter-Insurgency," *Anthropological Quarterly* 75, no. 2 (2002): 339–354.

26. See Aihwa Ong, "Colonialism and Modernity: Feminist Representations of Women in Non-Western Societies," *Inscriptions* 3, no. 4 (1988): 79–93.

27. Steven Erlanger, "At Bonn Talks, 3 Women Push Women's Cause," *New York Times,* November 30, 2001.

28. Haleh Afshar, *Islam and Feminisms: An Iranian Case-Study* (New York: St. Martin's Press, 1998); Pardis Mahdavi, *Passionate Uprisings: Iran's Sexual Revolution* (Stanford, Calif.: Stanford University Press, 2009); Ziba Mir-Hosseini, *Islam and Gender: The Religious Debate in Contemporary Iran*, Princeton Studies in Muslim Politics (Princeton, N.J.: Princeton University Press, 1999); Haideh Moghissi, *Feminism and Islamic Fundamentalism: The Limits of Postmodern Analysis* (London: Zed Books, 1999); Afsaneh Najmabadi, "Feminisms

in an Islamic Republic," in *Islam, Gender, and Social Change,* ed. Yvonne Yazbeck Haddad and John Esposito (Oxford: Oxford University Press, 1998); Arzoo Osanloo, *The Politics of Women's Rights in Iran* (Princeton, N.J.: Princeton University Press, 2009).

29. Lila Abu-Lughod, "'Orientalism' and Middle East Feminist Studies," *Feminist Studies* 27, no. 1 (2001): 101–113.

30. Lila Abu-Lughod, "Dialects of Women's Empowerment: The International Circuitry of the Arab Human Development Report," *International Journal of Middle East Studies* 41, no. 1 (2009): 83–103.

31. Saba Mahmood, "Feminist Theory, Embodiment, and the Docile Agent: Some Reflections on the Egyptian Islamic Revival," *Cultural Anthropology* 16, no. 2 (2001): 223.

32. Annie Van Sommer and Samuel Zwemer, *Our Moslem Sisters: A Cry of Need from Lands of Darkness Interpreted by Those Who Heard It* (New York: F. H. Revell, 1907). For a historical study, see Ellen Fleischmann, "'Our Moslem Sisters': Women of Greater Syria in the Eyes of American Protestant Missionary Women," *Islam and Christian-Muslim Relations* 9, no. 3 (1998): 307–323.

33. Annie Van Sommer, "Hagar and Her Sisters," in Van Sommer and Zwemer, *Our Moslem Sisters,* 16.

34. Samuel Zwemer, introduction to Van Sommer and Zwemer, *Our Moslem Sisters,* 5.

35. See the excellent film by Liz Mermin, *Beauty Academy of Kabul* (Sma Distribution, 2006); for a good analysis of the film and the project, see Mimi Thi Nguyen, "The Biopower of Beauty: Humanitarian Imperialisms and Global Feminisms in an Age of Terror," *Signs* 36, no. 2 (2011): 359; and for an account by one of the American participants, see Deborah Rodriguez and Kristin Ohlson, *Kabul Beauty School: An American Woman Goes behind the Veil* (New York: Random House, 2007).

36. Christine J. Walley, "Searching for 'Voices': Feminism, Anthropology, and the Global Debate over Female Genital Operations," *Cultural Anthropology* 12, no. 3 (1997): 405–438.

37. Deniz Kandiyoti, "Old Dilemmas or New Challenges? The Politics of Gender and Reconstruction in Afghanistan," *Development and Change* 38, no. 2 (2007): 176.

38. Kandiyoti, "Old Dilemmas or New Challenges?"

39. Ibid., 180.

40. Deniz Kandiyoti, "The Lures and Perils of Gender Activism in Afghanistan" (Anthony Hyman Memorial Lecture, School of Oriental and African Studies, University of London, 2009), mrzine.monthlyreview.org/2009/kandiyoti041109p.html.

41. Aryn Baker, "Afghan Women and the Return of the Taliban," *Time*, August 9, 2010, www.time.com/time/world/article/0,8599,2007238-4,00 .html.

42. Cynthia Enloe has examined these closely, including for Afghanistan; see Enloe, *The Curious Feminist* (Berkeley: University of California Press, 2004) and *Globalization and Militarism* (New York: Rowman and Littlefield, 2007).

2. THE NEW COMMON SENSE

1. Nicholas D. Kristof and Sheryl WuDunn, *Half the Sky: How to Change the World* (London: Virago, 2010), back cover.

2. Ibid., vii.

3. Ibid., back cover.

4. Anthony Appiah, *The Honor Code: How Moral Revolutions Happen* (New York: W. W. Norton, 2010). Found in places like Pakistan, though previously in places like Sicily, the form of violence against women that Appiah targets in particular is the so-called honor crime. This violence is explained as arising from the desire for men to control women. It happens that these men are Muslims. I discuss and dissect the "honor crime" in Chapter 4.

5. I was recently invited to contribute to a book, following a conference in Australia. To be called *In the Name of Honour*, it was being edited by Aisha Gill, Karl Roberts, and Carolyn Strange. For the "Shop Honour" campaign and tote bag offer, see theahafoundation.org/get-involved/honour/shop-honour/, accessed June 30, 2012.

6. Ayaan Hirsi Ali's three books are *The Caged Virgin: An Emancipation Proclamation for Women and Islam* (New York: Free Press, 2006); *Infidel* (New York: Free Press, 2007); and *Nomad: From Islam to America; A Personal Journey through the Clash of Civilizations* (New York: Free Press, 2010).

7. In response to those whom Hirsi Ali describes as performing "the emotional equivalent of patting my hand" because they believe that her battle is hopeless, she writes, "I choose not to adopt this defeatist approach." Hirsi Ali, *Nomad*, 232.

8. Kristof and WuDunn, *Half the Sky*, xviii.

9. Hirsi Ali, *Caged Virgin*.

10. Kristof and WuDunn, *Half the Sky*, xxiv.

11. Ibid., 261.

12. Christopher Leslie Brown, *Moral Capital: Foundations of British Abolitionism* (Chapel Hill: University of North Carolina Press, 2006), 452–455.

13. Ibid., 453.

14. Michelle Alexander, *The New Jim Crow* (New York: New Press, 2010). But even a decade ago, young black men were six to eight times more likely to serve time in prison than young white men. Since a staggering 30 percent of black men who have finished only high school and 60 percent of high school dropouts have been to prison, researchers conclude that "imprisonment has become a common life event for recent cohorts of black men who never went to college." This has dire consequences for their future opportunities. Becky Pettit and Bruce Western, "Mass Imprisonment and the Life Course: Race and Class Inequality in U.S. Incarceration," *American Sociological Review* 69, no. 2 (2004): 151.

15. Norbert Elias, *The Civilizing Process,* Mole editions (New York: Urizen Books, 1978).

16. Interestingly, the new Islamic feminists who are seeking gender equality through reform of Islamic family law also lay their hope for gender equality in the prior acceptance of slavery and its current rejection. For the activists in Musawah, however, gender equality must be achieved through internal reform, not external intervention. Their Framework for Action states: "The principles and ideals within the Qur'an lay out a path toward equality and justice in family laws and practices, as they did in ending the institution of slavery. As the injustices of slavery became increasingly recognised and the conditions emerged for its abolishment, laws and practices related to slavery were reconsidered and the classical fiqh rulings became obsolete. Similarly, our family laws—as well as practices that have not been codified into law—must evolve to reflect the Islamic values of equality and justice, reinforce universal human rights standards and address the lived realities of families in the twenty-first century." Musawah: For Equality in the Family, "The Musawah Framework for Action," 2009, musawah.org/sites/default/files/Musawah-Framework-EN_1.pdf.

17. Kristof and WuDunn, *Half the Sky,* xxiii.

18. Patricia Tjaden and Nancy Thoennes, *Extent, Nature, and Consequences of Rape Victimization: Findings from the National Violence against Women Survey,* Special Report (Washington, D.C.: National Institute of Justice and the Centers for Disease Control and Prevention, January 2006). The rates are the same for minority and nonminority women.

19. Peggy Reeves Sanday, *Fraternity Gang Rape: Sex, Brotherhood, and Privilege on Campus* (New York: New York University Press, 1990); never mind the scientific literature that pokes holes in pop attempts to explain social facts by sex hormones. For a cutting-edge critique of sex

in science, see Rebecca M. Jordan-Young, *Brain Storm: The Flaws in the Science of Sex Differences* (Cambridge, Mass.: Harvard University Press, 2010).

20. Kristof and WuDunn, *Half the Sky,* xvi.

21. Cynthia H. Enloe, *Bananas, Beaches, and Bases: Making Feminist Sense of International Politics* (Berkeley: University of California Press, 1990); Cynthia H. Enloe, *The Morning After: Sexual Politics at the End of the Cold War* (Berkeley: University of California Press, 1993).

22. Kristof and WuDunn, *Half the Sky,* 181. This is an intriguing image and I am curious to know whether Kristof here is deliberately calling up the "suitcase carriers" ("les porteurs de valises") of the Algerian War in the late 1950s and early 1960s. This was the name given in France to a group of people of different origins—some priests, some Marxists, and some others—who supported the Algerian struggle for independence and carried money collected by Algerians in France for the National Liberation Front, but who also assisted with forging false identity papers and finding safe houses for the National Liberation Front militants (Alain Gresh, personal communication, April 17, 2011).

23. Appiah, *Honor Code,* 99.

24. Dorothy Ko, "Footbinding and Anti-Footbinding in China: The Subject of Pain in the Nineteenth and Early Twentieth Centuries," in *Discipline and the Other Body: Correction, Corporeality, Colonialism,* ed. Steven Pierce and Anupama Rao (Durham, N.C.: Duke University Press, 2006), 215–217.

25. Dorothy Ko, *Cinderella's Sisters: A Revisionist History of Footbinding,* Philip E. Lilienthal Asian Studies Imprint (Berkeley: University of California Press, 2005).

26. Carma Hinton and Richard Gordon, *Small Happiness* (Ronin Films, 1984); Gail Hershatter, *The Gender of Memory: Rural Women and China's Collective Past* (Berkeley: University of California Press, 2011). For a pathbreaking book on Chinese feminism that disrupts such narratives of tradition, modernity, and western influence, see Lydia H. Liu, Rebecca E. Karl, and Dorothy Ko, eds., *The Birth of Chinese Feminism: Essential Texts in Transnational Theory* (New York: Columbia University Press, 2013).

27. A few of the key works to consult are Margery Wolf, *Revolution Postponed: Women in Contemporary China* (Stanford, Calif.: Stanford University Press, 1985); Margery Wolf, "Women and Suicide in China," in *Women in Chinese Society,* ed. Margery Wolf and Roxane Witke (Stanford, Calif.: Stanford University Press, 1975); Ko, *Cinderella's Sisters;* Ko, "Footbinding and Anti-Footbinding in China"; Lisa Rofel,

Other Modernities: Gendered Yearnings in China after Socialism (Berkeley: University of California Press, 1999); Hershatter, *Gender of Memory*; Emily Honig and Gail Hershatter, *Personal Voices: Chinese Women in the 1980's* (Stanford, Calif.: Stanford University Press, 1988); Delia Davin, "Women in the Countryside of China," in Wolf and Witke, *Women in Chinese Society*.

28. Ko, *Cinderella's Sisters*.

29. Ko, "Footbinding and Anti-Footbinding in China," 235.

30. Kristof and WuDunn, *Half the Sky*, xxii.

31. It has often been noted that Americans do not accept that human rights law should apply to the United States. It is also often said but forgotten that the United States is one of the few countries that has not ratified the Convention on the Elimination of All Forms of Discrimination against Women (CEDAW). There are many reasons for this—guarding national sovereignty and political and economic concerns might be among them; Republicans don't help.

32. Catherine Lutz, *Homefront: A Military City and the American Twentieth Century* (Boston: Beacon Press, 2001).

33. Kristof and WuDunn, *Half the Sky*, 211. Studies of microcredit have actually shown that interest rates are far higher and that there are serious problems with microcredit schemes for women. Lamia Karim, *Microfinance and Its Discontents: Women in Debt in Bangladesh* (Minneapolis: University of Minnesota Press, 2011); Ananya Roy, *Poverty Capital* (New York: Routledge, 2010).

34. Kristof and WuDunn, *Half the Sky*, 24.

35. Ibid., 23.

36. Ibid., 20.

37. She subtitles one of her books "A Woman's Cry for Reason" and another "A Personal Journey through the Clash of Civilizations." For more on Hirsi Ali from her days in the Netherlands, see Erik Snel and Femke Stock, "Debating Cultural Differences: Ayaan Hirsi Ali on Islam and Women," in *Immigrant Families in Multicultural Europe: Debating Cultural Difference*, ed. Ralph Grillo (Amsterdam: Amsterdam University Press, 2008); Halleh Ghorashi, "Ayaan Hirsi Ali: Daring or Dogmatic? Debates on Multiculturalism and Emancipation in the Netherlands," in *Multiple Identifications and the Self*, ed. Henk Driessen and Toon van Meijl (Utrecht, Netherlands: Stichting Focaal, 2003).

38. The extent of this political patronage for Ayaan Hirsi Ali, like Irshad Manji and Azar Nafisi is well documented in Saba Mahmood, "Feminism, Democracy, and Empire: Islam and the War of Terror," in *Women's Studies on the Edge*, ed. Joan Wallach Scott (Durham, N.C.: Duke

University Press, 2008). For an analysis of the key role of women in the construction of the "moderate Muslim" who denounces Islam, see Elora Shehabuddin's "Gender and the Figure of the 'Moderate Muslim,'" in *The Question of Gender: Joan W. Scott's Critical Feminism*, ed. Judith Butler and Elizabeth Weed (Bloomington: Indiana University Press, 2011).

39. Hirsi Ali invents the country of "Islamistan" as the setting of her film script for *Submission*, directed by Theo Van Gogh (2004).

40. Hirsi Ali, *Caged Virgin*, 2.

41. Kristof and WuDunn, *Half the Sky*, 175.

42. Appiah, *Honor Code*, 153.

43. Kristof and WuDunn, *Half the Sky*, xii.

44. He used the same techniques in his earlier cause, the Save Darfur campaign. See Rosemary R. Hicks and Jodi Eichler-Levine, "'As Americans against Genocide': The Crisis in Darfur and Interreligious Political Activism," *American Quarterly* 59, no. 3 (2007): 711–735.

45. Kristof and WuDunn, *Half the Sky*, 171.

46. Elaine H. Pagels, *The Gnostic Gospels* (New York: Random House, 1979).

47. Kathryn Joyce, *Quiverfull: Inside the Christian Patriarchy Movement* (Boston: Beacon Press, 2009); "QuiverFull," n.d., quiverfull.com/.

48. Appiah quotes from Leviticus and Deuteronomy.

49. Nadia Abu El-Haj, *The Genealogical Science* (Chicago: University of Chicago Press, 2012).

50. See Letty Cottin Pogrebin, "Gloria Steinem," in *Jewish Women: A Comprehensive Historical Encyclopedia—Jewish Women's Archive*, March 20, 2009, jwa.org/encyclopedia/article/steinem-gloria.

51. Hirsi Ali, *Nomad*, 247. She writes this without a footnote to the Crusades, whose castles attract busloads of tourists across the Middle East, not to mention a hundred years of nineteenth- and twentieth-century colonial missionary work in the Arab world that produced some good schools but only managed to convert some Eastern Orthodox Christians to Protestantism.

52. miriam cooke, "The Muslimwoman," *Contemporary Islam* 1, no. 2 (2007): 139–154.

53. Hirsi Ali, *Nomad*, 129.

54. As is standard practice, I use pseudonyms to protect the anonymity of people about whom I write.

55. One of the best analyses of the link between social visiting and family honor is in Anne Meneley, *Tournaments of Value: Sociability and Hierarchy in a Yemeni Town* (Toronto: University of Toronto Press, 1996).

56. Appiah writes about a Pakistan he does not know, relying on websites and journalism for his analysis. I try to imagine what a philosopher from Iran would say about what Americans should do if he based his knowledge of the United States on American newspapers, studies of women in shelters and jails, legal briefs on child welfare, or on advertisements in magazines. Would we trust his analysis of gender relations based on tabloid coverage of kidnappings or serial killers?

57. Hirsi Ali, *Nomad*, 25–26. I borrow the term "contingent" to describe the specifics from Shehabuddin, "Gender and the Figure of the 'Moderate Muslim,'" 126.

58. Janet Halley et al., "From the International to the Local in Feminist Legal Responses to Rape, Prostitution/Sex Work, and Sex Trafficking: Four Studies in Contemporary Governance Feminism," *Harvard Journal of Law & Gender* 29 (2006): 335–509.

59. Karen Halttunen, "Humanitarianism and the Pornography of Pain in Anglo-American Culture," *American Historical Review* 100, no. 2 (1995): 303–334.

60. The term "pulp nonfiction" comes from Dohra Ahmad, "Not Yet beyond the Veil: Muslim Women in American Popular Literature," *Social Text* 27, no. 99 (2009): 105.

3. AUTHORIZING MORAL CRUSADES

1. Ratna Kapur, "The Tragedy of Victimization Rhetoric: Resurrecting the Native Subject in International/Postcolonial Feminist Legal Politics," *Harvard Human Rights Law Journal* 15 (2002): 1.

2. Kristof and WuDunn humbly announce that they feel honored to have sat at the feet of some amazing women. Nicholas D. Kristof and Sheryl WuDunn, *Half the Sky: How to Change the World* (London: Virago, 2010), acknowledgments, 287.

3. Catharine A. MacKinnon, *Are Women Human? And Other International Dialogues* (Cambridge, Mass.: Harvard University Press, 2006), 41–43; Charlotte Bunch, "Women's Rights as Human Rights: Toward a Re-Vision of Human Rights," *Human Rights Quarterly* 12, no. 4 (1990): 486–498; Susan Moller Okin, *Is Multiculturalism Bad for Women?*, ed. Joshua Cohen, Matthew Howard, and Martha Craven Nussbaum (Princeton, N.J.: Princeton University Press, 1999); Martha Craven Nussbaum, *Women and Human Development: The Capabilities Approach*, John Robert Seeley Lectures (Cambridge: Cambridge University Press, 2000).

4. MacKinnon, *Are Women Human?*, 43.

5. Bunch, "Women's Rights as Human Rights," 491.

6. Okin, *Is Multiculturalism Bad for Women?*, 10.

7. Wendy Brown, *Regulating Aversion: Tolerance in the Age of Identity and Empire* (Princeton, N.J.: Princeton University Press, 2006), 190.

8. Both the rights and the capabilities approaches use cultural arguments to explain sex-subordinating practices in other places, and religion usually comes in for special opprobrium. In blaming culture or religion, as Leti Volpp has noted, liberals obscure the degree to which many women's problems around the world are rooted in forces beyond their individual cultures or communities—for example, in international structures of inequality, novel forms of patriarchy related to politicized religious movements, and flows of transnational capital. They direct attention away from issues affecting women that are separate from what are considered sexist cultural or religious practices—problems that they might share with others, including men. Meanwhile, as I argue in Chapter 4, they divert our gaze from the sexism "indigenous" to the contemporary United States or Europe, or to the middle classes. Leti Volpp, "Feminism versus Multiculturalism," *Columbia Law Review* 101, no. 5 (2001): 1204.

9. Okin, *Is Multiculturalism Bad for Women?*, 23; As one of her critics objects, why assume the public sphere is neutral? Brown asks, "What if male superordination is inscribed in liberalism's core values of liberty—rooted in autonomy and centered on self-interest—and equality—defined as sameness and confined to the public sphere?" Brown, *Regulating Aversion*, 194.

10. Okin, *Is Multiculturalism Bad for Women?*, 16. See Dipesh Chakrabarty, *Provincializing Europe: Postcolonial Thought and Historical Difference*, Princeton Studies in Culture/Power/History (Princeton, N.J.: Princeton University Press, 2000), 27.

11. Martha Nussbaum, "Non-Relative Virtues: An Aristotelian Approach," in *The Quality of Life*, ed. Martha Nussbaum and Amartya Sen, Studies in Development Economics (Oxford: Oxford University Press, 1993), 265.

12. Nussbaum, *Women and Human Development*, 97.

13. Nussbaum may be correct that the capabilities approach has not been tainted by its association with the West in the same way that human rights has, despite multiple attempts to also locate such rights within particular and "non-Western" traditions (as evidenced in the International Islamic Declaration of Human Rights, the Cairo Declaration of Human Rights in Islam, and the Islamic Human Rights Commission in Iran). For a discussion of these, see, for example, Ridwan al-Sayyid, "The Question of Human Rights in Contemporary Islamic Thought," in

Human Rights in Arab Thought: A Reader, ed. Salma Khadra Jayyusi (London: I. B. Tauris, 2009), 257–273; For Iran, see Arzoo Osanloo, *The Politics of Women's Rights in Iran* (Princeton, N.J.: Princeton University Press, 2009); and Arzoo Osanloo, "The Measure of Mercy: Islamic Justice, Sovereign Power, and Human Rights in Iran," *Cultural Anthropology* 21, no. 4 (2006): 570–602.

14. Nussbaum, *Women and Human Development,* 99–100. To convey the contrast between the universalistic rhetoric she deploys and the extreme cultural particularity of the elements she presents as universal, we need to look at how she describes these human capabilities. Talal Asad argues that hers is "a thick account of what being human is," quoting the most blatantly value-laden of these. Talal Asad, "Redeeming the 'Human' through Human Rights," in *Formations of the Secular: Christianity, Islam, Modernity,* Cultural Memory in the Present Series (Stanford: Stanford University Press, 2003), 127–158. I seized on the same capability and unpacked the values in Lila Abu-Lughod, "Against Universals: The Dialects of (Women's) Human Rights and Human Capabilities," in *Rethinking the Human,* ed. J. Michelle Molina, Don Swearer, and Susan Lloyd McGarry (Cambridge, Mass.: Center for the Study of World Religions, Harvard Divinity School, Harvard University Press, 2010), 69–93.

15. Universal Declaration of Human Rights, General Assembly Resolution 217 A (III) (Geneva: UN Official Records, December 10, 1948), 71–79. The text of the Universal Declaration of Human Rights is available in 360 different languages on the website of the UN Office of the High Commissioner for Human Rights, ohchr.org/EN/Pages/Welcome Page.aspx. An English version of the resolution is available from that website at ohchr.org/EN/UDHR/Pages/Language.aspx?LangID=eng.

16. Postcolonial scholars urge us to ask what historical processes made certain notions of "universal" human progress seem self-evident, well beyond the places where they originated; Chakrabarty, *Provincializing Europe,* 43. And how might they have been developed not just in Europe but also in the non-West, which was some kind of laboratory for centuries? See Timothy Mitchell, "The Stage of Modernity," in *Questions of Modernity,* ed. Timothy Mitchell (Minneapolis: University of Minnesota Press, 2000), 1–34. Historians of colonialism have taught us that a focus on race, culture, and, most importantly, religion as impediments to modernization deflected attention away from many illiberal forms of governance that characterized imperial rule. Steven Pierce and Anupama Rao, eds., *Discipline and the Other Body: Correction, Corporeality, Colonialism* (Durham, N.C.: Duke University Press, 2006).

17. See Chakrabarty, *Provincializing Europe,* 27. For elaboration of these arguments about the particularity of universality, see Abu-Lughod, "Against Universals," 69–93.

18. As Talal Asad has put it, human rights builds on a thick description of the human that is culturally and historically specific and thus parochial; it also seeks to impose this version of the human by force. Asad, "Redeeming the 'Human' through Human Rights"; Lila Abu-Lughod, "Against Universals."

19. Dohra Ahmad, "Not Yet beyond the Veil: Muslim Women in American Popular Literature," *Social Text* 27, no. 99 (2009): 105.

20. Meyda Yegenoglu, *Colonial Fantasies: Towards a Feminist Reading of Orientalism* (Cambridge: Cambridge University Press, 1998); Malek Alloula, *The Colonial Harem* (Minneapolis: University of Minnesota Press, 1986); Annie Van Sommer and Samuel Zwemer, *Our Moslem Sisters: A Cry of Need from Lands of Darkness Interpreted by Those Who Heard It* (New York: F. H. Revell, 1907); Linda Nochlin, "The Imaginary Orient," *Art in America,* May 1983; Edward W. Said, *Orientalism* (New York: Vintage Books, 1979); Rana Kabbani, *Europe's Myths of Orient* (Bloomington: Indiana University Press, 1986).

21. Saba Mahmood, "Feminism, Democracy, and Empire: Islam and the War of Terror," in *Women's Studies on the Edge,* ed. Joan Wallach Scott (Durham, N.C.: Duke University Press, 2008).

22. Leti Volpp, "Blaming Culture for Bad Behavior," *Yale Journal of Law and the Humanities* 12 (2000): 89–116.

23. Young Hee Kwon, "Searching to Death for 'Home': A Filipina Immigrant Bride's Subaltern Rewriting," *NWSA Journal* 17, no. 2 (2005): 69–85.

24. This association has been reinforced twenty years later in the spare best-selling "memoir" titled *I am Nujood, Age 10 and Divorced.* Like other books in the genre, this is an "as told to" story. It is written by Delphine Minoui, a prizewinning French journalist. Like other victim/heroines, this girl has been lionized in the West and the association of barbarity with IslamLand reinforced in an era in which Yemen has become intimately associated with terrorism and Al-Qaeda. Nujood Ali and Delphine Minoui, *I am Nujood, Age 10 and Divorced* (New York: Crown Publishing Group, 2010).

25. Miriam Ali with Jana Wain, *Without Mercy: A Mother's Struggle against Modern Slavery* (London: Little, Brown, 1995): 88–89.

26. Islamic feminists have taken up the issue as well. In late 2012, I received an e-mail questionnaire about "forced marriage" from the

Women's Islamic Initiative in Spirituality and Equality (WISE) of the American Society for Muslim Advancement that I discuss in Chapter 6.

27. Leila, with the collaboration of Marie-Thérèse Cuny, *Married by Force*, trans. Sue Rose, 2nd ed. (London: Portrait, 2006), 215.

28. Leila, *Married by Force*, 216. She presses charges and gets a restraining order, but still he won't leave. She then locks him in the apartment for an apocalyptic battle, which ends in an orgy of violence that sends her into a guilty psychotic episode and attempted suicide. Yet between the lines, we can see that for her husband, this marriage has been terrible. "He began to strike himself, screaming, 'I'm sick to death of this girl, I'm sick to death of this girl! I want to make a success of my life. I don't want my son to grow up all alone and my mother isn't here!' He punched himself so badly that his face and eyes were swollen . . . he was banging his head against the walls, rolling around on the floor . . . I had to call the neighbours for help, and then an ambulance." Leila, *Married by Force*, 222–223.

29. Jean Sasson, *Desert Royal* (London: Bantam Books, 2004), 124.

30. Ibid., 130.

31. Ibid., 29.

32. Ibid., 292–293.

33. Ibid., 297. Sultana obviously hadn't read Kristof.

34. To cite just a sample, I would mention Anne Meneley, *Tournaments of Value: Sociability and Hierarchy in a Yemeni Town* (Toronto: University of Toronto Press, Inc., 1996); Soraya Altorki, *Women in Saudi Arabia: Ideology and Behavior among the Elite* (New York: Columbia University Press, 1986); Christine Eickelman, *Women and Community in Oman* (New York: New York University Press, 1984); Elizabeth Warnock Fernea, *Guests of the Sheik: An Ethnography of an Iraqi Village*, 3rd ed. (New York: Anchor Books, 1995); Deborah Kapchan, *Gender on the Market* (Philadelphia: University of Pennsylvania Press, 1996); Saba Mahmood, *Politics of Piety: The Islamic Revival and the Feminist Subject* (Princeton, N.J.: Princeton University Press, 2005); and Lara Deeb, *An Enchanted Modern: Gender and Public Piety in Shi'i Lebanon* (Princeton, N.J.: Princeton University Press, 2008).

35. Hannah Shah, *The Imam's Daughter* (London: Rider, 2009), 270.

36. For good analyses of this controversy, see Talal Asad, Wendy Brown, Judith Butler, and Saba Mahmood, *Is Critique Secular? Blasphemy, Injury, and Free Speech* (Berkeley: University of California Press, 2009).

37. Jean P. Sasson, *Desert Royal* (London: Bantam, 1999), 16.

38. Ali and Wain, *Without Mercy,* 274, 285; Zana Muhsen with Andrew Crofts, *Sold: A Story of Modern-Day Slavery* (London: Little, Brown Book Group: 1991).

39. See Nacira Guénif-Souilamas, "The Other French Exception: Virtuous Racism and the War of the Sexes in Postcolonial France," *French Politics, Culture & Society* 24, no. 3 (2006): 23–41; Miriam Ticktin, *Casualties of Care: Immigration and the Politics of Humanitarianism in France* (Berkeley: University of California Press, 2011); Mayanthi Fernando, "Reconfiguring Freedom: Muslim Piety and the Limits of Secular Law and Public Discourse in France," *American Ethnologist* 37, no. 1 (2010): 19.

40. Leila, *Married by Force,* 193. It is worth noting that recent statistical studies conducted by the French National Institute for Demographic Studies and the National Institute for Statistics and Economic Studies show the complexity of questions of consent and the number of fewer forced marriages among immigrant women and their daughters. Christelle Hamel, "Fewer Forced Marriages among Immigrant Women and Daughters of Immigrants." *Population and Societies* 479 (2011): 1–4. I thank Nisrin Abu Amara, who has done the research for this study, for bringing the findings to my attention, including her own analysis both of the rarity of "forced marriages" and their lack of connection to obtaining immigration documents.

41. Miriam Ticktin, "Sexual Violence as the Language of Border Control: Where French Feminist and Anti-immigrant Rhetoric Meet," *Signs* 33, no. 41 (2008): 863–889. She expands on the case of Zina in Ticktin, *Casualties of Care.* The quote from Sarkozy is on p. 128.

42. Mukhtar Mai, *In the Name of Honor: A Memoir,* trans. Linda Coverdale (New York: Washington Square Press, 2006).

43. See Carole S. Vance, "Thinking Trafficking, Thinking Sex," *GLQ: A Journal of Lesbian and Gay Studies* 17, no. 1 (2011): 135–143, for nineteenth-century melodrama themes in trafficking debates; see also Elizabeth Bernstein, "Militarized Humanitarianism Meets Carceral Feminism: The Politics of Sex, Rights, and Freedom in Contemporary Antitrafficking Campaigns," *Signs* 36, no. 1 (2010): 45.

44. Amazon.co.uk, "Disgraced: Forced to Marry a Stranger, Betrayed by My Own Family, Sold My Body to Survive, This Is My Story: Amazon.co.uk: Saira Ahmed and Andrew Crofts: Books," 2011, amazon .co.uk/Disgraced-Forced-Stranger-Betrayed-Survive/dp/0755318188/ref =sr_1_1?ie=UTF8&qid=1322254584&sr=8–1.

45. Amazon.co.uk, "Belonging: Amazon.co.uk: Sameem Ali: Books,"
2011, amazon.co.uk/Belonging-Sameem-Ali/dp/071956462X/ref=sr_
1_1?s=books&ie=UTF8&qid=1322254797&sr=1-1.
46. Shah, *The Imam's Daughter,* viii.
47. Ibid., 80–81.
48. This freedom is not always secular. I was surprised to find Shah,
The Imam's Daughter advertised on a website called ChristianBooks
(christianbook.com/the-imams-daughter-hannah-shah/9780310325758/
pd/325758?event=1036SPF|527742|1036), where it was described as "a
true story of a courageous woman who broke free of cultural oppression
and embraced a new life in Christ . . . She married who she wanted. An
amazing account of God's saving grace."
49. She wrote the script for this film and made it with Theo Van
Gogh, a Dutch filmmaker known for his sharp tongue and relish for
controversy (including, but not limited to, racist remarks he made about
Muslim immigrants). For excellent discussions, see the work by Dutch
anthropologists: Annelies Moors, "Submission," *ISIM Review* 15
(2005); and Marc de Leeuw and Sonja van Wichelen, "Please, Go Wake
Up!," *Feminist Media Studies* 5, no. 3 (2005), 329.
50. As Annelies Moors pointed out about Ayaan Hirsi Ali in response to her film *Submission,* "Hirsi Ali has been seen as a lone voice
willing to take great personal risks to reveal the cruelty Islam inflicts on
women that others had tried to cover up. It is certainly true that she has
taken great risks, but the presentation of her position in Dutch society
as a lone voice is remarkable. Whereas she does not have much support
amongst Muslims, men or women, she finds herself in the company of
very powerful players." Moors, "Submission," 9. Halleh Ghorashi, another scholar based in the Netherlands, describes her as "a welcome
mouthpiece for the dominant discourse on Islam in the Netherlands
that pictures Islamic migrants as problems and enemies of the nation."
Ghorashi, "Ayaan Hirsi Ali: Daring or Dogmatic?" *Focaal: European
Journal of Anthropology* 42 (2003): 163–173. Iveta Jusová, a scholar
who was in the Netherlands at the time the film came out, noted how
unconcerned Hirsi Ali seemed about making alliances with Dutch Muslim women or checking the appropriation of her film for Islamophobes.
To the contrary, Jusová writes, "By depicting Muslim women in the film
as victims with no agency, by quoting from the Qur'an selectively and
only those verses that represent its autocratic voice, and by ignoring
the tradition of Muslim women's efforts to forge new readings of the
Qur'an appropriate for the 21st century, in fact by the whole way the

film's argument is expressed, *Submission* lends itself easily to appropriation by the Islamophobic discourse." Iveta Jusová, "Hirsi Ali and van Gogh's *Submission*: Reinforcing the Islam vs. Women Binary," *Women's Studies International Forum* 31, no. 2 (2008): 154.

51. De Leeuw and van Wichelen, "Please, Go Wake Up!," 329.

52. Moors, "Submission," 8.

53. Hirsi Ali, *Caged Virgin*, 141–150.

54. Marcus Wood, *Slavery, Empathy, and Pornography* (Oxford: Oxford University Press, 2002), 87.

55. Ibid., 96.

56. See also Carolyn J. Dean, "Empathy, Pornography, and Suffering," *Differences: A Journal of Feminist Cultural Studies* 14, no. 1 (2003): 88–124.

57. Jay M. Bernstein, "Bare Life, Bearing Witness: Auschwitz and the Pornography of Horror," *Parallax* 10, no. 1 (2004): 12.

58. Wood, *Slavery, Empathy, and Pornography*, 102–103.

59. For other discussions, see Ahmad, "Not Yet beyond the Veil"; Laila Lalami, "The Missionary Position," *Nation,* June 19, 2006, thenation.com/article/missionary-position; and Roksana Bahramitash, "The War on Terror, Feminist Orientalism and Orientalist Feminism: Case Studies of Two North American Bestsellers," *Critique: Critical Middle Eastern Studies* 14, no. 2 (2005): 221–235.

60. Saba Mahmood, "Feminism, Democracy, and Empire: Islam and the War of Terror," in *Women's Studies on the Edge,* ed. Joan Wallach Scott (Durham, N.C.: Duke University Press, 2008), 92–93. She notes that like Ayaan Hirsi Ali, this "native" who takes us inside a country in the "axis of evil" has been celebrated by Western feminists as well as the neoconservative men and women who people the American Enterprise Institute.

61. Sherene H. Razack, "Stealing the Pain of Others: Reflections on Canadian Humanitarian Responses," *Review of Education, Pedagogy, and Cultural Studies* 29, no. 4 (2007): 375–394.

62. Ayaan Hirsi Ali, *Infidel* (New York: Free Press), 85.

63. Ibid., 207–208.

64. Ibid., 209.

65. See Abu-Lughod, "Against Universals."

66. Veena Das, "National Honor and Practical Kinship: Unwanted Women and Children," in *Conceiving the New World Order: The Global Politics of Reproduction,* ed. Faye D. Ginsburg and Rayna R. Rapp (Berkeley: University of California Press, 1995); Ritu Menon and Kamla Bhasin, *Borders & Boundaries: Women in India's Partition* (New

Brunswick, N.J.: Rutgers University Press, 1998); Urvashi Butalia, *The Other Side of Silence: Voices from the Partition of India* (Durham, N.C.: Duke University Press, 2000).

67. I am grateful to Partha Chatterjee for this insight.

4. SEDUCTIONS OF THE "HONOR CRIME"

1. For details, see a longer and earlier version of this chapter published as Lila Abu-Lughod, "Seductions of the 'Honor Crime'," *Differences: A Journal of Feminist Cultural Studies* 22, no. 1 (2011):17–63.

2. I take this term from James Ferguson's now classic study of the work of the development industry in the Third World. James Ferguson, *The Anti-Politics Machine: Development, Depoliticization, and Bureaucratic Power in Lesotho* (Minneapolis: University of Minnesota Press, 1994).

3. Amnesty International, *Culture of Discrimination: A Fact Sheet on "Honor" Killings* (New York: Amnesty International, July 20, 2005).

4. As Kristof informs us, "the hymen—fragile, rarely seen, and pretty pointless—remains an object of worship among many religions and societies around the world." Nicholas D. Kristof and Sheryl WuDunn, *Half the Sky: How to Change the World* (London: Virago, 2010), 90.

5. Lila Abu-Lughod, *Writing Women's Worlds: Bedouin Stories* (Berkeley: University of California Press, 1993), 192, 184.

6. For a particularly compelling story in which love poems were even credited for causing a death, see Lila Abu-Lughod, "Shifting Politics in Bedouin Love Poetry," in *Language and the Politics of Emotion,* ed. Catherine Lutz and Lila Abu-Lughod (New York: Cambridge University Press, 1990), 24–45. For a beautiful Romeo and Juliet type traditional romance, in which the fronds of trees growing from the graves of a pair of tragic lovers cross high in the sky, see Lila Abu-Lughod, *Veiled Sentiments: Honor and Poetry in a Bedouin Society* (Berkeley: University of California Press, 1986), 249–250.

7. Anthony Appiah, *The Honor Code: How Moral Revolutions Happen* (New York: W. W. Norton, 2010), 172.

8. Unni Wikan, *In Honor of Fadime: Murder and Shame* (Chicago: University of Chicago Press, 2008), 62.

9. Ibid., 117.

10. Ibid., 110.

11. Ibid., 236.

12. Ibid., 167.

13. Ibid., 275.

14. Riemers's analysis of the Swedish media coverage of the event has revealed the patterns. As she notes, "The newspapers represented Fadime

Sahindal as a martyr for the Swedish way of living, which is signified by equality, modernity, freedom, and enlightenment. This representation was founded on, and thereby reiterated, cultural racism, sexism, and class prejudice." These representations exaggerated differences among Swedish and immigrant cases of violence against women. Eva Riemers, "Representations of an Honor Killing: Intersections of Discourses on Culture, Gender, Equality, Social Class, and Nationality," *Feminist Media Studies* 7, no. 3 (2007): 239–255, quote on 252. Rema Hammami kindly brought this article to my attention after I had completed my analysis. For a sharp critique of the way this incident was represented in Canada by Wikan, see Sherene Razack, *Casting Out: The Eviction of Muslims from Western Law and Politics* (Toronto: University of Toronto Press, 2008).

15. Annie Van Sommer and Samuel Zwemer, *Our Moslem Sisters: A Cry of Need from Lands of Darkness Interpreted by Those Who Heard It* (New York: F. H. Revell, 1907), 16.

16. Norma Khouri, *Forbidden Love*, 2nd ed. (New York: Bantam Books, 2004), 8, 10–11.

17. Rana Husseini, *Murder in the Name of Honour: The True Story of One Woman's Heroic Fight against an Unbelievable Crime* (Oxford: Oneworld, 2009).

18. In 2007, a fascinating documentary film called *Forbidden Lie$*, by Anna Broinowski, was released about Norma Khouri. It features interviews with the Australian journalist who broke the story, Malcolm Knox, and many others who reveal, among other things, the support for Khouri's asylum case at the highest levels of the Bush administration. For further discussions of the case and the newspaper coverage, see Saba Mahmood "Feminism, Democracy, and Empire: Islam and the War of Terror," in *Women's Studies on the Edge*, ed. Joan Wallach Scott (Durham, N.C.: Duke University Press, 2008); Husseini, *Murder in the Name of Honour;* Joseph R. Slaughter, *Human Rights, Inc.: The World Novel, Narrative Form, and International Law* (New York: Fordham University Press, 2007).

19. It is certainly to be read cautiously, as an Australian historian and specialist on memoirs has argued. Thérèse Taylor, "Truth, History, and Honor Killing: A Review of *Burned Alive*," *AntiWar.com*, May 2, 2005, antiwar.com/orig/ttaylor.php?articleid=5801.

20. Souad and Marie-Thérèse Cuny, *Burned Alive* (London: Bantam, 2004), 68.

21. Wikan, *In Honor of Fadime*, 24.

22. E-mail communication, September 8, 2007. The parent site, Mideast Youth, was set up in 2005 as "a platform for dialogue between

Iranian and Arab youth." It has since expanded to cover minority rights and many other issues, garnering international awards for cyberactivism. Al-Azraq had to give up his volunteer work with the "No Honor" site because he got busy organizing dialogues between Jordanians and Danes, trying to convince the U.S. Embassy to sponsor a similar Jordanian-American youth dialogue project, and helping teach a virtual course for American college students interested in international relations and the Middle East. The website, accessed November 3, 2010, is no longer live.

23. Human Rights Watch, *A Question of Security: Violence against Palestinian Women and Girls,* November 11, 2006, unhcr.org/refworld /docid/4565dd724.html. I discuss this report in Chapter 5.

24. Dicle Koğacioğlu, "The Tradition Effect: Framing Honor Crimes in Turkey," *Differences: A Journal of Feminist Cultural Studies* 15, no. 2 (2004): 119, 141.

25. For a critique of the association of tradition with honor, see Ayse Parla, "The 'Honor' of the State," *Feminist Studies* 27, no. 1 (2001): 65–88.

26. Khaled Fahmy, "Women, Medicine, and Power in Nineteenth Century Egypt," in *Remaking Women: Feminism and Modernity in the Middle East,* ed. Lila Abu-Lughod, Princeton Studies in Culture/Power/ History (Princeton, N.J.: Princeton University Press, 1998); Liat Kozma, "Negotiating Virginity: Narratives of Defloration from Late Nineteenth-Century Egypt," *Comparative Studies of South Asia, Africa and the Middle East* 24, no. 1 (2004): 57–69; Mario M. Ruiz, "Virginity Violated: Sexual Assault and Respectability in Mid- to Late-Nineteenth-Century Egypt," *Comparative Studies of South Asia, Africa and the Middle East* 25, no. 1 (2005): 214–226.

27. Nadera Shalhoub-Kevorkian and Suhad Daher-Nashif, "The Politics of Killing Women in Colonized Contexts," *Jadaliyya,* December 17, 2012, jadaliyya.com/pages/contributors/110635.

28. Human Rights Watch, *A Question of Security,* 49.

29. Katherine Pratt Ewing, *Stolen Honor: Stigmatizing Muslim Men in Berlin* (Stanford, Calif.: Stanford University Press, 2008), chap. 5.

30. Ibid., 153.

31. Ibid., 154.

32. As Miriam Ticktin argues in her analysis of the hyperconcern in France about rapes in the slums and sexual soliciting on the street, "Put in the larger context of debates in France about immigration, national security, and a growing Europe-wide form of Islamophobia, the focus on sexuality—and sexual violence, more specifically—can be explained

NOTES TO PAGES 134–142

by the fact that it has become the discourse of border control and the way borders are policed." Miriam Ticktin, "Sexual Violence as the Language of Border Control: Where French Feminist and Anti-immigrant Rhetoric Meet," *Signs* 33, no. 4 (2008): 864.

33. Nacira Guénif-Souilamas, "The Other French Exception: Virtuous Racism and the War of the Sexes in Postcolonial France," *French Politics, Culture & Society* 24, no. 3 (2006): 27.

34. Jacqueline Rose, "A Piece of White Silk," *London Review of Books* 31, no. 21 (2009): 5–8.

35. Anna C. Korteweg and Gökçe Yurdakul, "Religion, Culture and the Politicization of Honour-Related Violence," Paper No. 12, *Gender and Development Programme,* UN Research Institute for Social Development, October 2010.

36. Fadwa El Guindi, *Veil: Modesty, Privacy, and Resistance,* Dress, Body, Culture (Oxford: Berg, 1999); Saba Mahmood, *Politics of Piety: The Islamic Revival and the Feminist Subject* (Princeton, N.J.: Princeton University Press, 2005).

37. Lara Deeb and Mona Harb, *Leisurely Islam* (Princeton, N.J.: Princeton University Press, 2013); Lara Deeb and Mona Harb, "Sanctioned Pleasures: Youth, Piety and Leisure in Beirut," *Middle East Report* 245 (2007): 12–19; Frances Susan Hasso, *Consuming Desires: Family Crisis and the State in the Middle East* (Stanford, Calif.: Stanford University Press, 2011).

38. Homa Hoodfar, *Between Marriage and the Market: Intimate Politics and Survival in Cairo* (Berkeley: University of California Press, 1997); Arlene Elowe Macleod, *Accommodating Protest: Working Women, the New Veiling, and Change in Cairo* (New York: Columbia University Press, 1991); Mahmood, *Politics of Piety.*

39. Lama Abu-Odeh, "Crimes of Honour and the Construction of Gender in Arab Societies," in *Feminism and Islam: Legal and Literary Perspectives,* ed. Mai Yamani and Andrew Allen (New York: New York University Press, 1996).

40. As Saba Mahmood writes, "No discursive object occupies a simple relation to the reality it purportedly denotes. Rather, representations of facts, objects, and events are profoundly mediated by the fields of power in which they circulate and through which they acquire their precise shape and form." Saba Mahmood, "Feminism, Democracy, and Empire: Islam and the War of Terror," in *Women's Studies on the Edge,* ed. Joan W. Scott (Durham, N.C.: Duke University Press, 2008), 97.

41. Janet Halley, Prabha Kotiswaran, Hila Shamir, and Chantal Thomas, "From the International to the Local in Feminist Legal

Responses to Rape, Prostitution/Sex Work, and Sex Trafficking: Four Studies in Contemporary Governance Feminism," *Harvard Journal of Law and Gender* 29 (2006): 335–423.

5. THE SOCIAL LIFE OF MUSLIM WOMEN'S RIGHTS

1. Arjun Appadurai, ed., *The Social Life of Things: Commodities in Cultural Perspective* (Cambridge: Cambridge University Press, 1988), has alerted us to the circulation of objects through his notion of the social life of things; Sally Engle Merry, *Human Rights and Gender Violence: Translating International Law into Local Justice,* Chicago Series in Law and Society (Chicago: University of Chicago Press, 2006), has introduced the idea of vernacularization for women's human rights; and Bruno Latour, "Circulating Reference: Sampling the Soil in the Amazon Forest," in *Pandora's Hope: Essays on the Reality of Science Studies* (Cambridge, Mass.: Harvard University Press, 1999) and other ethnographers of science have taught us to look at the instruments through which concepts are mediated. For another ethnographic approach to rights that focuses on the arts, see Susan Slyomovics, *The Performance of Human Rights in Morocco* (Philadelphia: University of Pennsylvania Press, 2005).

2. Though my examples are drawn from the Arab world because that is where I have done my research, I am keenly aware of how this skewing perpetuates the association of Islam with the Arab world when, in fact, Muslims are found around the world. For a good critical analysis of the "Muslimwoman," see miriam cooke, "The Muslimwoman," *Contemporary Islam* 1, no. 2 (2007): 139–154; for counterweights to the focus on the Arab world, see Elora Halim Chowdhury, Leila Farsakh, and Rajini Srikanth, "Introduction-Engaging Islam," *International Feminist Journal of Politics* 10, no. 4 (2008): 439–454.

3. For more on early Egyptian and Middle Eastern feminism, see Lila Abu-Lughod, ed., *Remaking Women: Feminism and Modernity in the Middle East,* Princeton Studies in Culture/Power/History (Princeton, N.J.: Princeton University Press, 1998); Margot Badran, *Feminists, Islam, and Nation: Gender and the Making of Modern Egypt* (Princeton, N.J.: Princeton University Press, 1995); Beth Baron, *Egypt as a Woman: Nationalism, Gender, and Politics* (Berkeley: University of California Press, 2005); Marilyn Booth, *May Her Likes Be Multiplied: Biography and Gender Politics in Egypt* (Berkeley: University of California Press, 2001); Afsaneh Najmabadi, "Crafting an Educated Housewife in Iran," in Abu-Lughod, *Remaking Women;* Hoda El Sadda, 'Imad Abu Ghazi, and Jabir 'Usfur, *Significant Moments in the History of Egyptian*

256 NOTES TO PAGES 148-150

Women (Cairo, Egypt: National Council for Women, Committee for Culture and Media, 2001).

4. For state feminism, see Laura Bier, *Revolutionary Womanhood: Feminisms, Modernity, and the State in Nasser's Egypt* (Stanford, Calif.: Stanford University Press, 2011); Mervat F. Hatem, "Economic and Political Liberation in Egypt and the Demise of State Feminism," *International Journal of Middle East Studies* 24, no. 2 (1992): 231–251; Mervat F. Hatem, "In the Eye of the Storm: Islamic Societies and Muslim Women in Globalization Discourses," *Comparative Studies of South Asia, Africa and the Middle East* 26, no. 1 (2006): 22–35; Cynthia Nelson, *Doria Shafik, Egyptian Feminist: A Woman Apart* (Gainesville: University Press of Florida, 1996); El Sadda, Abu Ghazi, and 'Usfur, *Significant Moments*.

5. Maha M. Abdelrahman, *Civil Society Exposed: The Politics of NGOs in Egypt,* Library of Modern Middle East Studies (London: Tauris Academic, 2004), 54; Maha M. Abdelrahman, "The Nationalisation of the Human Rights Debate in Egypt," *Nations and Nationalism* 13, no. 2 (2007): 285–300.

6. Nadje Sadig Al-Ali, *Iraqi Women: Untold Stories from 1948 to the Present* (London: Zed Books, 2007); Siham 'Abd al-Salam, *Al-munazzamat al-ahliyya al-saghira al-'amila fi majal al-mar'a* [Small civil society organizations working on women's issues] (Cairo, Egypt: Dar al-'ayn li al-nashr, 2005).

7. For a sharp analysis of the structure of and impediments to women's activism in Egypt, see Rabab El Mahdi, "Does Political Islam Impede Gender-Based Mobilization? The Case of Egypt," *Totalitarian Movements and Political Religions* 11, no. 3 (2010):379–396.

8. Nadje Sadig Al-Ali, *Secularism, Gender, and the State in the Middle East: The Egyptian Women's Movement,* Cambridge Middle East Studies (Cambridge: Cambridge University Press, 2000), 20.

9. Abdelrahman, *Civil Society Exposed,* 182–183.

10. The literature is fast growing and the debates continue to rage about the implications of the "Arab Spring" for women. For an early assessment that was critical of media representations, see Lila Abu-Lughod and Rabab El Mahdi, "Beyond the 'Woman Question' in the Egyptian Revolution," *Feminist Studies* 37, no. 3 (2012): 683–691. Mona El Tahawy's "Why Do They Hate Us? The Real War on Women is in the Middle East," in *Foreign Policy,* Sex Issue, May/June 2013, ignited controversy; foreignpolicy.com/articles/2012/04/23/why_do_they_hate_us.

11. For an ethnographic consideration of the way the "revolution" was experienced in Fayruz and 'Aysha's village, see Lila Abu-Lughod,

"In Every Village a Tahrir: Rural Youth in Moral Revolution," in *Public Space and Revolt: Tahrir Square 2011*, ed. Elena Tzelepis and Sherene Seikaly (Cairo, Egypt: American University in Cairo Press, forthcoming); and Lila Abu-Lughod, "Living the 'Revolution' in an Egyptian Village: Moral Action in a National Space," *American Ethnologist* 39, no. 1 (2012): 16–20.

12. Naomi Sakr, "Friend or Foe? Dependency Theory and Women's Media Activism in the Arab Middle East," *Critique: Critical Middle Eastern Studies* 13, no. 2 (2004): 166.

13. Nationalist campaigns to discredit the smaller nongovernmental organizations (NGOs) for their foreign links must be seen, as Sakr argues, as "a diversionary tactic." Given that Egypt is the second-largest recipient of U.S. aid, Sakr concludes that it "seems perverse to suggest that NGOs were more to blame than the government for prolonging dependency on foreign powers," ibid., 172; for more on the complicated scene of such organizations, see Sheila Carapico, "NGOs, INGOs, GO-NGOs and DO-NGOs: Making Sense of Non-Governmental Organizations," *Middle East Report* 214 (2000): 12–15.

14. United Nations Egypt, *United Nations Development Assistance Framework 2007–2011 Egypt: Moving in the Spirit of the Millennium Declaration: The DNA of Progress* (Egypt: United Nations, 2006), 22. Similarly, the annual report on the European Neighbourhood Policy by the Commission of the European Communities notes that 17 million euros were earmarked in 2008 for human rights, women's rights, and children's rights projects in Egypt. Commission of the European Communities (CEC), *Implementation of the European Neighbourhood Policy in 2008: Progress Report Egypt* (Cairo, Egypt: CEC, 2009), 22, ec.europa.eu/world/enp/pdf/progress2009/sec09_523_en.pdf.

15. This strategy of setting up a government body to advance rights that were formerly the bailiwick of more critical NGOs while trying to discredit them by presenting them as part of a foreign plot, was copied, it seems, in the case of human rights. Three years after the creation of the National Council for Women (NCW), a National Council for Human Rights was established. As Maha Abdelrahman has argued, with serious restrictions on NGOs and a campaign to misrepresent "human rights and the organisations that attempt to promote these rights as mouthpieces of Western imperialist powers," the regime tarred human rights organizations as a threat to Egypt's national security and reputation. Meanwhile, the regime "has gained a degree of legitimacy in the eyes of the public by representing itself as the protector of national interests. More recently . . . since the debate on and the foundation of the

National Council for Human Rights in 2003, the state has refined its discourse on the role of civil society and human rights organisations by promoting an image of itself as the true patron of civil society organisations and the 'official agent' of a more nationalistically defined human rights movement." Abdelrahman, "Nationalisation of the Human Rights Debate in Egypt," 287.

16. Janet Halley et al., "From the International to the Local in Feminist Legal Responses to Rape, Prostitution/Sex Work, and Sex Trafficking: Four Studies in Contemporary Governance Feminism," *Harvard Journal of Law & Gender* 29 (2006): 335–509. Similar trends of governmental control over substantial funds for women's empowerment and rights have been observed in Jordan and Syria. See Mayssoun Sukarieh, "The First Lady Phenomenon: Women's Empowerment and the Colonial Present in the Contemporary Arab World," paper presented at the Boas Seminar, Columbia University, March 27, 2013.

17. Association for the Development and Enhancement of Women, "History of ADEW," 2008, adew.org/en/?action=10000&sub=1.

18. Funders include one Egyptian (Sawiris Foundation for Development) and one Arab (Arab Gulf Program for United Nations Development Organization, or AG Fund), and the rest is a who's who of foreign or UN foundations or agencies: the Delegation of the European Commission to Egypt, Swiss Development Fund, Ford Foundation, Embassy of Japan, Royal Netherlands Embassy, Dutch Organization for International Development Cooperation (NOVIB), German Technical Cooperation (GTZ), Italian Debt Swap Program, United Nations Development Program (UNDP), Australian Embassy, and Embassy of Finland.

19. Naela Rifaat, personal communication, Cairo, March 2008.

20. The Center for Egyptian Women's Legal Assistance (CEWLA) is sought after as a partner by many, including the School of Oriental and African Studies at the University of London when it was conducting a multiyear project on honor crimes. See Lynn Welchman and Sara Hossein, *Honour: Crimes, Paradigms and Violence against Women* (London: Zed Press, 2005). CEWLA also commissioned its own study.

21. Both Coptic and Muslim NGOs have long provided services to women in Egypt, though Iman Bibars, an Egyptian scholar and activist, has criticized them for their rigid expectations about gender roles and, in the case of Muslim welfare groups, their bias toward women who are heavily veiled and who present themselves as "lonely, sick and poor." Iman Bibars, *Victims and Heroines: Women, Welfare and the Egyptian State* (London: Zed, 2001); and Abdelrahman, *Civil Society Exposed*, 116.

NOTES TO PAGES 154-156

22. Seham Ali interview, 2008. The director of CEWLA, Azza Sleiman, is also part of a transnational network of Muslim feminists who launched an organization called Musawah in Kuala Lumpur in February 2009, dedicated to seeking justice and equality within Islamic family law. For more on this organization, see Chapter 6.

23. United Nations Egypt, *United Nations Development Assistance Framework 2007–2011 Egypt;* for more on the alliance of the state and Al-Azhar in Egypt, see Malika Zeghal, "Religion and Politics in Egypt: The Ulema of Al-Azhar, Radical Islam, and the State (1952–94)," *International Journal of Middle East Studies* 31, no. 3 (1999): 371–399; and Tamir Moustafa, "Conflict and Cooperation between the State and Religious Institutions in Contemporary Egypt," *International Journal of Middle East Studies* 32, no. 1 (2000): 3–22.

24. Bibars was interviewed on Al-Jazeera by Riz Khan. Ashoka, "Iman Bibars and Sakeena Yacoobi on Al Jazeera," Ashoka: Innovators for the Public, September 22, 2008, ashoka.org/video/5007.

25. Ashoka, "Support Social Entrepreneurs," Ashoka: Innovators for the Public, n.d., ashoka.org/support. The Ashoka Middle East and North Africa fellows program, like ADEW (perhaps because both are directed by Bibars), has also taken advantage of the opportunity to partner with Columbia University's School of International and Public Affairs. Students in the development program in 2008–2009 were commissioned to evaluate a girls' sports program in Upper Egypt sponsored by Nike and run by an Ashoka fellow. For a critical analysis of the role of sports in imagining the liberation of village girls in Egypt, see Rania Kassab Sweis, "Saving Egypt's Village Girls: Humanity, Rights, and Gendered Vulnerability in a Global Youth Initiative," *Journal of Middle East Women's Studies* 8, no. 2 (2012): 26–50.

26. A report on the Egyptian Center for Women's Rights's campaigns against sexual harassment, which have taken new forms to respond to the harassment of women protesters that have been orchestrated since the events in Tahrir Square in 2011, can be found on their website. See ecwronline.org/blog/2012/12/16/publications-of-sexual-harassment-campaign/.

27. The Egyptian Center for Women's Rights (ECWR) appropriated the slogan "The Street Is Ours" from a more radical coalition formed in the summer of 2005 after the scandalous attack on women protesters by thugs with police approval/instigation at a peaceful prodemocracy demonstration by the political movement Kefaya (Enough) (Rabab El Mahdi, personal communication, 2008). See El Mahdi, "Does Political Islam Impede Gender-Based Mobilization? The Case of Egypt." Such

attacks were seen again across our television screens in the initial days
of the revolt in Tahrir Square on January 28, 2011, but this time without succeeding in stopping the demonstrators. The ECWR's campaign
against anonymous sexual harassment delinks the problems from the
ugly politics of government repression and violence by the security
forces and their successors.

28. For the results of this initiative, see harassmap.org.

29. Mona Abaza, *Changing Consumer Cultures of Modern Egypt:
Cairo's Urban Reshaping,* Social, Economic, and Political Studies of the
Middle East and Asia (Leiden, Netherlands: Brill, 2006); Diane Singer-
man and Paul Ammar, eds., *Cairo Cosmopolitan: Politics, Culture, and
Urban Space in the Globalized Middle East* (Cairo, Egypt: American
University in Cairo Press, 2006); Anouk De Koning, *Global Dreams:
Class, Gender, and Public Space in Cosmopolitan Cairo* (Cairo, Egypt:
American University in Cairo Press, 2009). For a major study of con-
temporary Cairo that focuses instead on informal development across
the social classes, see David Sims, *Understanding Cairo: The Logic of
a City Out of Control* (Cairo, Egypt: American University in Cairo,
2011).

30. Sally Engle Merry has shown that since the 1990s, violence has
been the main issue on the agenda of the transnational feminist community, a focus not without its suspicious critics. Merry, *Human Rights
and Gender Violence.*

31. One in Three Women: A Global Campaign to Raise Awareness
about Violence against Women, Domestic Violence, Sexual Assault, Human Trafficking, n.d., oneinthreewomen.com/. The website indicates an
interesting mix of commerce and good works: It states, "One in Three
Women™ is a program of Moxie Company, Seattle, WA, founded by
Cheyla McCornack and Evelyn Brom. Moxie Company is a social enterprise supporting programs and organizations working to end violence
against women"; oneinthreewomen.com/index.cfm?action=about.

32. PeaceKeeper Cause-metics, "Women's Health Advocacy and Urgent Human Rights," 2013, iamapeacekeeper.com/peacekeeperadvoca
cyissuesnew.htm?

33. Women Living under Muslim Laws (WLUML), "Violence Is Not
Our Culture: The Global Campaign to Stop Violence against Women in
the Name of Culture," 2009, stop-stoning.org/.

34. See Valentine M. Moghadam, *Globalizing Women: Transnational
Feminist Networks,* Themes in Global Social Change (Baltimore, Md.:
Johns Hopkins University Press, 2005), 142–172, for an excellent de-
scription of WLUML's positions and history.

35. Women Living under Muslim Laws (WLUML), "The Global Campaign 'Stop Stoning and Killing Women!' Concept Paper," 2007, 2, wluml.org/english/news/stop_stoning _and _killing _ women%20_con cept_paper.pdf.

36. For example, see Robert Spencer and Phyllis Chesler, *The Violent Oppression of Women in Islam* (Los Angeles: David Horowitz Freedom Center, 2007).

37. Amnesty International, *Israeli Army Used Flechettes against Civilians* (New York: Amnesty International, January 27, 2009), amnesty .org/en/news-and-updates/news/israeli-used-flechettes-against-gaza-civilians-20090127; James Hider, "Names of Commanders to Be Kept Secret as Gaza Weapons Inquiry Begins," *Times of London: TimesOnline,* January 22, 2009, timesonline.co.uk/tol/news/world/middle_east /article5563082.ece.

38. New evidence of this has emerged in the report of the United Nation Fact Finding Mission on the Gaza Conflict, submitted in September 2009. For the "Goldstone Report," see United Nations Human Rights Council (UN/HRC), *Human Rights in Palestine and Other Occupied Arab Territories: Report of the United Nations Fact Finding Mission on the Gaza Conflict,* September 15, 2009. www2.ohchr.org/english/ bodies/hrcouncil/specialsession/9/FactFindingMission.htm. Although Goldstone disavowed the report under pressure, other members of the commission did not.

39. Carapico, "NGOs, INGOs, GO-NGOs and DO-NGOs"; Sari Hanafi and Linda Tabar, *The Emergence of a Palestinian Globalized Elite: Donors, International Organizations and Local NGOs* (Ramallah, Palestine: Institute of Jerusalem Studies; Muwatin, Palestinian Institute for the Study of Democracy, 2005); Islah Jad, "Between Religion and Secularism: Islamist Women of Hamas," in *On Shifting Ground: Muslim Women in the Global Era,* ed. Fereshteh Nouraie-Simone (New York: Feminist Press at the City University of New York, 2005); Islah Jad, "The Demobilization of the Palestinian Women's Movement in Palestine: From Empowered Active Militants to Powerless and Stateless 'Citizens,'" *MIT Electronic Journal of Middle East Studies* 8 (Spring 2008): 94–111; Penny Johnson, "Violence All Around Us: Dilemmas of Global and Local Agendas Addressing Violence against Palestinian Women, an Initial Intervention," *Cultural Dynamics* 20, no. 2 (2008): 119–131.

40. For good analyses, see Nadera Shalhoub-Kevorkian, *Militarization and Violence against Women in Conflict Zones in the Middle East: A Palestinian Case-Study,* Cambridge Studies in Law and Society (Cam-

262

NOTES TO PAGES 159–161

bridge: Cambridge University Press, 2009); Nahla Abdo, *Women in Israel: Race, Gender and Citizenship* (London: Zed Books, 2011).

41. Nadera Shalhoub-Kevorkian, "Conceptualizing Voices of the Oppressed in Conflict Areas," in *Women, Armed Conflict and Loss: The Mental Health of Palestinian Women in the Occupied Territories,* ed. Khawla Abu Baker (Jerusalem: Women's Studies Centre, 2004), published with Swedish funding: Kvinna Till Kvinna (Woman to Woman) and Sida (Swedish International Development Cooperation Agency).

42. Ibid., 17–31.

43. For a subtle analysis of the impact of human rights on Palestinian politics, representations, and subjectivity, see Lori Allen, "Martyr Bodies in the Media: Human Rights, Aesthetics, and the Politics of Immediation in the Palestinian Intifada," *American Ethnologist* 36, no. 1 (2009): 161. Didier Fassin also comments on the depoliticizing focus on trauma during the second intifada; see his *Humanitarian Reason* (Berkeley: University of California Press, 2012). Islah Jad, based at Birzeit University in Palestine, chose to coauthor the UNDP's *Arab Human Development Report 2005: Towards the Rise of Women in the Arab World.* Scholar-activists, including Nadera Shalhoub-Kevorkian, assisted Human Rights Watch (HRW) in preparing *A Question of Security,* its 2006 report on violence against Palestinian women and girls.

44. Johnson, "Violence All Around Us," 125.

45. These kinds of critiques are different from ones that focus on the way the Human Rights Report played in the American media. The reception of the report returns us to the dense terrain surrounding the focus of the campaign to "stop killing and stoning women"—the transnational terrain "Muslim women's rights" traverses. According to some analysts, the U.S. reportage on violence in Palestine is skewed: of eighty reports documenting human rights abuses in the Palestinian-Israeli conflict since 2000, only two of the seventy-six that were primarily critical of Israel were featured in the *New York Times,* while two of the four that were primarily critical of Palestinians received coverage, including the 2006 Human Rights Watch report on *Domestic Security.* Moreover, HRW 2006 was represented selectively to reinforce the impression that Muslim women need saving because they are passive victims of patriarchy and family violence. Also, as these commentators note, by failing to quote a single Palestinian women's rights activist of the twenty-one mentioned in the report, the *New York Times* coverage also made it seem as if only foreigners could identify women's problems and help resolve them. This was not HRW's position. Patrick O'Connor and Rachel Roberts, "The *New York Times* Marginalizes Palestinian Women

and Palestinian Rights," *Electronic Intifada,* November 17, 2006, elec
tronicintifada.net/content/new-york-times-marginalizes-palestinian-wo
men-and-palestinian-rights/6544#.TsHn0HERpq4.

46. Jad, "Demobilization of the Palestinian Women's Movement in
Palestine."

47. Islah Jad, "Between Religion and Secularism: Islamist Women of
Hamas;" Islah Jad, "The Politics of Group Weddings in Palestine: Political and Gender Tensions," *Journal of Middle East Women's Studies* 5,
no. 3 (2009): 36–53.

48. Sama Aweidah, "A Glimpse into the Women's Stories," in Abu
Baker, *Women, Armed Conflict and Loss,* 102.

49. I acknowledge the dangers of picking out individual cases; I do
so here neither to present such women as victims in order to solicit aid
or justify good works, nor to cast them as unsung heroines resisting
patriarchy in far-flung places, as critics charge is commonly the case in
NGO work or feminist ethnography; see Marnia Lazreg, "Development: Feminist Theory's Cul-de-Sac," in *Feminist Post-Development
Thought: Rethinking Modernity, Post-Colonialism and Representation,*
ed. Kriemild Saunders, Zed Books on Women and Development (London: Zed, 2002); Sangtin Writers and Richa Nagar, *Playing with Fire:
Feminist Thought and Activism through Seven Lives In India,* 1st ed.
(Minneapolis: University of Minnesota Press, 2006). I use their voices
here to speak to those concerned with "Muslim women's rights" and
therefore to insert these village women into the discourses and practices
that constitute them as subjects of "women's rights."

50. For more on Arab women and education, see Fida Adely, *Gen-
dered Paradoxes* (Chicago: University of Chicago Press, 2012); Adely,
"Educating Women for Development: The Arab Human Development
Report 2005 and the Problem with Women's Choices," *International
Journal of Middle East Studies* 41 (2009): 105–122; for more on educa-
tion in the village, see Lila Abu-Lughod, *Dramas of Nationhood: The
Politics of Television in Egypt,* Lewis Henry Morgan Lectures 2001
(Chicago: University of Chicago Press, 2005).

51. She explained to me this element of Islamic law: the man takes
two portions of the inheritance and the woman takes one.

52. This is confirmed by Rachida Chih's study of this and other Sufis
of the Khalwatiyya Brotherhood in Upper Egypt. Based on research in
the 1990s, she argues, "Women, like men, want to meet the Shaykh for
his baraka, for spiritual counseling but also for his mediation and protection against a ruthless husband or to escape a forced marriage . . .
The Shaykh's mediation is so popular that the population of the village

has called it hukm hasani meaning for them a fair and quick justice that compensates the victims and prevents vendettas." Rachida Chih, "The Khalwatiyya Brotherhood in Rural Upper Egypt and in Cairo," in *Upper Egypt: Identity and Change,* ed. Nicholas Hopkins and Reem Saad (Cairo, Egypt: American University in Cairo Press, 2004), 162.

53. Rania Kassab Sweis, "Saving Egypt's Village Girls." As Sweis argues, in this project of "saving village girls," crafting "the adolescent girl body as mobile, healthy, and rights bearing in these ways is viewed as imperative to the overall construction of a healthy national population in line with developmentalist models," 37.

54. For more on the response of the villagers to the uprisings, see Lila Abu-Lughod, "In Every Village a Tahrir: Rural Youth in Moral Revolution."

55. Christine Walley, "What We Women Want: An Ethnography of Transnational Feminism" (Unpublished book manuscript).

56. Mark Goodale, "Introduction to 'Anthropology and Human Rights in a New Key,'" *American Anthropologist* 108, no. 1 (2006): 3; Richard Ashby Wilson, "Afterword to 'Anthropology and Human Rights in a New Key': The Social Life of Human Rights," *American Anthropologist* 108, no. 1 (2006): 81.

57. Smadar Lavie, "Mizrahi Feminism and the Question of Palestine," *Journal of Middle East Women's Studies* 7, no. 2 (2011): 56.

6. AN ANTHROPOLOGIST IN THE TERRITORY OF RIGHTS

1. I draw some implications of feminist ethnography for debates about rights in the preface to the 15th anniversary edition of my ethnography, Lila Abu-Lughod, *Writing Women's Worlds: Bedouin Stories* (Berkeley: University of California Press, 2008).

2. I am referencing Clifford Geertz, of course. Clifford Geertz, *The Interpretation of Cultures: Selected Essays* (New York: Basic Books, 1973). George E. Marcus picked this up in the title of his book, *Ethnography through Thick and Thin* (Princeton, N.J.: Princeton University Press, 1998).

3. Sally Engle Merry, *Human Rights and Gender Violence: Translating International Law into Local Justice,* Chicago Series in Law and Society (Chicago: University of Chicago Press, 2006).

4. Feminist anthropologists have tended instead to observe the workings of women's rights in particular contexts, whether the UN Convention on the Elimination of All Forms of Discrimination against Women (CEDAW) Commission hearings or local women's organizations. The development of such organizations is often accompanied by tensions

between what elite nationals, transnational feminists, and donor orga-nizations want, and the women's priorities in their communities. See Dorothy L. Hodgson, "'These Are Not Our Priorities': Maasai Women, Human Rights and the Problem of Culture," in *Gender and Culture at the Limit of Rights*, ed. Dorothy Hodgson (Philadelphia: University of Pennsylvania Press, 2011); Christine J. Walley, "What We Women Want: An Ethnography of Transnational Feminism," unpublished manuscript.

5. Taking both conceptual and practical rights as their objects, anthropologists have considered everything from rights as cultural and performative to the ways that rights talk is mobilized (Dorothy L. Hodgson, "Women's Rights as Human Rights: Women in Law and De-velopment in Africa [WiLDAF]," *Africa Today* 49, no. 2 [2002]: 3–26; Dorothy L. Hodgson, "Introduction: Comparative Perspectives on the Indigenous Rights Movement in Africa and the Americas," *American Anthropologist* 104, no. 4 [2002]: 1037–1049; and Hodgson, "'These Are Not Our Priorities.'") They have studied the dynamics of trans-plantation and vernacularization of rights frames and the social ma-chinery of the production and reproduction of rights: see especially Merry, *Human Rights and Gender Violence;* Peggy Levitt and Sally En-gle Merry, "Making Women's Human Rights in the Vernacular: Navi-gating the Culture/Rights Divide," in *Gender and Culture at the Limit of Rights*, ed. Dorothy Hodgson (Philadelphia: University of Pennsylva-nia Press, 2011). Others have invoked human rights to find ways to as-sist indigenous communities: Elsa Stamatopoulou and Bruce Robbins, "Reflections on Culture and Cultural Rights," *South Atlantic Quarterly* 103, nos. 2–3 (2004): 419–434. In an important contribution aptly titled "Rights Inside Out," Riles has shown the peculiar way women's groups in Fiji adopted "women's rights as human rights" as a frame-work, despite their own doubts, convinced of the efficacy of a discourse that they imagined others "out there" found persuasive. See Annelise Riles, "Rights Inside Out: The Case of the Women's Human Rights Campaign," *Leiden Journal of International Law* 15, no. 2 (2002): 285–305.

6. Elizabeth Povinelli, *The Cunning of Recognition: Indigenous Al-terities and the Making of Australian Multiculturalism* (Durham, N.C.: Duke University Press, 2002).

7. See Harri Englund, *Prisoners of Freedom: Human Rights and the African Poor* (Berkeley: University of California Press, 2006), writing on Malawi; and Michael Jackson, *Existential Anthropology: Events, Exigencies and Effects* (New York: Berghahn Books, 2005), writing on Sierra Leone. See also James Ferguson and Akhil Gupta, "Spatializing

States: Toward an Ethnography of Neoliberal Governmentality," *American Ethnologist* 29, no. 4 (2002): 98–110.

8. Lori Allen, "Martyr Bodies in the Media: Human Rights, Aesthetics, and the Politics of Immediation in the Palestinian Intifada," *American Ethnologist* 36, no. 1 (2009): 161. See also Didier Fassin, *Humanitarian Reason: A Moral History of the Present* (Berkeley: University of California Press, 2011); Peter Redfield, "Doctors, Borders, and Life in Crisis," *Cultural Anthropology* 20, no. 3 (2005): 328–361; Miriam Ticktin, *Casualties of Care* (Berkeley: University of California Press, 2011); Ticktin, "Where Ethics and Politics Meet: The Violence of Humanitarianism in France," *American Ethnologist* 33, no. 1 (2006): 33–49.

9. Wendy Brown, "'The Most We Can Hope For . . .': Human Rights and the Politics of Fatalism," *South Atlantic Quarterly* 103, nos. 2–3 (2004): 451–463. Robert Meister, *After Evil: A Politics of Human Rights* (New York: Columbia University Press, 2011).

10. Ratna Kapur, "The Tragedy of Victimization Rhetoric: Resurrecting the 'Native' Subject in International/Post-Colonial Feminist Legal Politics," *Harvard Human Rights Journal* 15 (2002): 1–38; Inderpal Grewal, "'Women's Rights as Human Rights': The Transnational Production of Global Feminist Subjects," in *Transnational America: Feminisms, Diasporas, Neoliberalisms,* ed. Inderpal Grewal, Next Wave (Durham, N.C.: Duke University Press, 2005), 125.

11. As Norani Othman, one of the founders of Sisters in Islam explains, "The experience of many women's groups operating in Muslim countries these past two decades demonstrates that in their daily battles a great deal more progress is achieved by working with their religious and cultural paradigm." Norani Othman, "Grounding Human Rights Arguments in Non-Western Culture: Shari'a and the Citizenship Rights of Women in a Modern Islamic State," in *The East Asian Challenge for Human Rights,* ed. Joanne R. Bauer and Daniel A. Bell (Cambridge: Cambridge University Press, 1999).

12. The focus will be on one of the key "violations" of women's human rights that has mobilized the transnational community in recent years: domestic violence. See Grewal, "'Women's Rights as Human Rights'"; for a questioning of the capacity of legal language to capture the experience of violence, see Kirsten Hastrup, "Violence, Suffering and Human Rights: Anthropological Reflections," *Anthropological Theory* 3, no. 3 (2003): 309–323.

13. Those concerned with women's rights realized that for the "grassroots"—their objects of concern and intended beneficiaries—the moral appeal of fidelity to Islam had never wavered and in fact has been

enhanced in the past few decades with the spread of education, media, and the growing funding of Islamic education and proselytizing.

14. Irshad Manji is a good example, discussed by Saba Mahmood, "Feminism, Democracy, and Empire: Islam and the War of Terror," in *Women's Studies on the Edge*, ed. Joan Wallach Scott (Durham, N.C.: Duke University Press, 2008). Ayaan Hirsi Ali is another.

15. An interesting new mix is represented by Nazreen Nawaz, media spokesperson for Hizb ut-Tahrir's 2012 launch of an international campaign called "The Khilafah: A Shining Model for Women's Rights and Political Role," which fuses women's rights language with a radical vision of a "ruling system based purely upon Islamic laws and principles," hizb-ut-tahrir.info/info/english.php/contents_en/entry_16414.

16. According to some accounts, Sisters in Islam (SIS) catalyzed when theologian Dr. Amina Wadud, having since become famous through her books like *Inside the Gender Jihad* (Oxford: Oneworld, 2008) and through leading a mixed congregation prayer, came to teach in Malaysia; Madhavi Sunder, "Reading the Quran in Kuala Lumpur," *University of Chicago Law School Faculty Blog*, February 16, 2009, uchicagolaw .typepad.com/faculty/2009/02/reading-the-quran-in-kuala-lumpur.html. For other important arguments about achieving women's rights through feminist interpretations of the Qur'an, see Zainah Anwar, "Sisters in Islam and the Struggle for Women's Rights," in *On Shifting Ground: Muslim Women in the Global Era*, ed. Fereshteh Nouraie-Simone (New York: Feminist Press at the City University of New York, 2005); Asma Barlas, "Globalizing Equality: Muslim Women, Theology, and Feminism," in *On Shifting Ground: Muslim Women in the Global Era*, ed. Fereshteh Nouraie-Simone (New York: Feminist Press at the City University of New York, 2005); Azizah al-Hibri, "Deconstructing Patriarchal Jurisprudence in Islamic Law: A Faithful Approach," in *Global Critical Race Feminism: An International Reader*, ed. Adrien Katherine Wing (New York: New York University Press, 2000); and Azizah al-Hibri, "Muslim Women's Rights in the Global Village: Challenges and Opportunities," *Journal of Law and Religion* 15, nos. 1–2 (2000): 37–66. For an overview of issues, see Margot Badran, *Feminism in Islam: Secular and Religious Convergences* (Oxford: Oneworld, 2009).

17. But Basarudin, writing her dissertation about SIS, describes the organization more neutrally as those "working from within their religious and cultural frameworks." Azza Basarudin, "Musawah Movement: Seeking Equality and Justice in Muslim Family Law," *CSW Update Newsletter, UCLA*, March 1, 2009, repositories.cdlib.org/csw/newsletter /Mar09_Basarudin.

18. Musawah: For Equality in the Family, "Musawah Framework for Action," 2009, musawah.org/sites/default/files/Musawah-Framework -EN_1.pdf.

19. The statement continued, "Today's Muslim family laws are human interpretations of the Shari'ah, based on juristic theories and assumptions. Therefore, they can change in accordance with the changing realities of time and place and contemporary notions of justice."

20. Musawah: For Equality in the Family, "Musawah Framework for Action."

21. Ziba Mir-Hosseini's contribution to Musawah's resource book is "Towards Gender Equality: Muslim Family Laws and the Shari'ah," in *Wanted: Equality and Justice in the Muslim Family,* ed. Zainah Anwar (Selangor, Malaysia: Musawah, 2009), musawah.org/background_papers.asp, but she has published widely on such issues, starting with her excellent piece "Stretching the Limits: A Feminist Reading of the Shari'a in post-Khomeini Iran," in *Feminism and Islam: Legal and Literary Perspectives,* ed. Mai Yamani and Andrew Allen (New York: New York University Press, 1996), and extending to her essay: Ziba Mir-Hosseini, "Muslim Women's Quest for Equality: Between Islamic Law and Feminism," *Critical Inquiry* 32, no. 4 (2006): 629-645.

22. The latter article is by Khaled Abou Fadl, named in Mahmood's article as one of the "good Muslims," the moderate Muslim thinkers with whom the U.S. government wishes to partner, even if they are more or less critical of U.S. policy in the Middle East.

23. Saba Mahmood, "Secularism, Hermeneutics, and Empire: The Politics of Islamic Reformation," *Public Culture* 18, no. 2 (2006): 323-347.

24. Zainah Anwar, "Introduction: Why Equality and Justice Now?" in Anwar, *Wanted: Equality and Justice in the Muslim Family,* 3.

25. Basarudin has described the launch and the issues; she notes in the piece that a part of her dissertation will discuss Musawah and Sisters in Islam. Basarudin, "Musawah Movement."

26. Musawah, "CEDAW and Muslim Family Laws," December 12, 2011, musawah.org/cedaw-and-muslim-family-laws-search-common -ground.

27. Madhavi Sunder, "Reading the Quran in Kuala Lumpur"; for more on Nafisi, see Chapter 3 and Laila Lalami, "The Missionary Position," *Nation,* June 19, 2006, thenation.com/article/missionary-position; Roksana Bahramitash, "The War on Terror, Feminist Orientalism and Orientalist Feminism: Case Studies of Two North American Bestsellers," *Critique: Critical Middle Eastern Studies* 14, no. 2 (2005): 221-235;

Hamid Dabashi, "Native Informers and the Making of the American Empire," *Al-Ahram Weekly Online*, June 1, 2006, weekly.ahram.org .eg/2006/797/special.htm; Mahmood, "Feminism, Democracy, and Empire."

28. A third issue to consider in Musawah's construction of its reform project is its family resemblance to some political efforts from which it would distance itself unequivocally. In Saba Mahmood's provocative article "Secularism, Hermeneutics, and Empire: The Politics of Islamic Reformation," she has drawn attention to the awkward relationship between liberalism and U.S. imperial projects directed at the Muslim world. As she notes, somewhat surprisingly for a secular state, "the United States has embarked upon an ambitious theological campaign aimed at shaping the sensibilities of ordinary Muslims whom the State Department deems to be too dangerously inclined toward fundamentalist interpretations of Islam" (Mahmood, "Secularism, Hermeneutics, and Empire," 329). She argues that "secular normativity" is not, as it avers, about separating church and state or promoting tolerance of differences, but about "remaking religious subjectivities," ibid., 328. This can be seen in the targets of U.S. fears (the "traditionalist Muslim"), the goal of their reform efforts (encouraging "moderate Islam"), and their methods, which are, as Mahmood describes them, theological. She notes, for example, that a portion of the $1.3 billion allocated to the Muslim World Outreach initiative has gone into training Islamic preachers, establishing Islamic schools that could counter the "madrasas" (a word that means "school," but that Western media now use to designate conservative religious schools that produce, it is believed, extremists), and shaping the content of religious debate in the media. This is perfectly in line with the media efforts of states like Egypt to drive a wedge between a good moderate enlightened Islam and bad and wrongheaded extremism; Lila Abu-Lughod, *Dramas of Nationhood: The Politics of Television in Egypt*, Lewis Henry Morgan Lectures 2001 (Chicago: University of Chicago Press, 2005). What Mahmood argues, however, is that the partners these U.S. initiatives have sought to encourage are those who consider themselves moderate Muslim reformers who are distinguished by the fact that they agree with the "diagnosis that the central problem haunting Muslim societies lies in their inability to achieve critical distance between the divine text and the world." So it is not just ideology or practice but hermeneutics that distinguishes the reformers to be encouraged and the rest of society that is dangerously literalist, ritual-bound, and therefore in danger of being attracted by the messages of extremists; Mahmood, "Secularism, Hermeneutics, and Empire," 330–331.

29. Ziba Mir-Hosseini, "Beyond 'Islam' vs. 'Feminism,'" *IDS Bulletin* 42, no. 1 (2011): 67–77, esp. 71.

30. Ibid., 75.

31. Their sophisticated new website is Women's Islamic Initiative in Spirituality and Equality (WISE), "WISE Muslim Women," wisemuslimwomen.org/.

32. See "The Cordoba Initiative," cordobainitiative.org/; see also Rosemary R. Hicks, "Translating Culture, Transcending Difference? Cosmopolitan Consciousness and Sufi Sensibilities in New York City after 2001," *Journal of Islamic Law and Culture* 10, no. 3 (2008): 281–306. For more on the cosmopolitan ideology of Sufis in New York and the work of Imam Feisal, see Rosemary R. Hicks, "Creating an 'Abrahamic America' and Moderating Islam: Cold War Political Economy and Cosmopolitan Sufis in New York After 2001" (Ph.D. diss., New York: Columbia University, 2010).

33. Wendy Brown, *Regulating Aversion: Tolerance in the Age of Identity and Empire* (Princeton, N.J.: Princeton University Press, 2006) shows that contemporary liberal tolerance discourse masks some unsavory politics. Despite Abdel Raouf's insistent liberalism, his bid to set up a cultural center near Ground Zero in New York set off vitriolic protests by Islamophobes.

34. Even the visions of femininity were multiple. Some capitalized on the fact that the acronym WISE had a meaning: some of the women present spoke about women's wisdom as a source of authority. Others were uncomfortable with the essentialization of femininity sometimes invoked.

35. See poster on website: Women's Islamic Initiative in Spirituality and Equality (WISE), *Jihad against Violence: Muslim Women's Struggle for Peace*, July 2009, wisemuslimwomen.org/pdfs/jihad-report.pdf.

36. The ideological positioning of one of the most forceful women in the group placed her squarely in the camp that Mahmood calls reformist. Her biographical sketch notes that she "has spent the past decade assisting moderate Muslim communities around the world to resist the ideological onslaught of Islamic extremism. She advises both government and civic leaders on the threat posed by the extremists, as well as on policies to transform stifled Muslim societies into progressive participants of a free society."

37. What follows in the compact is a series of declarations about exactly what, in these six domains, WISE women are dedicated to: in the sphere of protecting religion, for example, the compact states, "We are dedicated to advancing Muslim women's positions as religious and

spiritual authorities." In the sphere of the intellect, "We are dedicated to defending Muslim women's freedom to interpret, think, and express, especially concerning Islam's primary texts." Under property, they support "Muslim women's financial independence." And under dignity, "We are dedicated to empowering Muslim women to make dignified personal, familial, and career choices." Women's Islamic Initiative in Spirituality and Equality (WISE), "Resources," n.d., wisemuslimwomen .org/resources/.

38. Ironically, at the same time, one of the more extraordinary recent scholarly ventures dedicated to research on Islam and the Muslim world, the Institute for the Study of Islam in the Modern World (ISIM), lost its funding from the Dutch government.

39. Interestingly, the American Society of Muslim Advancement's (ASMA's) other big initiative is to train young leaders.

40. Sally Engle Merry's ethnography, *Human Rights and Gender Violence,* describes the transnational feminists who attend the meetings in New York, Geneva, and Beijing where the Commission on the Status of Women holds its hearings on CEDAW and where documents and platforms are tortuously composed to produce consent by delegates from many nations.

41. In addition to the major competitive grant from the Dutch Ministry of Foreign Affairs, WISE lists an impressive group of supporters: the United Nations Population Fund, the William and Mary Greve Foundation, Rockefeller Brothers Fund, the Sister Fund, Ford Foundation, Global Fund for Women, Danny Kaye and Sylvia Fine Kaye Foundation, Graham Charitable Foundation, Deak Family Foundation, Henry Luce Foundation, the Elizabeth Foundation, and the Ms. Foundation. The Malaysian-based organization Sisters in Islam has also been successful in fund-raising, although again, a good deal of hard volunteer work has gone into it for years. Since 2005, for example, it has been a grantee of the Sigrid Rausing Trust, which claims to fund international human rights work; the current 100,000 pound sterling grant they have seems to be for establishing Musawah.

An intriguing initiative out of North Africa that has received extensive European government funding has produced something more concrete and defined: a way to try to guarantee women's rights through a legitimate instrument within the Islamic tradition, the prenuptial contract. The Model Marriage Contract, published in 2008, was developed out of coordinated efforts in Morocco, Tunisia, and Algeria through partnering with Global Rights, self-described as a thirty-year-old international human rights advocacy organization (globalrights.org). The

North African feminists who developed the Model Marriage Contract consulted with a wide range of ordinary women about their experiences and desires in marriage and the published contract is "intended to guide future spouses as they draft their marriage contract by providing suggestions for topics to discuss as well as examples of clauses to stipulate." The booklet recognizes that contracts must be tailored to individual situations, but insists that they should be "rights protective for women" and should promote "equality within marriage." Like so many of the feminist projects of the past decade and a half that work for reform within an Islamic framework, the project found enthusiastic funding from outsiders: the United Kingdom Foreign Commonwealth Office Global Opportunities Fund, the British Embassy in Rabat, the Norwegian Royal Ministry of Foreign Affairs, and the Norwegian Embassy in Rabat are thanked. In turn, the drafters' expertise was sought by Musawah. Global Rights, *Conditions, Not Conflict: Promoting Women's Human Rights in the Maghreb through Strategic Use of the Marriage Contract* (Rabat, Morocco: Global Rights, September 2008).

42. This bill presented to the Judiciary Committee would amend the Immigration and Nationality Act. It was proposed by Congressman Tom Tancredo. I thank Mahmood Mamdani for bringing this to my attention. This was followed by an equally silly motion in Oklahoma to ban Shari'a law, as if there were any threat that "it" could be installed.

43. Naomi Sakr, "Friend or Foe? Dependency Theory and Women's Media Activism in the Arab Middle East," *Critique: Critical Middle Eastern Studies* 13, no. 2 (2004): 153–174; Maha M. Abdelrahman, *Civil Society Exposed: The Politics of NGOs in Egypt*, Library of Modern Middle East Studies (London: Tauris Academic, 2004); Maha M. Abdelrahman, "The Nationalisation of the Human Rights Debate in Egypt," *Nations and Nationalism* 13, no. 2 (2007): 285–300.

44. Their range of issues is admirable and much broader, however. See WISE, wisemuslimwomen.org/currentissues/.

45. Naz K. Modirzadeh, "Taking Islamic Law Seriously: INGOs and the Battle for Muslim Hearts and Minds," *Harvard Human Rights Journal* 19 (2006): 192.

46. Ibid., 207.

47. Modirzadeh's presentation was at the workshop, "Who's Afraid of Shari'a?" held at the Center for the Critical Analysis of Social Difference (cosponsored by the Institute for the Study of Religion, Culture, and Public Life) at Columbia University, October 3, 2008. I am grateful to Katherine Franke for bringing this job advertisement to our attention.

Posted in 2007, it was for an "Advisor on Sharia in the Women's Rights Division." This person was to provide Human Rights Watch (HRW) "with advice on the application of sharia as a legal system, the variations in its employment by states and other agents in different regions of the world, and how it is used to advance or restrict women's human rights, in areas including civil and political rights, family law, and sexuality." The qualifications included "deep expertise in Islamic jurisprudence and history" and "a history of involvement with women's organizations and human rights organizations in Muslim communities." Also required was an advanced degree, work experience, and fluency in English and advanced Arabic. Described as "beneficial" were other linguistic talents: "knowledge of one or more of the languages of countries in Asia, Africa, or the Middle East with substantial Muslim populations" and "knowledge of international human rights law and experience with field research, report writing, advocacy, and media work," in other words, the transnational language of rights—a tall order. A couple of feminist anthropologists who work on Islamic law or Muslim societies were rejected for the position; they believed that HRW had a very specific kind of candidate in mind: a more "authentic" Muslim woman trained in Islamic legal studies, perhaps wearing a hijab. This just might be the kind of woman that the Women's Shura Council has envisioned training and that, as the president of Union Theological Seminary, Reverend Serene Jones, announced at their conference in Kuala Lumpur in 2009, her institution was prepared to help train. Rasha Elass, "Conference Told of Plan for Female Muftis," *National,* July 20, 2009, thenational.ae/news /uae-news/conference-told-of-plan-for-female-muftis.

48. For various treatments of women in/and Islamist parties, see Lara Deeb, *An Enchanted Modern: Gender and Public Piety in Shi'i Lebanon,* Princeton Studies in Muslim Politics (Princeton, N.J.: Princeton University Press, 2006); Sherine Hafez, *An Islam of Her Own: Reconsidering Religion and Secularism in Women's Islamic Movements* (New York: New York University Press, 2011); Islah Jad, "Between Religion and Secularism: Islamist Women of Hamas," in *On Shifting Ground: Muslim Women in the Global Era,* ed. Fereshteh Nouraie-Simone (New York: Feminist Press at the City University of New York, 2005); Zakia Salime, *Between Feminism and Islam: Human Rights and Sharia Law in Morocco* (Minneapolis: University of Minnesota Press, 2011); and Elora Shehabuddin, *Reshaping the Holy: Democracy, Development, and Muslim Women in Bangladesh* (New York: Columbia University Press, 2008). For more on nongovernmental organizations (NGOs) and the introduction of debate about Shari'a in Egypt, see the

longer version of Chapter 5, published as Lila Abu-Lughod, "The Active Social Life of 'Muslim Women's Rights': A Plea for Ethnography, Not Polemic, with Cases from Egypt and Palestine," *Journal of Middle East Women's Studies* 6, no. 1 (2010): 1–45.

49. As Merry notes of successful social work projects against domestic violence in Hawai'i, anger management for men and police training are among the practices that have been transplanted to that locale that may help women develop "rights consciousness." Merry, *Human Rights and Gender Violence*.

50. For more examples of such projects in Egypt and Palestine, see Abu-Lughod, "The Active Social Life of 'Muslim Women's Rights.'"

51. I am not arguing with the Egyptian feminist, scholar, and wouldbe parliamentarian Iman Bibars, who anticipates criticisms of her focus on battering in her study of the urban poor by saying, "I could be accused of applying my Westernized middle-class biases in assessing, interpreting, and analyzing the stories of the women interviewed in this study," but the issues came from them. "Wife-battering is a violent and humiliating experience, as stated by the women themselves in their own words." Then she quotes one informant, who said, "I felt like dying. I hate him and hated my life." Iman Bibars, *Victims and Heroines: Women, Welfare and the Egyptian State* (London: Zed, 2001). The question I ask, instead, is how the things these women say about their husbands or brothers or fathers are translated into the language of women's rights through the medium of reports and projects by rights advocates, and how the re-embedding transforms their own readings. I am aware that my own rendering of Khadija's situation as an ethnographic case study may make her stories part of the rights discourse too. For a critique of this problem, see Marnia Lazreg, "Development: Feminist Theory's Cul-de-Sac," in *Feminist Post-Development Thought: Rethinking Modernity, Post-Colonialism and Representation*, ed. Kriemild Saunders, Zed Books on Women and Development (London: Zed, 2002).

52. Enloe has drawn our attention to the shifting gender dynamics produced from mass tourism by European and North American women. Cynthia H. Enloe, *Bananas, Beaches, and Bases* (Berkeley: University of California Press, 2000).

53. Timothy Mitchell, *Rule of Experts: Egypt, Technopolitics, Modernity* (Berkeley: University of California Press, 2002); Timothy Mitchell, "Worlds Apart: An Egyptian Village and the International Tourism Industry," *Middle East Report* 196 (September–October 1995): 8–23;

Kees Van Der Spek, *The Modern Neighbors of Tutankhamun: History, Life, and Work in the Villages of the Theban West Bank* (Cairo, Egypt: American University in Cairo Press, 2011).

CONCLUSION: REGISTERS OF HUMANITY

1. Talal Asad, "Redeeming the 'Human' through Human Rights," in *Formations of the Secular* (Stanford, Calif.: Stanford University Press, 2003), 140.

2. For a reflection on my relationship with Gateefa and her husband, see Lila Abu-Lughod, "A Kind of Kinship," in *Being There: Learning to Live Cross-Culturally*, ed. Sarah H. Davis and Melvin Konner (Cambridge, Mass.: Harvard University Press, 2011), 8–21.

3. Division for the Advancement of Women, Department of Economic and Social Affairs, *Convention on the Elimination of All Forms of Discrimination against Women*, "General Recommendations Made by the Committee on the Elimination of Discrimination against Women," June 12, 2009, un.org/womenwatch/daw/cedaw/recommenda tions/recomm.htm.

4. This is discussed in Chapter 6. In many countries, age of consent or age of marriage has been the focus of campaigns by conservative Muslim clerics as well as feminists. The long genealogy of the debate over age begins with British colonial rule. Flavia Agnes, "Interrogating 'Consent' and 'Agency' across the Complex Terrain of Family Laws in India," *Social Difference Online* 1 (2011): 1–16, socialdifference.co lumbia.edu/publications/social-differences-vol-1.

5. I quote from the young woman's essay and commentary in my ethnography, Lila Abu-Lughod, *Writing Women's Worlds: Bedouin Stories* (Berkeley: University of California Press, 1993), 211–213.

6. Gregory Starrett, *Putting Islam to Work: Education, Politics, and Religious Transformation in Egypt* (Berkeley: University of California Press, 1998).

7. Lila Abu-Lughod, "The Romance of Resistance: Tracing Transformations of Power through Bedouin Women," *American Ethnologist* 17, no. 1 (1990): 41–55.

8. Brinkley Messick, "Interpreting Tears: A Marriage Case from Imamic Yemen," in *The Islamic Marriage Contract: Case Studies in Islamic Family Law*, ed. Asifa Quraishi and Frank E. Vogel (Cambridge, Mass.: Harvard Law School, Islamic Legal Studies Program, 2008); Lynn Welchman, "Consent: Does the Law Mean What It Says?" *Social Difference Online* (2011), socialdifference.org/publications.

9. As I describe in Abu-Lughod, *Writing Women's Worlds,* her father eventually arranged a marriage for her to someone who fit all her criteria, except that he was of Bedouin origin.

10. This is still the ideal in her community, where women do not work or live independently. For more on women and work, see Lila Abu-Lughod, "Dialects of Women's Empowerment: The International Circuitry of the Arab Human Development Report." *International Journal of Middle East Studies* 41, no. 1 (2009): 83–103.

11. Frances Susan Hasso, *Consuming Desires: Family Crisis and the State in the Middle East* (Stanford, Calif.: Stanford University Press, 2011).

12. The idea of the individual we work with today was developed, as Émile Durkheim so nicely suggested, as part of the cult of the individual personality that grew up with the modern division of labor or, as Marcel Mauss put it in 1979, as a product of social evolution. Anthropologists have pursued this idea of different senses of the individual in many societies. For India, McKim Marriott called this the "dividual" rather than the individual. Dorothy Lee was an early thinker on this subject, but Shelley Rosaldo also contributed. Marcel Mauss, *Sociology and Psychology: Essays* (London: Routledge, 1979); Marriott, referenced in E. Valentine Daniel, *Fluid Signs: Being a Person the Tamil Way* (Berkeley: University of California Press, 1984); Dorothy Lee, *Freedom and Culture* (Prospect Heights, Ill.: Waveland Press, 1987); Michelle Zimbalist Rosaldo, *Knowledge and Passion: Ilongot Notions of Self and Social Life* (Cambridge: Cambridge University Press, 1980).

13. Clifford Geertz, *The Interpretation of Cultures: Selected Essays* (New York: Basic Books, 1973).

14. See Lila Abu-Lughod, *Veiled Sentiments: Honor and Poetry in a Bedouin Society* (Berkeley: University of California Press, 1986); Abu-Lughod, *Writing Women's Worlds;* Lila Abu-Lughod, "Against Universals: The Dialects of (Women's) Human Rights and Human Capabilities," in *Rethinking the Human,* ed. J. Michelle Molina, Donald K. Swearer, and Susan Lloyd McGarry (Cambridge, Mass.: Center for the Study of World Religions, Harvard Divinity School, Harvard University Press, 2010).

15. Judith Butler, "Sexual Consent: Some Thoughts on Psychoanalysis and Law," *Columbia Journal of Gender and the Law* 21, no. 2 (2011): 405–429.

16. Human rights and human capabilities talk is part of this "universal reason" that needs to be parochialized, not in order to dismiss it as Western or to make peace with it by asserting that other religious or

cultural traditions share the same values, but to ask what historical processes and what institutional arrangements from nation-states to the flourishing forms of transnational governance, advocacy, and humanitarianism have installed this dialect of universality in so many places. And to follow Talal Asad, to ask who has the political power to redeem humanity (including women) from "traditional cultures" or to reclaim for them their inalienable rights, which he says, "comes down in the end to the same thing." Asad, "Redeeming the 'Human' through Human Rights," 154.

17. I am referring here to the famous photography exhibit that traveled the world, first shown at the Museum of Modern Art (MOMA) in 1952. The curator had been, as O'Brian notes, "a member of a UNESCO [United Nations Educational, Scientific, and Cultural Organization] committee established 'to study the problem of how the Visual Arts can contribute to the dissemination of information on the Universal Declaration of Human Rights.'" Meant to stress the "universal elements and aspects of human relations and experiences common to all mankind," the exhibit censored photographs of lynching and the effects of the atom bomb in Japan and was used as part of American propaganda in the Cold War setting. See John O'Brian, "The Nuclear Family of Man," *Asia-Pacific Journal: Japan Focus* (July 11, 2008). japanfocus.org/_John _O_Brian-The_Nuclear_Family_of_Man. I am arguing that family must be understood differently.

18. For an example of the range of this rethinking, see Sarah Franklin and Susan McKinnon, eds., *Relative Values: Reconfiguring Kinship Study* (Durham, N.C.: Duke University Press, 2001).

19. After I had written this section, I was pleased to find that Marshall Sahlins noted on p. 44 of his pamphlet *The Western Illusion of Human Nature* (Chicago: Prickly Paradigms Press, 2008) that "the Western tradition has long harbored an alternative conception of order and being, of the kind anthropologists have often studied: kinship community. True that in the West this is the unmarked human condition, despite that (or perhaps because) family and kindred relations are sources of our deepest sentiments and attachments." He does not, however, consider the family as a complex mixture of power and attachment.

20. Roland Barthes, "The Great Family of Man," in *Mythologies*, trans. Annette Lavers (New York: Hill and Wang, 1972 [1957]), 100–102.

21. For example, see Alice Ann Munro, *Runaway* (Toronto: McClelland & Stewart Limited, 2004). For an elaboration of the argument about the importance of ethnography of the particular, see the introduction to Abu-Lughod, *Writing Women's Worlds*.

22. I am not the first to suggest the inadequacy of "women's rights" as a gloss or solution even in Egypt. In her study of poor urban women in Cairo, Heba El-Kholy also refuses this concept because of "the subtle, elusive, overlapping, and diffuse nature of the constraints on women, the intermeshing of exploitation and reciprocity, the fluctuations of their power due to life cycle changes, and the lack of a clear person, group, or class to confront." Heba Aziz El-Kholy, *Defiance and Compliance: Negotiating Gender in Low-Income Cairo,* New Directions in Anthropology (New York: Berghahn Books, 2002), 25-26.

23. Rania Kassab Sweis, "Saving Egypt's Village Girls: Humanity, Rights, and Gendered Vulnerability in a Global Youth Initiative," *Journal of Middle East Women's Studies* 8, no. 2 (2012): 29.

24. This was the slogan of the Save Darfur campaign, which Mahmood Mamdani has called "the humanitarian face of the War on Terror." He contrasts his argument to the motto of the Save Darfur campaign, which is to act even before you know. "Rather than a call to act in the face of moral certainty, it is an argument against those who substitute moral certainty for knowledge, and who feel virtuous even when acting on the basis of total ignorance. Indeed, the lesson of Darfur is a warning to those who would act first and understand later. Only those possessed of disproportionate power can afford to assume that knowing is irrelevant, thereby caring little about the consequences of their actions." Mahmood Mamdani, *Saviors and Survivors: Darfur, Politics, and the War on Terror* (New York: Pantheon, 2009), 6.

25. For some Middle Eastern cases, see Lila Abu-Lughod, ed., *Remaking Women: Feminism and Modernity in the Middle East* (Princeton, N.J.: Princeton University Press, 1998).

BIBLIOGRAPHY

Abaza, Mona. *Changing Consumer Cultures of Modern Egypt: Cairo's Urban Reshaping.* Social, Economic, and Political Studies of the Middle East and Asia. Leiden, Netherlands: Brill, 2006.

'Abd al-Salam, Siham. *Al-munazzamat al-ahliyya al-saghira al-'amila fi majal al-mar'a* [Small civil society organizations working on women's issues]. Cairo, Egypt: Dar al-'ayn li al-nashr, 2005.

Abdelrahman, Maha M. *Civil Society Exposed: The Politics of NGOs in Egypt.* Library of Modern Middle East Studies. London: I. B. Tauris, 2004.

———. "The Nationalisation of the Human Rights Debate in Egypt." *Nations and Nationalism* 13, no. 2 (2007): 285–300.

Abdo, Nahla. *Women in Israel: Race, Gender and Citizenship.* London: Zed Books, 2011.

Abu El-Haj, Nadia. *The Genealogical Science.* Chicago: University of Chicago Press, 2012.

Abu-Lughod, Lila. "The Active Social Life of 'Muslim Women's Rights': A Plea for Ethnography, Not Polemic, with Cases from Egypt and Palestine." *Journal of Middle East Women's Studies* 6, no. 1 (2010): 1–45.

———. "Against Universals: The Dialects of (Women's) Human Rights and Human Capabilities." In *Rethinking the Human,* edited by J. Michelle Molina, Donald K. Swearer, and Susan Lloyd McGarry. Cambridge, Mass.: Center for the Study of World Religions, Harvard Divinity School, Harvard University Press, 2010.

————. "The Debate about Gender, Religion and Rights: Thoughts of a Middle East Anthropologist." *PMLA* 121, no. 5 (2006): 1621–1630.

————. "Dialects of Women's Empowerment: The International Circuitry of the Arab Human Development Report." *International Journal of Middle East Studies* 41, no. 1 (2009): 83–103.

————. *Dramas of Nationhood: The Politics of Television in Egypt.* Lewis Henry Morgan Lectures, 2001. Chicago: University of Chicago Press, 2005.

————. "In Every Village a Tahrir: Rural Youth in Moral Revolution." In *Public Space and Revolt: Tahrir Square 2011*, edited by Elena Tzelepis and Sherene Seikaly. Cairo, Egypt: American University in Cairo Press, forthcoming.

————. "A Kind of Kinship." In *Being There: Learning to Live Cross-Culturally,* edited by Sarah H. Davis and Melvin Konner. Cambridge, Mass.: Harvard University Press, 2011.

————. "Living the 'Revolution' in an Egyptian Village: Moral Action in a National Space." *American Ethnologist* 39, no. 1 (2012): 16–20.

————. "'Orientalism' and Middle East Feminist Studies." *Feminist Studies* 27, no. 1 (2001): 101–113.

————, ed. *Remaking Women: Feminism and Modernity in the Middle East.* Princeton Studies in Culture/Power/History. Princeton, N.J.: Princeton University Press, 1998.

————. "The Romance of Resistance: Tracing Transformations of Power through Bedouin Women." *American Ethnologist* 17, no. 1 (1990): 41–55.

————. "Seductions of the 'Honor Crime'." *Differences: A Journal of Feminist Cultural Studies* 22, no. 1 (2011): 17–63.

————. "Shifting Politics in Bedouin Love Poetry." In *Language and the Politics of Emotion,* edited by Catherine Lutz and Lila Abu-Lughod. New York: Cambridge University Press, 1990.

————. *Veiled Sentiments: Honor and Poetry in a Bedouin Society.* Berkeley: University of California Press, 1986.

————. *Writing Women's Worlds: Bedouin Stories.* Berkeley: University of California Press, 1993. 15th anniv. ed., 2008.

Abu-Lughod, Lila, and Rabab El-Mahdi. "Beyond the 'Woman Question' in the Egyptian Revolution." *Feminist Studies* 37, no. 3 (2011): 683–691.

Abu-Odeh, Lama. "Crimes of Honour and the Construction of Gender in Arab Societies." In *Feminism and Islam: Legal and Literary Perspectives,* edited by Mai Yamani and Andrew Allen. New York: New York University Press, 1996.

Adely, Fida J. "Educating Women for Development: The Arab Human Development Report 2005 and the Problem with Women's Choices." *International Journal of Middle East Studies* 41 (2009): 105–122.
———. *Gendered Paradoxes: Educating Jordanian Women in Nation, Faith, and Progress.* Chicago: University of Chicago Press, 2012.
Afshar, Haleh. *Islam and Feminisms: An Iranian Case-Study.* New York: St. Martin's Press, 1998.
Agnes, Flavia. "Interrogating 'Consent' and 'Agency' across the Complex Terrain of Family Laws in India." *Social Difference Online* 1 (2011): 1–16.
Agostín, Laura A. "The Soft Side of Imperialism." *Counterpunch*, January 25, 2012. counterpunch.org/2012/01/25/the-soft-side-of-imperialism/.
Ahmad, Dohra. "Not Yet beyond the Veil: Muslim Women in American Popular Literature." *Social Text* 27, no. 99 (2009): 105–131.
Ahmed, Leila. *A Quiet Revolution: The Veil's Resurgence, from the Middle East to America.* New Haven, Conn.: Yale University Press, 2011.
———. *Women and Gender in Islam: Historical Roots of a Modern Debate.* New Haven, Conn.: Yale University Press, 1992.
Al-Ali, Nadje Sadig. *Iraqi Women: Untold Stories from 1948 to the Present.* London: Zed Books, 2007.
———. *Secularism, Gender, and the State in the Middle East: The Egyptian Women's Movement.* Cambridge Middle East Studies. Cambridge: Cambridge University Press, 2000.
Al-Ali, Nadje Sadig, and Nicola Pratt. *What Kind of Liberation? Women and the Occupation of Iraq.* Berkeley: University of California Press, 2009.
Alexander, Michelle. *The New Jim Crow: Mass Incarceration in the Age of Color-Blindness.* New York: New Press, 2010.
al-Hibri, Azizah. "Deconstructing Patriarchal Jurisprudence in Islamic Law: A Faithful Approach." In *Global Critical Race Feminism: An International Reader,* edited by Adrien Katherine Wing. Critical America. New York: New York University Press, 2000.
———. "Muslim Women's Rights in the Global Village: Challenges and Opportunities." *Journal of Law and Religion* 15, nos. 1–2 (2000): 37–66.
Ali, Miriam, and Jana Wain. *Without Mercy: A Woman's Struggle against Modern Slavery.* London: Warner, 1995.

Ali, Nujood, and Delphine Minoui. *I Am Nujood, Age 10 and Divorced.* New York: Crown, 2010.

Allen, Lori. "Martyr Bodies in the Media: Human Rights, Aesthetics, and the Politics of Immediation in the Palestinian Intifada." *American Ethnologist* 36, no. 1 (2009): 161.

Alloula, Malek. *The Colonial Harem.* Minneapolis: University of Minnesota Press, 1986.

al-Sayyid, Ridwan. "The Question of Human Rights in Contemporary Islamic Thought." In *Human Rights in Arab Thought: A Reader,* edited by Salma Khadra Jayyusi. London: I. B. Tauris, 2009.

Altorki, Soraya. *Women in Saudi Arabia: Ideology and Behavior among the Elite.* New York: Columbia University Press, 1986.

Amazon.co.uk. "Belonging: Amazon.co.uk: Sameem Ali: Books." 2011. amazon.co.uk/Belonging-Sameem-Ali/dp/071956462X/ref=sr_1_1 ?s=books&ie=UTF8&qid=1322254797&sr=1-1.

———. "Disgraced: Forced to Marry a Stranger, Betrayed by My Own Family, Sold My Body to Survive, This Is My Story: Amazon.co.uk: Saira Ahmed and Andrew Crofts: Books." 2011. amazon.co.uk /Disgraced-Forced-Stranger-Betrayed-Survive/dp/0755318188/ref=s r_1_1?ie=UTF8&qid=1322254584&sr=8-1.

Amnesty International. *Culture of Discrimination: A Fact Sheet on "Honor" Killings.* New York: Amnesty International, 2005.

———. *Israeli Army Used Flechettes against Civilians.* New York: Amnesty International, 2009. amnesty.org/en/news-and-updates /news/israeli-used-flechettes-against-gaza-civilians-20090127.

Angelou, Maya. *The Complete Collected Poems of Maya Angelou.* New York: Random House, 1994.

———. *I Know Why the Caged Bird Sings.* New York: Bantam Books, 1993.

Anwar, Zainah. "Introduction: Why Equality and Justice Now?" In *Wanted: Equality and Justice in the Muslim Family,* edited by Zainah Anwar. Selangor, Malaysia: Musawah, 2009. musawah.org /sites/default/files/Wanted-EN-intro.pdf.

———. "Sisters in Islam and the Struggle for Women's Rights." In *On Shifting Ground: Muslim Women in the Global Era,* edited by Fereshteh Nouraie-Simone. New York: Feminist Press at the City University of New York, 2005.

Appadurai, Arjun. "Putting Hierarchy in Its Place." *Cultural Anthropology* 3, no. 1 (1988): 36–49.

———, ed. *The Social Life of Things: Commodities in Cultural Perspective.* Cambridge: Cambridge University Press, 1988.

Appiah, Anthony. *The Honor Code: How Moral Revolutions Happen.* New York: W. W. Norton, 2010.

Asad, Talal. "Redeeming the 'Human' through Human Rights." In *Formations of the Secular: Christianity, Islam, Modernity.* Cultural Memory in the Present. Stanford, Calif.: Stanford University Press, 2003.

Asad, Talal, Wendy Brown, Judith Butler, and Saba Mahmood. *Is Critique Secular? Blasphemy, Injury, and Free Speech.* Berkeley: University of California Press, 2009.

Ashoka. "Iman Bibars and Sakeena Yacoobi on Al Jazeera." Ashoka: Innovators for the Public, 2008. ashoka.org/video/5007.

Association for the Development and Enhancement of Women. "History of ADEW." 2008. adew.org/en/?action=10000&sub=1.

Aweidah, Sama. "A Glimpse into the Women's Stories." In *Women, Armed Conflict and Loss: The Mental Health of Palestinian Women in the Occupied Territories,* edited by Khawla Abu Baker. Jerusalem: Women's Studies Centre, 2004.

Badran, Margot. *Feminism in Islam: Secular and Religious Convergences.* Oxford: Oneworld, 2009.

———. *Feminists, Islam, and Nation: Gender and the Making of Modern Egypt.* Princeton, N.J.: Princeton University Press, 1995.

Bahramitash, Roksana. "The War on Terror, Feminist Orientalism and Orientalist Feminism: Case Studies of Two North American Bestsellers." *Critique: Critical Middle Eastern Studies* 14, no. 2 (2005): 221–235.

Baker, Aryn. "Afghan Women and the Return of the Taliban." *Time,* August 9, 2010. time.com/time/world/article/0,8599,2007238 -4,00.html.

Barlas, Asma. "Globalizing Equality: Muslim Women, Theology, and Feminism." In *On Shifting Ground: Muslim Women in the Global Era,* edited by Fereshteh Nouraie-Simone. New York: Feminist Press at the City University of New York, 2005.

Baron, Beth. *Egypt as a Woman: Nationalism, Gender, and Politics.* Berkeley: University of California Press, 2005.

Barthes, Roland. "The Great Family of Man." In *Mythologies,* translated by Annette Lavers. New York: Hill and Wang, 1972 [1957].

Basarudin, Azza. "Musawah Movement: Seeking Equality and Justice in Muslim Family Law." *CSW Update Newsletter, UCLA,* March 1, 2009. repositories.cdlib.org/csw/newsletter/Mar09 _Basarudin.

Bernstein, Elizabeth. "Militarized Humanitarianism Meets Carceral
    Feminism: The Politics of Sex, Rights, and Freedom in Contempo-
    rary Antitrafficking Campaigns." *Signs* 36, no. 1 (2010): 45–71.
Bernstein, Jay M. "Bare Life, Bearing Witness: Auschwitz and the
    Pornography of Horror." *Parallax* 10, no. 1 (2004): 2–16.
Bibars, Iman. *Victims and Heroines: Women, Welfare and the Egyptian
    State.* London: Zed, 2001.
Bieber, Jodi. "Jodi Bieber Speaking about Her Bibi Aisha Photograph."
    Audio clip, n.d. audioboo.fm/
    boos/350494-jodi-bieber-speaking-about-her-bibi-aisha-
    photograph.
Bier, Laura. *Revolutionary Womanhood: Feminisms, Modernity, and
    the State in Nasser's Egypt.* Stanford, Calif.: Stanford University
    Press, 2011.
Booth, Marilyn. *May Her Likes Be Multiplied: Biography and Gender
    Politics in Egypt.* Berkeley: University of California Press, 2001.
Brenner, Suzanne April. "Reconstructing Self and Society: Javanese
    Muslim Women and 'the Veil.'" *American Ethnologist* 23, no. 4
    (1996): 673–697.
Brown, Christopher Leslie. *Moral Capital: Foundations of British
    Abolitionism.* Chapel Hill: University of North Carolina Press,
    2006.
Brown, Wendy. "Civilizational Delusions: Secularism, Tolerance,
    Equality." *Theory and Event* 15, no. 2 (2012).
———. "'The Most We Can Hope For . . .': Human Rights and the
    Politics of Fatalism." *South Atlantic Quarterly* 103, nos. 2–3
    (2004): 451–463.
———. *Regulating Aversion: Tolerance in the Age of Identity and
    Empire.* Princeton, N.J.: Princeton University Press, 2006.
Bunch, Charlotte. "Women's Rights as Human Rights: Toward a
    Re-Vision of Human Rights." *Human Rights Quarterly* 12, no. 4
    (1990): 486–498.
Burton, Antoinette. "The White Woman's Burden." In *Western Women
    and Imperialism,* edited by Nupur Chaudhuri and Margaret
    Strobel. Bloomington: Indiana University Press, 1992.
Bush, Laura. "Radio Address by Mrs. Bush." *The American Presidency
    Project,* November 17, 2001. presidency.ucsb.edu/ws/index.
    php?pid=24992#axzz1Zh0bpVSX.
Butalia, Urvashi. *The Other Side of Silence: Voices from the Partition
    of India.* Durham, N.C.: Duke University Press, 2000.

Butler, Judith. "Sexual Consent: Some Thoughts on Psychoanalysis and Law." *Columbia Journal of Gender and the Law* 21, no. 2 (2011): 405–429.

Carapico, Sheila. "NGOs, INGOs, GO-NGOs and DO-NGOs: Making Sense of Non-Governmental Organizations." *Middle East Report* 214 (2000): 12–15.

Chakrabarty, Dipesh. *Provincializing Europe: Postcolonial Thought and Historical Difference.* Princeton Studies in Culture/Power /History. Princeton, N.J.: Princeton University Press, 2000.

Chih, Rachida. "The Khalwatiyya Brotherhood in Rural Upper Egypt and in Cairo." In *Upper Egypt: Identity and Change,* edited by Nicholas Hopkins and Reem Saad. Cairo, Egypt: American University in Cairo Press, 2004.

Chowdhury, Elora Halim. *Transnationalism Reversed: Women Organizing against Gendered Violence in Bangladesh.* SUNY Series, Praxis: Theory in Action. Albany: State University of New York Press, 2011.

Chowdhury, Elora Halim, Leila Farsakh, and Rajini Srikanth. "Introduction-Engaging Islam." *International Feminist Journal of Politics* 10, no. 4 (2008): 439–454.

Commission of the European Communities (CEC). *Implementation of the European Neighbourhood Policy in 2008: Progress Report Egypt.* Cairo, Egypt: CEC, 2009. ec.europa.eu/world/enp/pdf /progress2009/sec09_523_en.pdf.

Convention on the Elimination of All Forms of Discrimination against Women. "General Recommendations Made by the Committee on the Elimination of Discrimination against Women." Division for the Advancement of Women, Department of Economic and Social Affairs, 2009. un.org/womenwatch/daw/cedaw/recommendations /recomm.htm.

cooke, miriam. "The Muslimwoman." *Contemporary Islam* 1, no. 2 (2007): 139–154.

Cordoba Initiative. 2010. cordobainitiative.org/.

Crowe, Derrick. "*Time*'s Epic Distortion of the Plight of Women in Afghanistan." myFDL (FireDogLake), 2010. my.firedoglake.com /derrickcrowe/2010/08/02/time's-epic-distortion-of-the-plight-of -women-in-afghanistan/.

Dabashi, Hamid. "Native Informers and the Making of the American Empire." *Al-Ahram Weekly Online,* June 1–7, 2006. weekly.ahram .org.eg/2006/797/special.htm.

Daniel, E. Valentine. *Fluid Signs: Being a Person the Tamil Way.*
Berkeley: University of California Press, 1984.
Das, Veena. "National Honor and Practical Kinship: Unwanted
Women and Children." In *Conceiving the New World Order: The
Global Politics of Reproduction,* edited by Faye D. Ginsburg and
Rayna R. Rapp. Berkeley: University of California Press, 1995.
Davin, Delia. "Women in the Countryside of China." In *Women in
Chinese Society,* edited by Margery Wolf and Roxane Witke.
Stanford, Calif.: Stanford University Press, 1975.
Dean, Carolyn J. "Empathy, Pornography, and Suffering." *Differences:
A Journal of Feminist Cultural Studies* 14, no. 1 (2003): 88–124.
———. *The Fragility of Empathy after the Holocaust.* Ithaca, N.Y.:
Cornell University Press, 2004.
Deeb, Lara. *An Enchanted Modern: Gender and Public Piety in Shi'i
Lebanon.* Princeton Studies in Muslim Politics. Princeton, N.J.:
Princeton University Press, 2006.
Deeb, Lara, and Mona Harb. *Leisurely Islam.* Princeton, N.J.: Prince-
ton University Press, 2013.
———. "Sanctioned Pleasures: Youth, Piety and Leisure in Beirut."
Middle East Report 245 (2007): 12–19.
De Koning, Anouk. *Global Dreams: Class, Gender, and Public Space
in Cosmopolitan Cairo.* Cairo, Egypt: American University in Cairo
Press, 2009.
De Leeuw, Marc, and Sonja van Wichelen. "Please, Go Wake Up!
Submission, Hirsi Ali, and the 'War on Terror' in the Netherlands."
Feminist Media Studies 5, no. 3 (2005): 325–340.
Dusenbery, Maya. "Agency Is Easily Overlooked if You Actively Erase
It." Feministing, 2011. feministing.com/2011/04/14/
agency-is-easily-overlooked-if-you-actively-erase-it/.
Eickelman, Christine. *Women and Community in Oman.* New York:
New York University Press, 1984.
Elass, Rasha. "Conference Told of Plan for Female Muftis." *National,*
July 20, 2009. thenational.ae/news/uae-news/
conference-told-of-plan-for-female-muftis.
El Guindi, Fadwa. *Veil: Modesty, Privacy, and Resistance.* Oxford:
Berg, 1999.
Elias, Norbert. *The Civilizing Process.* Mole Editions. New York:
Urizen Books, 1978.
El-Kholy, Heba Aziz. *Defiance and Compliance: Negotiating Gender in
Low-Income Cairo.* New Directions in Anthropology. New York:
Berghahn Books, 2002.

El Mahdi, Rabab. "Does Political Islam Impede Gender-Based Mobilization? The Case of Egypt." *Totalitarian Movements and Political Religions* 11, no. 3 (2010): 379–396.

El Sadda, Hoda, 'Imad Abu Ghazi, and Jabir 'Usfur. *Significant Moments in the History of Egyptian Women.* Cairo, Egypt: National Council for Women, Committee for Culture and Media, 2001.

El Tahawy, Mona. "Why Do They Hate Us? The Real War on Women is in the Middle East." *Foreign Policy,* Sex Issue, May/June 2013. foreignpolicy.com/articles/2012/04/23/why_do_they_hate_us.

Englund, Harri. *Prisoners of Freedom: Human Rights and the African Poor.* California Series in Public Anthropology. Berkeley: University of California Press, 2006.

Enloe, Cynthia H. *Bananas, Beaches and Bases: Making Feminist Sense of International Politics.* Berkeley: University of California Press, 1990.

———. *The Curious Feminist.* Berkeley: University of California Press, 2004.

———. *Globalization and Militarism.* New York: Rowman and Littlefield, 2007.

———. *The Morning After: Sexual Politics at the End of the Cold War.* Berkeley: University of California Press, 1993.

Erlanger, Steven. "At Bonn Talks, 3 Women Push Women's Cause." *New York Times,* November 30, 2001.

Ewing, Katherine Pratt. *Stolen Honor: Stigmatizing Muslim Men in Berlin.* Stanford, Calif.: Stanford University Press, 2008.

Fahmy, Khaled. "Women, Medicine, and Power in Nineteenth Century Egypt." In *Remaking Women: Feminism and Modernity in the Middle East,* edited by Lila Abu-Lughod. Princeton Studies in Culture/Power/History. Princeton, N.J.: Princeton University Press, 1998.

Fakhraie, Fatemeh. "Just . . . Ugh." Muslimah Media Watch, 2011. http://muslimahmediawatch.org/2011/04/just-ugh/.

Farrell, Amy, and Patrice McDermott. "Claiming Afghan Women: The Challenge of Human Rights Discourse for Transnational Feminism." In *Just Advocacy? Women's Human Rights, Transnational Feminisms, and the Politics of Representation,* edited by Wendy S. Hesford and Wendy Kozol. New Brunswick, N.J.: Rutgers University Press, 2005.

Fassin, Didier. "Compassion and Repression: The Moral Economy of Immigration Policies in France." *Cultural Anthropology* 20, no. 3 (2005): 362–387.

————. *Humanitarian Reason*. Berkeley: University of California Press, 2012.

Ferguson, James. *The Anti-Politics Machine: Development, Depoliticization, and Bureaucratic Power in Lesotho*. Minneapolis: University of Minnesota Press, 1994.

Ferguson, James, and Akhil Gupta. "Spatializing States: Toward an Ethnography of Neoliberal Governmentality." *American Ethnologist* 29, no. 4 (2002): 98–110.

Fernando, Mayanthi. "Reconfiguring Freedom: Muslim Piety and the Limits of Secular Law and Public Discourse in France." *American Ethnologist* 37, no. 1 (2010): 19.

Fernea, Elizabeth Warnock. *Guests of the Sheik: An Ethnography of an Iraqi Village*. 3rd ed. New York: Anchor Books, 1995.

Fleischmann, Ellen. "'Our Moslem Sisters': Women of Greater Syria in the Eyes of American Protestant Missionary Women." *Islam and Christian-Muslim Relations* 9, no. 3 (1998): 307–323.

Franklin, Sarah, and Susan McKinnon, eds. *Relative Values: Reconfiguring Kinship Study*. Durham, N.C.: Duke University Press, 2001.

Fremson, Ruth. "Allure Must Be Covered: Individuality Peeks Through." *New York Times*, November 4, 2011.

Geertz, Clifford. *The Interpretation of Cultures: Selected Essays*. New York: Basic Books, 1973.

Ghorashi, Halleh. "Ayaan Hirsi Ali: Daring or Dogmatic? Debates on Multiculturalism and Emancipation in the Netherlands." In *Multiple Identifications and the Self*, edited by Henk Driessen and Toon van Meijl. Utrecht, Netherlands: Stichting Focaal, 2003.

Gilligan, Carol. *In a Different Voice*. Cambridge, Mass.: Harvard University Press, 1993.

Global Rights. *Conditions, Not Conflict: Promoting Women's Human Rights in the Maghreb through Strategic Use of the Marriage Contract*. Rabat, Morocco: Global Rights, 2008.

Goldenberg, Suzanne. "The Woman Who Stood Up to the Taliban." *Guardian*, January 23, 2002. guardian.co.uk/world/2002/jan/24/gender.uk1.

Goodale, Mark. "Introduction to 'Anthropology and Human Rights in a New Key.'" *American Anthropologist* 108, no. 1 (2006): 1–8.

Grewal, Inderpal. "On the New Global Feminism and the Family of Nations: Dilemmas of Transnational Feminist Practice." In *Talking Visions: Multicultural Feminism in a Transnational Age*, edited by Ella Shohat. Documentary Sources in Contemporary Art. Cambridge, Mass.: MIT Press, 1998.

———. "'Women's Rights as Human Rights': The Transnational Production of Global Feminist Subjects." In *Transnational America: Feminisms, Diasporas, Neoliberalisms*. Durham, N.C.: Duke University Press, 2005.

Guénif-Souilamas, Nacira. "The Other French Exception: Virtuous Racism and the War of the Sexes in Postcolonial France." *French Politics, Culture & Society* 24, no. 3 (2006): 23–41.

Hafez, Sherine. *An Islam of Her Own: Reconsidering Religion and Secularism in Women's Islamic Movements*. New York: New York University Press, 2011.

Halley, Janet, Prabha Kotiswaran, Hila Shamir, and Chantal Thomas. "From the International to the Local in Feminist Legal Responses to Rape, Prostitution/Sex Work, and Sex Trafficking: Four Studies in Contemporary Governance Feminism." *Harvard Journal of Law & Gender* 29 (2006): 335–509.

Halttunen, Karen. "Humanitarianism and the Pornography of Pain in Anglo-American Culture." *American Historical Review* 100, no. 2 (1995): 303–334.

Hanafi, Sari, and Linda Tabar. *The Emergence of a Palestinian Globalized Elite: Donors, International Organizations and Local NGOs*. Ramallah, Palestine: Institute of Jerusalem Studies; Muwatin, Palestinian Institute for the Study of Democracy, 2005.

Hasso, Frances Susan. *Consuming Desires: Family Crisis and the State in the Middle East*. Stanford, Calif.: Stanford University Press, 2011.

———. "Empowering Governmentalities rather than Women: The Arab Human Development Report 2005 and Western Development Logics." *International Journal of Middle East Studies* 41, no. 1 (2009): 63–82.

Hastrup, Kirsten. "Violence, Suffering and Human Rights: Anthropological Reflections." *Anthropological Theory* 3, no. 3 (2003): 309–323.

Hatem, Mervat F. "Economic and Political Liberation in Egypt and the Demise of State Feminism." *International Journal of Middle East Studies* 24, no. 2 (1992): 231–251.

———. "In the Eye of the Storm: Islamic Societies and Muslim Women in Globalization Discourses." *Comparative Studies of South Asia, Africa and the Middle East* 26, no. 1 (2006): 22–35.

Hershatter, Gail. *The Gender of Memory: Rural Women and China's Collective Past*. Berkeley: University of California Press, 2011.

Hesford, Wendy S. *Spectacular Rhetorics: Human Rights Visions, Recognitions, Feminisms.* Durham, N.C.: Duke University Press, 2011.

Hicks, Rosemary R. "Creating an 'Abrahamic America' and Moderating Islam: Cold War Political Economy and Cosmopolitan Sufis in New York after 2001." Ph.D. diss., Columbia University, New York, 2010.

————. "Translating Culture, Transcending Difference? Cosmopolitan Consciousness and Sufi Sensibilities in New York City after 2001." *Journal of Islamic Law and Culture* 10, no. 3 (2008): 281–306.

Hicks, Rosemary R., and Jodi Eichler-Levine. "'As Americans against Genocide': The Crisis in Darfur and Interreligious Political Activism." *American Quarterly* 59, no. 3 (2007): 711–735.

Hider, James. "Names of Commanders to Be Kept Secret as Gaza Weapons Inquiry Begins." *Times of London: TimesOnline*, January 22, 2009. timesonline.co.uk/tol/news/world/middle_east/arti cle5563082.ece.

Hinton, Carma, and Richard Gordon. *Small Happiness.* Ronin Films, 1984.

Hirschkind, Charles, and Saba Mahmood. "Feminism, the Taliban, and the Politics of Counter-Insurgency." *Anthropological Quarterly* 75, no. 2 (2002): 339–354.

Hirsi Ali, Ayaan. *The Caged Virgin: An Emancipation Proclamation for Women and Islam.* New York: Free Press, 2006.

————. *Infidel.* New York: Free Press, 2007.

————. *Nomad: From Islam to America; A Personal Journey through the Clash of Civilizations.* New York: Free Press, 2010.

————. *Submission.* Directed by Theo Van Gogh. 2004.

Hochschild, Adam. *King Leopold's Ghost: A Story of Greed, Terror, and Heroism in Colonial Africa.* Boston: Houghton Mifflin, 1998.

Hodgson, Dorothy L. "Introduction: Comparative Perspectives on the Indigenous Rights Movement in Africa and the Americas." *American Anthropologist* 104, no. 4 (2002): 1037–1049.

————. "'These Are Not Our Priorities': Maasai Women, Human Rights and the Problem of Culture." In *Gender and Culture at the Limit of Rights,* edited by Dorothy L. Hodgson. Philadelphia: University of Pennsylvania Press, 2011.

————. "Women's Rights as Human Rights: Women in Law and Development in Africa (WiLDAF)." *Africa Today* 49, no. 2 (2002): 3–26.

Honig, Emily, and Gail Hershatter. *Personal Voices: Chinese Women in the 1980's.* Stanford, Calif.: Stanford University Press, 1988.

Hoodfar, Homa. *Between Marriage and the Market: Intimate Politics and Survival in Cairo.* Berkeley: University of California Press, 1997.

Human Rights Watch. *A Question of Security: Violence against Palestinian Women and Girls.* November 11, 2006. unhcr.org/refworld/docid/4565dd724.html.

Husseini, Rana. *Murder in the Name of Honour: The True Story of One Woman's Heroic Fight against an Unbelievable Crime.* Oxford: Oneworld, 2009.

Hyneman, Esther. "Staying Honest about Afghanistan." *HuffPost-World,* September 20, 2010. huffingtonpost.com/esther-hyneman/staying-honest-about-afgh_b_732185.html.

Jackson, Michael. *Existential Anthropology: Events, Exigencies and Effects.* Methodology and History in Anthropology. New York: Berghahn Books, 2005.

Jad, Islah. "Between Religion and Secularism: Islamist Women of Hamas." In *On Shifting Ground: Muslim Women in the Global Era,* edited by Fereshteh Nouraie-Simone. New York: Feminist Press at the City University of New York, 2005.

———. "The Demobilization of the Palestinian Women's Movement in Palestine: From Empowered Active Militants to Powerless and Stateless 'Citizens.'" *MIT Electronic Journal of Middle East Studies* 8 (2008): 94–111.

Johnson, Penny. "Violence All Around Us: Dilemmas of Global and Local Agendas Addressing Violence against Palestinian Women, an Initial Intervention." *Cultural Dynamics* 20, no. 2 (2008): 119–131.

Jones, Ann. "Afghan Women Have Already Been Abandoned." *Nation,* August 12, 2010. thenation.com/article/154020/afghan-women-have-already-been-abandoned.

Jordan-Young, Rebecca M. *Brain Storm: The Flaws in the Science of Sex Differences.* Cambridge, Mass.: Harvard University Press, 2010.

Joyce, Kathryn. *Quiverfull: Inside the Christian Patriarchy Movement.* Boston: Beacon Press, 2009.

Jusová, Iveta. "Hirsi Ali and Van Gogh's *Submission*: Reinforcing the Islam vs. Women Binary." *Women's Studies International Forum* 31, no. 2 (2008): 148–155.

Kabbani, Rana. *Europe's Myths of Orient.* Bloomington: Indiana University Press, 1986.

Kandiyoti, Deniz. "The Lures and Perils of Gender Activism in Afghanistan." Presented at the Anthony Hyman Memorial Lecture, School of Oriental and African Studies, University of London, 2009. mrzine.monthlyreview.org/2009/kandiyoti041109p.html.

———. "Old Dilemmas or New Challenges? The Politics of Gender and Reconstruction in Afghanistan." *Development and Change* 38, no. 2 (2007): 169–199.

Kapchan, Deborah. *Gender on the Market.* Philadelphia: University of Pennsylvania Press, 1996.

Kapur, Ratna. "The Tragedy of Victimization Rhetoric: Resurrecting the 'Native' Subject in International/Post-Colonial Feminist Legal Politics." *Harvard Human Rights Law Journal* 1 (2002): 1–38.

Karim, Lamia. *Microfinance and Its Discontents: Women in Debt in Bangladesh.* Minneapolis: University of Minnesota Press, 2011.

Khouri, Norma. *Honor Lost: Love and Death in Modern-Day Jordan.* New York: Atria Books, 2003.

Ko, Dorothy. *Cinderella's Sisters: A Revisionist History of Footbinding.* Philip E. Lilienthal Asian Studies Imprint. Berkeley: University of California Press, 2005.

———. "Footbinding and Anti-Footbinding in China: The Subject of Pain in the Nineteenth and Early Twentieth Centuries." In *Discipline and the Other Body: Correction, Corporeality, Colonialism,* edited by Steven Pierce and Anupama Rao. Durham, N.C.: Duke University Press, 2006.

Koğacioğlu, Dicle. "The Tradition Effect: Framing Honor Crimes in Turkey." *Differences: A Journal of Feminist Cultural Studies* 15, no. 2 (2004).

Korteweg, Anna C., and Gökçe Yurdakul. "Religion, Culture and the Politicization of Honour-Related Violence." Paper No. 12, Gender and Development Programme, UN Research Institute for Social Development, October 2010.

Kozma, Liat. "Negotiating Virginity: Narratives of Defloration from Late Nineteenth-Century Egypt." *Comparative Studies of South Asia, Africa and the Middle East* 24, no. 1 (2004): 55–65.

Kristof, Nicholas D. Foreword to *In the Name of Honor: A Memoir* by Mukhtar Mai, translated by Linda Coverdale. New York: Atria Books, 2006.

Kristof, Nicholas D., and Sheryl WuDunn. *Half the Sky: How to Change the World.* London: Virago, 2010.

Kwon, Young Hee. "Searching to Death for 'Home': A Filipina Immigrant Bride's Subaltern Rewriting." *NWSA Journal* 17, no. 2 (2005): 69–85.

Lalami, Laila. "The Missionary Position." *Nation*, June 19, 2006. thenation.com/article/missionary-position.

Latour, Bruno. "Circulating Reference: Sampling the Soil in the Amazon Forest." In *Pandora's Hope: Essays on the Reality of Science Studies*. Cambridge, Mass.: Harvard University Press, 1999.

Lavie, Smadar. "Mizrahi Feminism and the Question of Palestine." *Journal of Middle East Women's Studies* 7, no. 2 (2011): 56–88.

Lazreg, Marnia. "Development: Feminist Theory's Cul-de-Sac." In *Feminist Post-Development Thought: Rethinking Modernity, Post-Colonialism and Representation*, edited by Kriemild Saunders. Zed Books on Women and Development. London: Zed, 2002.

———. *The Eloquence of Silence: Algerian Women in Question*. New York: Routledge, 1994.

Lee, Dorothy. *Freedom and Culture*. Prospect Heights, Ill.: Waveland Press, 1987.

Leila, and Marie-Thérèse Cuny. *Married by Force*. Translated by Sue Rose. London: Portrait, 2006.

Levitt, Peggy, and Sally Engle Merry. "Making Women's Human Rights in the Vernacular: Navigating the Culture/Rights Divide." In *Gender and Culture at the Limit of Rights*, edited by Dorothy Hodgson. Philadelphia: University of Pennsylvania Press, 2011.

Library of Congress. "Bill Text, 110th Congress (2007–2008), H.R.6975.IH." September 18, 2008. thomas.loc.gov/cgi-bin/query /z?c110:H.R.6975:.

Liu, Lydia H., Rebecca E. Karl, and Dorothy Ko, eds. *The Birth of Chinese Feminism: Essential Texts in Transnational Theory*. New York: Columbia University Press, 2013.

Lutz, Catherine. *Homefront: A Military City and the American Twentieth Century*. Boston: Beacon Press, 2001.

MacKinnon, Catharine A. *Are Women Human? And Other International Dialogues*. Cambridge, Mass.: Harvard University Press, 2006.

Macleod, Arlene Elowe. *Accommodating Protest: Working Women, the New Veiling, and Change in Cairo*. New York: Columbia University Press, 1991.

Mahdavi, Pardis. *Passionate Uprisings: Iran's Sexual Revolution*. Stanford, Calif.: Stanford University Press, 2009.

Mahmood, Saba. "Feminism, Democracy, and Empire: Islam and the War of Terror." In *Women's Studies on the Edge,* edited by Joan Wallach Scott. Durham, N.C.: Duke University Press, 2008.

———. "Feminist Theory, Embodiment, and the Docile Agent: Some Reflections on the Egyptian Islamic Revival." *Cultural Anthropology* 16, no. 2 (2001): 202–236.

———. *Politics of Piety: The Islamic Revival and the Feminist Subject.* Princeton, N.J.: Princeton University Press, 2004.

———. "Secularism, Hermeneutics, and Empire: The Politics of Islamic Reformation." *Public Culture* 18, no. 2 (2006): 323–347.

Mahmoud, Shatha. "Princess Basma Calls for End to Violence against Women." UN Women: United Nations Entity for Gender Equality and the Empowerment of Women, 2008. unifem.org.jo/pages/article details.aspx?aid=1246.

Mamdani, Mahmood. *Saviors and Survivors: Darfur, Politics, and the War on Terror.* New York: Pantheon Books, 2009.

Mani, Lata. "Contentious Traditions: The Debate on Sati in Colonial India." *Cultural Critique* 7, The Nature and Context of Minority Discourse II (1987): 119–156.

Marcus, George E. *Ethnography through Thick and Thin.* Princeton, N.J.: Princeton University Press, 1998.

Mauss, Marcel. *Sociology and Psychology: Essays.* London: Routledge, 1979.

Meister, Robert. *After Evil: A Politics of Human Rights.* New York: Columbia University Press, 2011.

Meneley, Anne. *Tournaments of Value: Sociability and Hierarchy in a Yemeni Town.* Toronto: University of Toronto Press, 1996.

Menon, Ritu, and Kamla Bhasin. *Borders and Boundaries: Women in India's Partition.* New Brunswick, N.J.: Rutgers University Press, 1998.

Mermin, Liz. *Beauty Academy of Kabul.* Sma Distribution, 2006.

Merry, Sally Engle. *Human Rights and Gender Violence: Translating International Law into Local Justice.* Chicago Series in Law and Society. Chicago: University of Chicago Press, 2006.

Messick, Brinkley. "Interpreting Tears: A Marriage Case from Imamic Yemen." In *The Islamic Marriage Contract: Case Studies in Islamic Family Law,* edited by Asifa Quraishi and Frank E. Vogel. Cambridge, Mass.: Islamic Legal Studies Program, Harvard Law School, 2008.

Mir-Hosseini, Ziba. "Beyond 'Islam' vs. 'Feminism.' " *IDS Bulletin* 42, no. 1 (2011): 67–77.

————. *Islam and Gender: The Religious Debate in Contemporary Iran.* Princeton Studies in Muslim Politics. Princeton, N.J.: Princeton University Press, 1999.

————. "Muslim Women's Quest for Equality: Between Islamic Law and Feminism." *Critical Inquiry* 32, no. 4 (2006): 629–645.

————. "Stretching the Limits: A Feminist Reading of the Shari'a in Post-Khomeini Iran." In *Feminism and Islam: Legal and Literary Perspectives,* edited by Mai Yamani and Andrew Allen. New York: New York University Press, 1996.

————. "Towards Gender Equality, Muslim Family Laws and the Shari'ah." In *Wanted: Equality and Justice in the Muslim Family,* edited by Zainah Anwar. Selangor, Malaysia: Musawah, 2009. musawah.org/background_papers.asp.

Mitchell, Timothy. *Rule of Experts: Egypt, Technopolitics, Modernity.* Berkeley: University of California Press, 2002.

————. "The Stage of Modernity." In *Questions of Modernity,* edited by Timothy Mitchell. Contradictions of Modernity, vol. 11. Minneapolis: University of Minnesota Press, 2000.

————. "Worlds Apart: An Egyptian Village and the International Tourism Industry." *Middle East Report* 196 (September–October 1995): 8–23.

Modirzadeh, Naz K. "Taking Islamic Law Seriously: INGOs and the Battle for Muslim Hearts and Minds." *Harvard Human Rights Journal* 19 (2006): 191–233.

Moghadam, Valentine M. *Globalizing Women: Transnational Feminist Networks.* Themes in Global Social Change. Baltimore, Md.: Johns Hopkins University Press, 2005.

Moghissi, Haideh. *Feminism and Islamic Fundamentalism: The Limits of Postmodern Analysis.* London: Zed Books, 1999.

Mohanty, Chandra Talpade. *Feminism without Borders: Decolonizing Theory, Practicing Solidarity.* Durham, N.C.: Duke University Press, 2003.

Moors, Annelies. "The Affective Power of the Face Veil: Between Disgust and Fascination." In *Things: Material Religion and the Topography of Divine Space,* edited by Birgit Meyer and Dick Houtman. New York: Fordham University Press, 2012.

————. "Submission." *ISIM Review* 15 (2005): 8–9.

Moustafa, Tamir. "Conflict and Cooperation between the State and Religious Institutions in Contemporary Egypt." *International Journal of Middle East Studies* 32, no. 1 (2000): 3–22.

Moyn, Samuel. *The Last Utopia: Human Rights in History.* Cambridge, Mass.: Harvard University Press, 2010.

Muhsen, Zana, and Andrew Crofts. *Sold: A Story of Modern-Day Slavery.* London: Sphere, 1991.

Munro, Alice Ann. *Runaway.* Toronto: McClelland & Stewart, 2004.

Musawah: For Equality in the Family. "Musawah Framework for Action." 2009. musawah.org/sites/default/files/Musawah -Framework-EN_1.pdf.

Mutua, Makau W. "Savages, Victims and Saviors: The Metaphor of Human Rights." *Harvard International Law Journal* 42, no. 1 (2001): 201–245.

Najmabadi, Afsaneh. "Crafting an Educated Housewife in Iran." In *Remaking Women: Feminism and Modernity in the Middle East,* edited by Lila Abu-Lughod. Princeton Studies in Culture/Power /History. Princeton, N.J.: Princeton University Press, 1998.

———. "Feminisms in an Islamic Republic." In *Islam, Gender, and Social Change,* edited by Yvonne Yazbeck Haddad and John Esposito. Oxford: Oxford University Press, 1998.

———. "(Un)Veiling Feminism." *Social Text* 18, no. 3 (2000): 29–45.

———. *Women with Mustaches and Men without Beards: Gender and Sexual Anxieties of Iranian Modernity.* Berkeley: University of California Press, 2005.

Nelson, Cynthia. *Doria Shafik, Egyptian Feminist: A Woman Apart.* Gainesville: University Press of Florida, 1996.

Nguyen, Mimi Thi. "The Biopower of Beauty: Humanitarian Imperialisms and Global Feminisms in an Age of Terror." *Signs* 36, no. 2 (2011): 359–383.

Nielsen, Hans Christian Korsholm. *The Danish Expedition to Qatar, 1959: Photos by Jette Bang and Klaus Ferdinand.* English-Arabic version. Moesgård Museum, 2009.

Nochlin, Linda. "The Imaginary Orient." *Art in America* 71, no. 5 (1983): 118–131, 187–191.

Nussbaum, Martha C. *Creating Capabilities: The Human Development Approach.* Cambridge, Mass.: Harvard University Press, 2011.

———. "Human Capabilities, Female Human Beings." In *Women, Culture, and Development: A Study of Human Capabilities,* edited by Martha Craven Nussbaum and Jonathan Glover. Oxford: Oxford University Press, 1995.

———. *The New Religious Intolerance: Overcoming the Politics of Fear in an Anxious Age.* Cambridge, Mass.: Harvard University Press, 2012.

BIBLIOGRAPHY 297

Parla, Ayse. "The 'Honor' of the State." *Feminist Studies* 27, no. 1 (2001): 65–88.

Pathak, Zakia, and Rajeswari Sunder Rajan. "Shahbano." *Signs* 14, no. 3 (1989): 558–582.

PeaceKeeper Cause-metics. "Women's Health Advocacy and Urgent Human Rights." 2013. iamapeacekeeper.com/peacekeeperadvocacy issuesnew.htm?

Pettit, Becky, and Bruce Western. "Mass Imprisonment and the Life Course: Race and Class Inequality in U.S. Incarceration." *American Sociological Review* 69, no. 2 (2004): 151.

Pierce, Steven, and Anupama Rao, eds. *Discipline and the Other Body: Correction, Corporeality, Colonialism.* Durham, N.C.: Duke University Press, 2006.

Povinelli, Elizabeth. *The Cunning of Recognition: Indigenous Alterities and the Making of Australian Multiculturalism.* Durham, N.C.: Duke University Press, 2002.

Puar, Jasbir, and Amit Rai. "Monster, Terrorist, Fag: The War on Terrorism and Production of Docile Patriots." *Social Text* 20, no. 3 (2002): 117–148.

"QuiverFull.com." 2010. quiverfull.com/.

Razack, Sherene H. *Casting Out: The Eviction of Muslims from Western Law and Politics.* Toronto: University of Toronto Press, 2008.

———. "Stealing the Pain of Others: Reflections on Canadian Humanitarian Responses." *Review of Education, Pedagogy, and Cultural Studies* 29, no. 4 (2007): 375–394.

Redfield, Peter. "Doctors, Borders, and Life in Crisis." *Cultural Anthropology* 20, no. 3 (2005): 328–361.

Riemers, Eva. "Representations of an Honor Killing: Intersections of Discourses on Culture, Gender, Equality, Social Class, and Nationality." *Feminist Media Studies* 7, no. 3 (2007): 239–255.

Riesman, Paul. *Freedom in Fulani Social Life: An Introspective Ethnography.* Chicago: University of Chicago Press, 1977.

Riles, Annelise. "Rights Inside Out: The Case of the Women's Human Rights Campaign." *Leiden Journal of International Law* 15, no. 2 (2002): 285–305.

Rodriguez, Deborah, and Kristin Ohlson. *Kabul Beauty School: An American Woman Goes behind the Veil.* New York: Random House Trade Paperbacks, 2007.

Rofel, Lisa. *Other Modernities: Gendered Yearnings in China after Socialism.* Berkeley: University of California Press, 1999.

Rosaldo, Michelle Zimbalist. *Knowledge and Passion: Ilongot Notions of Self and Social Life.* Cambridge: Cambridge University Press, 1980.

Rose, Jacqueline. "A Piece of White Silk." *London Review of Books* 31, no. 21 (2009): 5–8.

Roy, Ananya. *Poverty Capital: Microfinance and the Making of Development.* New York: Routledge, 2010.

Ruiz, Mario M. "Virginity Violated: Sexual Assault and Respectability in Mid- to Late-Nineteenth-Century Egypt." *Comparative Studies of South Asia, Africa and the Middle East* 25, no. 1 (2005): 214–227.

Sahlins, Marshall. *The Western Illusion of Human Nature.* Chicago: Prickly Paradigms Press, 2008.

Said, Edward W. *Orientalism.* New York: Vintage Books, 1979.

Sakr, Naomi. "Friend or Foe? Dependency Theory and Women's Media Activism in the Arab Middle East." *Critique: Critical Middle Eastern Studies* 13, no. 2 (2004): 153–174.

Salime, Zakia. *Between Feminism and Islam: Human Rights and Sharia Law in Morocco.* Minneapolis: University of Minnesota Press, 2011.

Sanday, Peggy Reeves. *Fraternity Gang Rape: Sex, Brotherhood, and Privilege on Campus.* New York: New York University Press, 1990.

Sangtin Writers, and Richa Nagar. *Playing with Fire: Feminist Thought and Activism through Seven Lives in India.* Minneapolis: University of Minnesota Press, 2006.

Sasson, Jean P. *Desert Royal.* London: Bantam, 1999.

Scott, Joan Wallach. *The Politics of the Veil.* Princeton, N.J.: Princeton University Press, 2007.

Shah, Hannah. *The Imam's Daughter.* London: Rider, 2009.

Shalhoub-Kevorkian, Nadera. "Conceptualizing Voices of the Oppressed in Conflict Areas." In *Women, Armed Conflict and Loss: The Mental Health of Palestinian Women in the Occupied Territories,* edited by Khawla Abu Baker. Jerusalem: Women's Studies Centre, 2004.

———. "Counter-Spaces as Resistance in Conflict Zones: Palestinian Women Recreating a Home." *Journal of Feminist Family Therapy* 17, no. 3 (2005): 109.

———. *Militarization and Violence against Women in Conflict Zones in the Middle East: A Palestinian Case-Study.* Cambridge Studies in Law and Society. Cambridge: Cambridge University Press, 2009.

———. "Voice Therapy for Women Aligned with Political Prisoners: A Case Study of Trauma among Palestinian Women in the Second Intifada." *Social Service Review* 79, no. 2 (2005): 322–343.

Shalhoub-Kevorkian, Nadera, and Suhad Daher-Nashif. "The Politics of Killing Women in Colonized Contexts." *Jadaliyya,* December 17, 2012, jadaliyya.com/pages/contributors/110635.

Shehabuddin, Elora. "Gender and the Figure of the 'Moderate Muslim': Feminism in the Twenty-First Century." In *The Question of Gender: Joan W. Scott's Critical Feminism,* edited by Judith Butler and Elizabeth Weed. Bloomington: Indiana University Press, 2011.

———. *Reshaping the Holy: Democracy, Development, and Muslim Women in Bangladesh.* New York: Columbia University Press, 2008.

Siapno, Jacqueline Aquino. "Shari'a Moral Policing and the Politics of Consent in Aceh." *Social Difference Online* 1 (2011): 17–29.

Siddiqi, Dina. "Crime and Punishment: Laws of Seduction, Consent, and Rape in Bangladesh." *Social Difference Online* 1 (2011): 46–53.

Sims, David. *Understanding Cairo: The Logic of a City Out of Control.* Cairo, Egypt: American University in Cairo, 2011.

Singerman, Diane, and Paul Ammar, eds. *Cairo Cosmopolitan: Politics, Culture, and Urban Space in the Globalized Middle East.* Cairo, Egypt: American University in Cairo Press, 2006.

Slaughter, Joseph R. *Human Rights, Inc.: The World Novel, Narrative Form, and International Law.* New York: Fordham University Press, 2007.

Slyomovics, Susan. *The Performance of Human Rights in Morocco.* Pennsylvania Studies in Human Rights. Philadelphia: University of Pennsylvania Press, 2005.

Snel, Erik, and Femke Stock. "Debating Cultural Differences: Ayaan Hirsi Ali on Islam and Women." In *Immigrant Families in Multicultural Europe: Debating Cultural Difference,* edited by Ralph Grillo. Amsterdam: Amsterdam University Press, 2008.

Sommers, Christina Hoff. "The Subjection of Islamic Women and the Fecklessness of American Feminism." *Weekly Standard,* May 21, 2007. weeklystandard.com/Content/Public/Articles/000/000/013/641szkys.asp.

Souad, and Marie-Thérèse Cuny. *Burned Alive.* London: Bantam, 2004.

Spencer, Robert, and Phyllis Chesler. *The Violent Oppression of Women in Islam*. Los Angeles: David Horowitz Freedom Center, 2007.

Spivak, Gayatri Chakravorty. "Can the Subaltern Speak?" In *Marxism and the Interpretation of Culture*, edited by Cary Nelson and Lawrence Grossberg. Urbana: University of Illinois Press, 1988.

Stamatopoulou, Elsa, and Bruce Robbins. "Reflections on Culture and Cultural Rights." *South Atlantic Quarterly* 103, nos. 2–3 (2004): 419–434.

Starrett, Gregory. *Putting Islam to Work: Education, Politics, and Religious Transformation in Egypt*. Berkeley: University of California Press, 1998.

Stengel, Richard. "The Plight of Afghan Women: A Disturbing Picture." *Time*, July 29, 2010. time.com/time/magazine/article/0,9171,2007415,00.html.

Strathern, Marilyn. "An Awkward Relationship: The Case of Feminism and Anthropology." *Signs* 12, no. 2 (1987): 276–292.

Suad, Joseph. "Elite Strategies for State Building." In *Women, Islam, and the State*, edited by Deniz Kandiyoti. Philadelphia: Temple University Press, 1991.

Sukarieh, Mayssoun. "The First Lady Phenomenon: Women's Empowerment and the Colonial Present in the Contemporary Arab World." Paper presented at the Boas Seminar, Columbia University, March 27, 2013.

———. "The Hope Crusades: Culturalism and Reform in the Arab World." *PoLAR: Political and Legal Anthropology Review* 35, no. 1 (2012): 115–134.

Sunder, Madhavi. "Reading the Quran in Kuala Lumpur." University of Chicago Law School Faculty Blog. 2009. uchicagolaw.typepad.com/faculty/2009/02/reading-the-quran-in-kuala-lumpur.html.

Sunder Rajan, Rajeswari. *Real and Imagined Women: Gender, Culture, and Postcolonialism*. London: Routledge, 1993.

Sweis, Rania Kassab. "Saving Egypt's Village Girls: Humanity, Rights, and Gendered Vulnerability in a Global Youth Initiative." *Journal of Middle East Women's Studies* 8, no. 2 (2012): 26–50.

Taylor, Thérèse. "Truth, History, and Honor Killing: A Review of *Burned Alive*." AntiWar.com. 2005. antiwar.com/orig/ttaylor.php?articleid=5801.

Ticktin, Miriam. *Casualties of Care: Immigration and the Politics of Humanitarianism in France*. Berkeley: University of California Press, 2011.

————. "Sexual Violence as the Language of Border Control: Where French Feminist and Anti-immigrant Rhetoric Meet." *Signs* 33, no. 41 (2008): 863–889.

————. "Where Ethics and Politics Meet: The Violence of Humanitarianism in France." *American Ethnologist* 33, no. 1 (2006): 33–49.

Tjaden, Patricia, and Nancy Thoennes. *Extent, Nature, and Consequences of Rape Victimization: Findings from the National Violence against Women Survey.* Special Report. Washington, D.C.: National Institute of Justice and the Centers for Disease Control and Prevention, 2006.

UN Development Programme, Regional Bureau for Arab States. *The Arab Human Development Report 2005: Towards the Rise of Women in the Arab World.* New York: United Nations Publications, 2006.

United Nations Egypt. *United Nations Development Assistance Framework 2007–2011 Egypt: Moving in the Spirit of the Millennium Declaration: The DNA of Progress.* Egypt: United Nations, 2006.

United Nations General Assembly, and 183rd Plenary Session. *Universal Declaration of Human Rights.* General Assembly Resolution 217 A (III). Geneva: UN Official Records, 1948.

United Nations Human Rights Council (UN/HRC). *Human Rights in Palestine and Other Occupied Arab Territories: Report of the United Nations Fact Finding Mission on the Gaza Conflict.* 2009. www2.ohchr.org/english/bodies/hrcouncil/specialsession/9/Fact FindingMission.htm.

Vance, Carole S. "Thinking Trafficking, Thinking Sex." *GLQ: A Journal of Lesbian and Gay Studies* 17, no. 1 (2011): 135–143.

Van Der Spek, Kees. *The Modern Neighbors of Tutankhamun: History, Life, and Work in the Villages of the Theban West Bank.* Cairo, Egypt: American University in Cairo Press, 2011.

Van Sommer, Annie, and Samuel Zwemer. *Our Moslem Sisters: A Cry of Need from Lands of Darkness Interpreted by Those Who Heard It.* New York: F. H. Revell, 1907.

Volpp, Leti. "Blaming Culture for Bad Behavior." *Yale Journal of Law & the Humanities* 12 (2000): 89–116.

————. "Feminism versus Multiculturalism." *Columbia Law Review* 101, no. 5 (2001): 1181–1218.

Walley, Christine J. "Searching for 'Voices': Feminism, Anthropology, and the Global Debate over Female Genital Operations." *Cultural Anthropology* 12, no. 3 (1997): 405–438.

———. "What We Women Want: An Ethnography of Transnational Feminism." Unpublished manuscript.

Welchman, Lynn. "Consent: Does the Law Mean What It Says?" *Social Difference Online* 1 (2011).

Welchman, Lynn, and Sara Hossein. *Honour: Crimes, Paradigms and Violence against Women.* London: Zed Press, 2005.

Wickett, Elizabeth. *For the Living and the Dead: The Funerary Laments of Upper Egypt, Ancient and Modern.* London: I. B. Tauris, 2010.

Wikan, Unni. *In Honor of Fadime: Murder and Shame.* Chicago: University of Chicago Press, 2008.

Wilson, Richard Ashby. "Afterword to 'Anthropology and Human Rights in a New Key': The Social Life of Human Rights." *American Anthropologist* 108, no. 1 (2006): 77–83.

Wimpelmann, Torunn. "The Price of Protection: Gender, Violence and Power in Afghanistan." Ph.D. diss., Department of Development Studies, School of Oriental and African Studies, University of London, 2013.

Wolf, Margery. *Revolution Postponed: Women in Contemporary China.* Stanford, Calif.: Stanford University Press, 1985.

———. "Women and Suicide in China." In *Women in Chinese Society,* edited by Margery Wolf and Roxane Witke. Stanford, Calif.: Stanford University Press, 1975.

Women Living under Muslim Laws (WLUML). "The Global Campaign 'Stop Stoning and Killing Women!' Concept Paper." 2007. wluml.org/english/news/stop_stoning _and _killing _ women%20 _concept_paper.pdf.

———. "Violence Is Not Our Culture: The Global Campaign to Stop Violence against Women in the Name of Culture." 2009. stop -stoning.org/.

Women's Islamic Initiative in Spirituality and Equality (WISE). *Jihad against Violence: Muslim Women's Struggle for Peace.* 2009. wisemuslimwomen.org/pdfs/jihad-report.pdf.

———. "Resources." 2010. wisemuslimwomen.org/resources/.

———. "WISE Muslim Women." 2010. wisemuslimwomen.org/.

Wood, Marcus. *Slavery, Empathy, and Pornography.* Oxford: Oxford University Press, 2002.

Woolf, Virginia. *A Room of One's Own.* London: Hogarth Press, 1929.

Wright, Melissa W. *Disposable Women and Other Myths of Global Capitalism.* New York: Routledge, 2006.

Yegenoglu, Meyda. *Colonial Fantasies: Towards a Feminist Reading of Orientalism*. Cambridge: Cambridge University Press, 1998.

Zeghal, Malika. "Religion and Politics in Egypt: The Ulema of Al-Azhar, Radical Islam, and the State (1952–94)." *International Journal of Middle East Studies* 31, no. 3 (1999): 371–399.

ACKNOWLEDGMENTS

How can one ever acknowledge all those who have contributed to one's thinking about a complex world? This book bears the traces of all those with whom I have thought and talked about women's rights during the past decade, including those I only know through their writings. I am grateful to them in ways I can never properly credit.

My debts to the women and men I have known in Egypt whose stories fill the pages of this book are immense. I would not have been so certain that we had to be so critical of the common discourses on women's rights and Muslim women if I had not been so warmly brought into their lives. They helped me to see the world through their eyes. I hope their experiences and perspectives and my analysis of their complex situations will shift the terms of the debates. I am sorry that I cannot name them here, but they will recognize what I have learned from them.

Colleagues and friends across the world, including at Columbia, which has been my intellectual home since 2000, commented on drafts, sent me clippings and citations, shared unpublished work, encouraged, and even inspired me. I want thank them all. Wendy Brown, Catherine Lutz, and Anupama Rao have been close interlocutors over many years; I cannot imagine my formation, or this book, without them. I owe them more than I can say, not just for their brilliance, political commitments, enthusiasm, and humor, but for giving me confidence. For their unique individual contributions, I also want to thank Nahla Abdo, Lori Allen, Soraya Altorki, Partha Chatterjee, Jane Cowan, Susan Crane, Lara

Deeb, Rabab El Mahdi, Hoda El Sadda, Katherine Ewing, Khaled Fahmy, Katherine Franke, Michael Gilsenan, Victoria de Grazia, Havva Guney-Ruebenacker, Janet Halley, Rema Hammami, Saidiya Hartman, Marianne Hirsch, Dorothy Hodgson, Jean Howard, Martha Howell, Rana Husseini, Islah Jad, Penny Johnson, Deniz Kandiyoti, Alice Kessler-Harris, Rashid Khalidi, Dorothy Ko, Nancy Kricorian, Saba Mahmood, Mahmood Mamdani, Sharon Marcus, Sally Engle Merry, Brinkley Messick, Ziba Mir-Hosseni, Mira Nair, Afsaneh Najmabadi, Elizabeth Povinelli, Naela Rifat, Susan Rogers, Reem Saad, Carol Sanger, Nadera Shalhoub-Kevorkian, Dina Mahnaz Siddiqi, Susan Slyomovics, Pamela Smith, Mayssoun Sukarieh, Neferti Tadiar, Miriam Ticktin, Leti Volpp, Boutros Wadieh, and Elizabeth Weed.

I have been deeply fortunate in students too. How can I capture what they have taught me? My graduate courses during the past few years through Columbia's Institute for Research on Women, Gender, and Sexuality have been invaluable intellectually—thanks to all the committed students who participated. The graduate students with whom I have worked most closely in the past fifteen years are especially precious interlocutors. Those who contributed in particularly helpful ways to the making of this book include Fida Adely, Amahl Bishara, Nadia Guessous, Sherine Hamdy, Rosemary Hicks, Maya Mikdashi, Ayse Parla, Sophia Stamatopoulou-Robbins, Shahla Talebi, Amina Tawasil, Christine Walley, Jessica Winegar, and Berna Yazici.

At every university where I have been invited to present my work-in-progress, I have encountered audiences who contributed to a better understanding of the issues I was addressing. I wish I could have done more with what they offered. Particularly memorable for me were conferences at Brown University's Pembroke Center (where the late Dicle Koğacıoğlu inspired us all), Duke University, the Harvard Center for World Religions, Harvard Law School, the Makerere Institute for Social Research, Rutgers, the University of Massachusetts-Boston, and the University of Wisconsin. Invitations to speak at the American University in Beirut, the British Academy, Cambridge University, CUNY, Mada al-Carmel, Simon Fraser University, the University of British Columbia, the University of California at Berkeley, the University of California at Santa Barbara, the University of Pennsylvania, the University of Washington, and Yale also allowed for productive exchanges. Thanks to those who invited me and those who engaged so constructively with my work.

Crucial to this project was the generous financial support I have received. Scholars depend on such support to do careful, long-term research; to carve out time to read, think, and write in the midst of teaching and administration; and to meet with colleagues to share ideas and learn from each other. I am grateful for fellowships from the American Council for Learned Societies and the Carnegie Foundation from 2007 to 2009. Columbia too was generous with research leaves. I will remain grateful to Nicholas Dirks for his support always.

Support from many quarters at Columbia for collaborative intellectual work was crucial for the development of my ideas. The Institute for Research on Women, Gender, and Sexuality was my perfect base, and out of it the Center for the Study of Social Difference. I have the best colleagues I could wish for there and have depended on them as well as the talented staff who make up our team, especially Laura Ciolkowski and Vina Tran. Enthusiastic support from the Institute for Social and Economic Research and Policy; from the Luce Foundation–funded initiative on religion and international affairs through the Center for Democracy, Toleration, and Religion; from the Institute for Religion, Culture, and Public Life; and most significantly from the Center for the Study of Social Difference, an advanced study center that nurtures intellectual work at Columbia, made it possible to set up faculty working groups and international workshops that advanced my thinking and connected me to wonderful scholars. I want to thank Toby Volkman at the Luce Foundation for her firm support and for being there both in Amman and in Paris for some of those workshops. None of these institutions or individuals is responsible for the views presented here.

Putting a book into production takes the good efforts of many. I am grateful to Elora Shehabuddin for making the connection with Sharmila Sen, my dynamic dream editor who understood in a flash what I was trying to do and gave me wise counsel (as well as pressuring me to finish). Heather Hughes shepherded the project in the most professional way. I am grateful to Brian Ostrander for meticulously overseeing the production and Fran Lyon for deftly clarifying my prose. Everyone I worked with at Harvard University Press contributed to making the process of bringing out this book so positive.

The labor of an embarrassing number of talented research assistants went into making this book a reality. I want to thank Ali Atif, Amina Ayad, Elisabeth Jacquette, Menna Khalil, Ana Maria Lebada, Sara Layton, Sarah Polefka, Leah Riviere, Mona Soleiman, Nikolas Sparks, and John Warner. My debt to Ana Maria Lebada for the index cannot be underestimated; it makes such a difference to have an intelligent and knowledgeable person constructing an index.

Earlier versions of sections of this book have been published. They are revised and used here with permission. Chapter 1 updates and expands "Do Muslim Women Really Need Saving? Anthropological Reflections on Cultural Relativism and Its Others," *American Anthropologist* 104, no. 3 (2002): 783–790. Chapter 4 is a revision and condensation of "Seductions of the 'Honor Crime,'" *Differences: A Journal of Feminist Cultural Studies* 22, no. 1 (2011): 17–63. Chapter 5 has been streamlined and updated from "The Active Social Life of 'Muslim Women's Rights': A Plea for Ethnography, not Polemic, with Cases from Egypt and Palestine," *Journal of Middle East Women's Studies* 6, no. 1 (Winter 2010): 1–45. Chapter 6 and parts of the conclusion are drawn from my 2009 Radcliffe-Brown Lecture in Social Anthropology, published as "Anthropology in the Territory of Rights, Human, Islamic, and Otherwise," *Proceedings of the British Academy* 167 (2010): 225–262.

Finally, I want to thank my family. Tim, Adie, and JJ have shared the life and times of this book. They have shaped both my everyday life and my thinking, not only by making the experiences and friendships we have had in Egypt and elsewhere a part of who we all are, but in having their own projects and visions that have expanded mine. I admire their talents, commitments, and integrity. I have been grateful for their various contributions to this book too, whether in reading chapters and helping me conceptualize issues, posing challenges, offering insights, or leading me to different parts of the world. I am grateful that they have lived with me in so many places, while giving me the space for this project to absorb and sometimes consume me. My wider family on both sides and of all generations has enriched my life, with a special thanks to Shahla and Raja.

I dedicate this book to my mother, Janet Abu-Lughod, who has watched keenly as I struggled to find the right place to stand, politically and intellectually. Her disagreements have sharpened my arguments, and her acumen about my relationship to this book, while sometimes taking me by surprise, has been a gift of the heart.

INDEX